Ari, Jackie & Maria
The Pirate, The Princess & The Diva

Onassis, Kennedy, Callas
The Love Triangle of
the 20th Century

Malcolm Turner

SunRise

First published in Great Britain in 2022 by SunRise

SunRise Publishing Ltd
Kemp House
152–160 City Road
London EC1V 2NX

ISBN 978-1-9144891-8-1

Copyright © Malcolm Turner

The right of Malcolm Turner to be identified as the author of this work has been asserted by him in accordance with the Copyright, Designs and Patents Act 1988.

All rights reserved. No part of this publication may be reproduced, stored in or introduced into a retrieval system, or transmitted, in any form, or by any means (electronic, mechanical, photocopying, recording or otherwise) without the prior written permission of the publisher. Any person who performs an unauthorised act in relation to this publication may be liable to criminal prosecution and civil claims for damages.

A CIP catalogue record for this book is available from the British Library.

Typeset in Minion Pro and Impact.

To Sue, who was, and is, always there for me.

Contents

CHAPTER 1	Jackie, How Could You?	7
CHAPTER 2	The Burning of Smyrna	15
CHAPTER 3	A Bad Omen	32
CHAPTER 4	A Country of Opportunity	44
CHAPTER 5	Pater Familias	55
CHAPTER 6	A Look of Destiny	66
CHAPTER 7	A Shipboard Romance	77
CHAPTER 8	A Marriage of Convenience	90
CHAPTER 9	Richer than Croesus	105
CHAPTER 10	A Turn of Providence	127
CHAPTER 11	A Man with a Compulsion	151
CHAPTER 12	Dukes, Princes and Kings	170
CHAPTER 13	Omertà	189
CHAPTER 14	A Formidable Clan	206
CHAPTER 15	The Baroness Who Would Not Be Bought	220
CHAPTER 16	A Son Is Lost	249
CHAPTER 17	The Aftermath	268
	Postscript	273
	References	274
	Bibliography	289
	Index	291

'They say I have no class. Fortunately, people with class are usually willing to overlook this flaw because I am very rich. You can't buy class, but you can buy tolerance for its absence.'

'If women didn't exist, all the money in the world would have no meaning.'

'The best deals, like the best sex, come out of exuberance.'

Aristotle Onassis 1906–1975

'Like Mark Anthony, Ari is a colossal child, capable of conquering the world, incapable of resisting a pleasure.'

Tina Onassis 1929–1974

'Glory goes to some people's heads, but not to mine. Glory terrifies me because it's quite uncomfortable up there.'

Maria Callas 1923–1977

'The first time you marry for love, the second for money, and the third for companionship.'

Jackie Kennedy 1929–1994

CHAPTER ONE

Jackie, How Could You?

The love triangle of Aristotle Onassis, Maria Callas and Jackie Kennedy was as volcanic as the eruption of Stromboli that staggered Aristotle and Maria at the beginning of their romance. Had they lived in the sixteenth century, Shakespeare would have written a play about them — it was too good a story to miss.

Betrothals are rarely well-kept secrets, especially when the intendeds are famous. Ordinarily, such pacts are market-tested long before they become official. Journalists will have been briefed, in advance, to ensure the public commentaries are as approving as the couple's reputations permit. Friends and family will have been forewarned and sweetened, lest a wayward relative or former lover should spoil the moment with an ill-timed memory or comment. Such precautions are wise as we, the public, generally have a warm corner of our hearts reserved for the nuptials of others, but we can be savagely critical of those who breach the unwritten but commonly understood rules of courtship.

All the more surprising then that five years after the assassination of John F Kennedy and weeks after the slaying of his brother, Bobby, an unsuspecting public would be dumbfounded by news of Jackie

Kennedy's engagement to Aristotle Onassis. On the streets of New York astonished passers-by, randomly interviewed by TV reporters, covered their mouths in horror and shook their heads in disbelief as though being told of a natural disaster, or the outbreak of war. Jackie Kennedy — the closest thing to a queen America had ever known — was to marry an ultra-rich, unbeautiful Greek who was her senior by twenty-three years. It was as if Camelot had subsided overnight, and vultures circled above. Ann Farber, a seventy-year-old Bronx resident, spoke for many when she told *The New York Times*, 'I'm terribly disappointed. She could have done better. To us she was royalty, a princess, and I think she should have married a prince. Or, at least, someone who looked like a prince.' In the same edition a *Times* op-ed noted, 'The reaction here is anger, shock and dismay,' while a Swedish newspaper demanded, 'Jackie, how could you?' Only New York's Greek community seemed to welcome the news.

The pair were as dissimilar as it is possible for a betrothed couple to be, sharing almost nothing except a love of luxury. Even their appearances were dramatically different: she was tall and slim while he was short and thickset.[1] She wore *haute couture* as confidently as any catwalk model, while he — despite buying expensive bespoke suits — often appeared dishevelled and unkempt. She looked younger than her years while he seemed older than his, and her beauty was sharply contrasted by his saturnine, almost reptilian looks. Jackie had, unaccountably, left Camelot for Caliban. The Onassis/Kennedy wedding — instantly dubbed *Beauty and the Beast* — filled

JACKIE, HOW COULD YOU?

Jackie Kennedy and Aristotle Onassis were about as dissimilar as it is possible for a betrothed couple to be, sharing almost nothing except a love of luxury.

newspapers across the world, and three decades would pass before another ill-starred marriage could rival it for publicity or obloquy.

President Kennedy and his wife had been anointed and crowned royalty long before they entered the White House. They were extremely rich, they had movie-star good looks, and both had unusual (and probably affected) accents. John F Kennedy's intonation has been described as pure Boston Brahmin: 'His distinctive trans-Atlantic tones, his dropped Rs, the faintest Boston-Irish twang, all identify him as the foremost member of America's most famous political clan.' [2] Jackie Kennedy's accent, often breathlessly delivered, was an early example of the mid-Atlantic English which would become vogueish throughout the 1960s. She also dropped her Rs — in what is sometimes known as a 'non-rhotic' affectation — and avoided obvious Americanisms.

In the months before the Kennedys' reign, *Camelot* — the Lerner and Loewe musical starring Richard Burton as King Arthur and Julie Andrews as Queen Guinevere — had become a huge Broadway success. When the Kennedys entered the White House in 1961, it did not take journalists long to link the Arthurian legends with contemporary Washington. The Kennedy White House would, henceforth, be known as Camelot.

Aristotle Onassis, while hardly royalty, had also built a dazzling public persona. During his long courtship of Maria Callas, he had often reminded people they were the two most famous Greeks in the world. When he sent red roses to the diva's dressing room, he signed the card 'from the other Greek'.

JACKIE, HOW COULD YOU?

In an age (unlike our own) where tycoons were expected to be flamboyant, Onassis was the most extravagant of them all. On his yacht, the *Christina* — then the most sumptuously appointed private vessel in the world — he entertained the great and good of America and Europe as lavishly as a Bourbon king. The engagement stunned the world, but only a handful of people knew that the couple had met more than a decade before, and that their affair may have pre-dated President Kennedy's death.

Aristotle Onassis, who had arrived in Argentina as a penniless teenage refugee, and built a shipping empire from nothing, had spent his life cultivating the rich, famous and powerful. He had always been drawn to them, but they had not always welcomed him. A succession of wives and mistresses had smoothed over his rough edges, but, in the eyes of many, he remained a 'shady' Levantine pirate. With this marriage to American royalty, however, he finally gained the social acceptance he had always craved, while decisively outshining his bitter, lifelong rival, Stavros Niarchos. The wedding should have been his crowning glory, but it would bring him some of his darkest hours and he would return to his former mistress, Maria Callas, eleven days after the ceremony.

Aristotle Onassis measured his success in column inches and had long employed all the black arts of PR, patronage and espionage to promote and manipulate his public image. Jackie Kennedy, contrastingly, had come to fear and loathe the paparazzi who pursued her and her children, and did all she could to avoid them. Consequently, it is Aristotle's version of history that we have come to accept.

Two myths have persisted in the decades since their marriage. The first is that Onassis was a rich but likeable rogue who avoided taxes but was otherwise, at heart, a decent and generous man. The second is that Jackie Onassis was a shameless gold-digger and spendthrift, motivated by little other than greed and personal ambition.

The truth was very different. Onassis was a vicious, drunken bully who beat his wives and mistresses until they were bloody and forced them to have abortions. When he tired of them, he smeared them in the media, tapped their phones and publicly humiliated them. His business empire was built largely on bribery, corruption and contempt for the law. He signed contracts in disappearing ink, reviled any politician who could not be bought, did business with dictators, and habitually lied. His children were so frightened in his presence that they peed themselves. His brutal treatment of his mistress, Maria Callas, led her to a suicide attempt and the abortion of her only child. Her early death at the age of only fifty-three was — in part — caused by the unhappiness that he inflicted on her.

It is true that Jackie Kennedy liked to spend money, but that was one of the reasons Onassis was attracted to her. When he had an affair with her sister, Lee, he boasted that she 'knew how to date a millionaire'; in other words, she happily accepted the clothes, jewellery and presents that he showered upon her. The carefully curated details of Jackie's spending which appeared in the media were deliberately leaked by his PR people to discredit her and pave the way to a divorce. He even used 'revenge porn' tactics against her, tipping off photographers that she was sunbathing naked on his 'private' island.

She had been raised by her mother to 'marry up', and learnt from the Kennedy matriarch, Rose, to respond to infidelity by spending extravagantly on her husband's account. When she agreed to marry Onassis, she was close to a mental breakdown following the murders of her husband and brother-in-law. At that moment, the sanctity of the Onassis yacht and island offered an irresistible escape from the goldfish bowl of America. It was naïve of her to believe that Onassis would treat her any better than he had treated her sister, or his first wife, or Maria Callas, but who has not been naïve in love?

'A Greek tragedy' is the cliché most often used to describe the love triangle of Aristotle, Maria and Jackie but none of them, in truth, were genuinely Greek. Both Aristotle and Maria had been born and raised outside Europe and chose to become naturalised Greeks, for legal reasons, later in life. Their 'Greekness' was a mantle they wore when it suited them and discarded when it did not. Jackie had tried hard to learn the Greek language and grasp Greek history and culture, but this only infuriated Aristotle, who thought her efforts were pretentious and unwifelike. The reality was that Onassis had created his own kingdom, first in Monaco and later on Skorpios, as well as aboard the *Christina*. He belonged to no other domain.

Their story is, however, a tragedy in all other senses. If you needed a cautionary tale on the themes of love, money, gender politics, and their association with happiness, then this would be it. Here you have passionate, life-changing love; breath-taking misogyny, fabulous amounts of money and no lasting happiness. Both Aristotle and Maria were wretched and miserable in their final years, if not before. Jackie eventually found contentment, but only after searing events which almost took her sanity. Aristotle's only surviving child, Christina, who inherited wealth beyond the dreams of avarice, was always a profoundly unhappy woman who repeatedly attempted suicide and died alone at the age of thirty-seven.

Remnants of the fairy tales we learn as children seem always to reside in our sub-conscious spirit. Even the most cynical of us can be enchanted by the notion of courtly love, and the rituals it requires. When, as so rarely happens, true life throws up a princess who seems worthy of a Prince Charming, we willingly suspend our disbelief. Such was the mood of America in the 1960s, the decade which changed everything.

CHAPTER TWO
The Burning of Smyrna

The characters, dreams and fears of the three had, as with most of us, formed in childhood, but their upbringings could not have been more different. Aristotle Socrates Onassis was born in 1906 in Karataş, a suburb of Smyrna (later renamed İzmir), in Anatolia. Karataş was, and remains, an affluent district with a fine beach, and the Onassis villa — one of the largest — was close to the sea with an unimpeded view. His parents, Socrates and Penelope, had underlined their child's Greekness by naming him after not merely one, but two of the greatest Greek philosophers. He was the son and heir of a wealthy family of tobacco merchants and, had history not intervened, he would have inherited both the business and a fortune. History, however, intervened spectacularly.

Today, the nation of Anatolia is largely forgotten, or remembered as Asia Minor. But for centuries it had been a vast territory stretching from the Black Sea to the Mediterranean encompassing most of modern Turkey; recently rebranded as Türkiye. This book is not a work of geopolitical history, but to understand Aristotle we need to know something of the seismic events in that region which would forge his character.

Anatolia was one of the first regions to convert to Christianity, and by the fourth century, western and central Anatolia were predominantly Christian and Greek-speaking. For hundreds of years Anatolia was the centre of the Hellenic world, but, by the eleventh century, Seljuk Turks from Central Asia had migrated into the region and become dominant. Anatolia began a slow transition from predominantly Christian and Greek-speaking, to predominantly Muslim and Turkish-speaking. The Greeks, however, remained numerous and retained their Christianity, their heritage, the Greek language and — as importantly — their identity.

By the end of the thirteenth century the Turkoman tribal leader, Osman I, had founded the Ottoman dynasty in the Anatolian town of Söğüt (modern-day Bilecik Province). By the fourteenth century the Ottomans had conquered the Balkans and created a transcontinental empire. In 1453, under their leader Mehmed the Conqueror, they decisively brought the Byzantine Empire to an end with their conquest of Constantinople. Suleiman the Magnificent would further expand the Ottoman Empire, and by the beginning of the seventeenth century, they controlled much of south-eastern Europe, western Asia, and northern Africa. For five centuries the Ottomans governed most of the Mediterranean and Near East from their capital in Constantinople.

While the seeds of decline had been sown by the nineteenth century, the fate of the empire would be sealed by a calamitous decision to support Germany during the First World War. The Allied victory meant the empire was partitioned and its Middle Eastern territories divided between the United Kingdom and France. The Turkish War of Independence, led by Mustafa Kemal Atatürk in 1923, created the modern Republic of Türkiye, and Anatolia disappeared from the maps.

Although Onassis always identified as Greek, both he and his father were, in truth, Greek-speaking Anatolians. The Turkish sultans admired the acumen of their Greek-speaking subjects and frequently promoted them to high office. The Anatolian Greeks were considered excellent businessmen and administrators and they dominated commerce and local government in Anatolia's major cities. Smyrna, then one of the largest and richest cities in Asia Minor, had a bigger Greek population than Athens. The respect of the pashas, however, did not extend to affection. The ethnic and religious tensions which had long simmered between Greeks and Turks were never far from the surface.

Socrates Onassis was a successful merchant who made a fortune from tobacco. He was a natural, self-made entrepreneur with a talent for languages: as well as Greek and Turkish he spoke French and a little English. Merchants who trade in a commodity to which they add little or no value are often the shrewdest of all businessmen; probably because they have little more than luck, courage and their wits to depend upon for profit. Socrates' newfound wealth enabled him to marry Penelope Dologlu, the seventeen-year-old daughter of another prosperous Anatolian-Greek family. Their first child was a daughter, Artemis. Two years later came a son, Aristotle, or Aristotélēs, as he was baptised. It was common practice among Greek-speaking Anatolians to name their children after figures from Greek antiquity. They were reminding their Turkish overlords — perhaps unwisely — that both their ethnicity and loyalty lay elsewhere.

The Greek population in Smyrna was tightly knit and fiercely protective of its culture. The young Aristotle, growing up in a Greek community surrounded by relatives and friends, would have been daily reminded of his heritage. In common with Greek custom, he was raised largely by his grandmother, Gethsemane, to whom he spoke only in Turkish. She was a deeply religious woman who tried to instil her faith in Aristotle, while simultaneously spoiling him. His closeness to her may have been a blessing because his mother died from a sudden illness when he was only six. At the funeral, as was the convention, he saw his mother in an open coffin but, as often happens when a young child loses a parent, it would take him many years to come to terms with her death.

Within eighteen months his father had remarried and Helen, his new wife, gave him two more daughters, Merope and Callirrhoe. Aristotle later remembered his stepmother with modest affection, stressing that she was a kind and 'obedient' wife. He had grown up in a society which was still strongly patriarchal with men seen very much as breadwinners and heads of the family, and women as homemakers and mothers. This had been a tradition in Greek society since ancient times. Xenophon had recorded that, for a girl, the ideal was 'to see the least possible, hear the least possible, and ask the least possible'. Obedience would, probably, remain for him an essential characteristic of any potential wife, and may be a clue to his failed relationships with so many women, including Maria Callas and Jackie Kennedy.

His bond with his grandmother and sister became closer. In fact, he and his sister, Artemis, were almost inseparable and would remain close for the rest of their lives. Whatever insecurities the death of his mother may have caused, the young Aristotle was outwardly self-confident, clever, and soon being groomed by Socrates to take over the family business. He developed an early interest in girls and later claimed to have been caught trying to seduce the daughter of a laundress at the age of only eleven. When his father rebuked him, it was on social rather than moral grounds: 'Never become involved with someone who can make you lose stature if the relationship becomes known. Sleep up.'[3] A few months later he successfully seduced his French tutor and conducted a year-long affair with her. For the rest of his life, he would speak very good French.

While Aristotle was ethnically Greek, many of his early influences were Turkish and he was always, essentially, a man of the Near East. The pashas of his youth still kept harems (they weren't abolished until 1927) and there were several in Smyrna. Prostitution was legal and the town had a prominent red-light district in Demiri Yolu. Aristotle grew up in a place and time where extra-marital sex was considered normal and unremarkable, especially among prominent men. Later in life, he would reminisce about the brass beds and brothels of Smyrna, along with the smell of civet and the feel of talcum powder. At the same time, he would have seen, riding at anchor outside the harbour, the splendid yacht of Mehmed VI, the last Ottoman Sultan. The notion that powerful men were surrounded by beautiful, subservient women and owned magnificent yachts, would remain with him for life.

By the age of twelve he was spending a few hours every day in the company offices or running errands for his father. At school, with his father's encouragement, he studied several languages but was, overall, a rebellious student who failed to graduate. The tumultuous political events of the early twentieth century would, however, dash all his parents' plans. No matter how secure and comfortable the Onassis household might have seemed, smouldering ethnic and political tensions were about to explode around them. The decay of empires can shake the world, and two had recently foundered: Austria-Hungary and the Ottoman Caliphate, neither of which survived the First World War. Relations between Greece and Türkiye had, anyway, been rancorous from 1830, the year in which Greece won its independence from the Ottomans. The two nations had already fought each other in the first Greco-Turkish War of 1897 and would fight again in the First Balkan War of 1912 to 1913.

Crucially, the Ottoman Empire backed the losing side in the First World War, and the aftermath would sweep away the old sultanate and the nation of Anatolia. During the hostilities the Greek Anatolians had publicly supported the Ottoman government when it joined the Central Powers of Germany, Austria-Hungary and Bulgaria. But this was mere lip service; secretly, they supported the Western Allies, especially Britain, France and, naturally, Greece. After the war the Turkish Nationalist Movement had emerged under the leadership of Mustafa Kemal Atatürk. He had been a Field Marshall during the fighting and had led the Turkish army to a crushing defeat of the Allies at the Battle of Gallipoli in 1915. Atatürk would later modernise and secularise Türkiye, but he would also continue a policy of Turkification which would contribute to genocide among the non-Turkish minorities. The holocaust had begun in 1915, under the Caliphate, when close to a million Armenians, mostly concentrated in eastern Anatolia, were rounded up and murdered, while others were forcibly converted to Islam.

The Gallipoli Campaign had convinced the Greek government that their long-held dream of a restored Greek Empire, with its capital in Constantinople, was in sight. Britain's wartime prime minister, Lloyd George, had offered Ottoman territory to Greece in exchange for their support, on the dubious grounds that Anatolia had been part of the ancient Greek and Byzantian empires. The result was the Greco-Turkish War of 1919–1922 in which Greek forces entered Smyrna and occupied most of western and north-western Anatolia. For the Onassis family, and other ethnic Greeks, this must have been a welcome intervention. For the first time in centuries, they were under Greek rule and no longer had to bow to their Turkish masters. It is doubtful, however, that they had any real presentiment of the horrors that lay before them following those three brief years of occupation.

The Greek invasion of Anatolia provoked a resurgence of nationalism in Türkiye and helped to sweep Atatürk and his Turkish Nationalist Movement into power. Turkish forces had checked the Greek army's advance by 1921, and defeated the Greeks altogether in 1922, finally driving them out of Smyrna in September of that year. When the crushed and demoralised Greeks retreated towards the coast, they began looting and murdering. As so often happens in war, their victims were rarely combatants but innocent civilians who were unable to flee. The advancing Turks came across villages where not a single house had been left standing, nor a single inhabitant left alive. By the time they reached Smyrna, they were determined to take revenge on not only the Greek army, but also the entire non-Turkish population.

As Smyrna fell, Turkish troops and irregulars began taking bloody recriminations against the Greeks and Armenians. In 1919–1922 the Greeks in Smyrna had numbered 150,000, forming just under half of the population and outnumbering the Turks by two to one.[4] Alongside Turks and Greeks, there were also sizeable Armenian, Jewish, and Levantine communities, but the genocide of 1922 would reduce the Greek population of the city to almost zero. Many of the wealthier Greeks, including Aristotle's uncle, Homer, saw the oncoming threat and fled while they could. For once, Socrates Onassis, who had balanced risk and security so carefully throughout his career, failed to see the danger. He held secret bank accounts in London and Geneva and could easily have escaped with enough money to start a new life, but he thought his friends in the Turkish hierarchy — carefully cultivated over many years — would protect him. He was wrong; the Onassis family were about to learn how quickly friendship can dissolve in the face of adversity. As Turkish troops entered Smyrna, they

THE BURNING OF SMYRNA

began to slaughter almost any Greek they came across. The retreating Greek army made little or no attempt to defend the city and their soldiers were evacuated as quickly as ships could take them away.

Many Greeks sought sanctuary in their churches but the buildings, often constructed of wood, were torched by Turkish soldiers who bayonetted anyone who tried to escape the flames. One of Aristotle's aunts, along with her husband and a child, died in this way. Other buildings were blown up and, when the wind changed to a south-easterly, more fires were lit causing an inferno which engulfed the Greek sections of the city but left Turkish areas largely intact. By the end of the first week of reoccupation more than 4,500 homes had been destroyed and 120,000 people had died. Those who were able to flee did so, and more than 1.5 million people became refugees.

Senior Turkish officers requisitioned grand houses for themselves, and the Onassis villa was taken over by a general. He knew Socrates Onassis's reputation and had read intelligence reports suggesting that he was a Greek sympathiser. Despite Socrates' protestations, he was fortunate to be sent to prison rather than summarily executed. Aristotle avoided jail because he was still a few weeks away from his seventeenth birthday, the age at which all Greek men were being sent to concentration camps.[5] Gethsemane, Helen and his three sisters were sent to evacuation camps to await transportation to Greece.

Over the next few months Aristotle Onassis, although still a young adolescent, showed the astonishing levels of opportunism, inventiveness, courage and sheer animal cunning that would make him one of the richest men on earth. Aristotle would later claim that, just a few days earlier, he had been preparing to leave Anatolia to become an undergraduate at Oxford University, but this seems unlikely as we know he was a poor student. Be that as it may, he now found himself and his family fighting to save their lives, never mind their property and fortune. In that moment he discovered he had a chameleon-like ability to adapt to changing circumstances, no matter how threatening, and it was to save not only his own life, but also that of his father and many members of his family. Although his education had been interrupted, he had already acquired one skill which, like his father, he would use masterfully throughout his life. He was fluent in four languages: Greek, Turkish, French, and English.

Another young man might have displayed only rage and hatred towards the officer who took his family's home and imprisoned his father. But Aristotle instantly understood that the best way, perhaps the *only* way to survive, was to make himself useful to the enemy. He offered to do household chores and run errands for the general and his *aide-de-camp* — a young lieutenant — explaining, in fluent Turkish, with the irresistible charm and humour that he had already developed, that the heating and plumbing were complicated, and he alone understood them.[6] The general agreed, allowing Aristotle to remain in the house and sending him back and forth across the city with messages and missions.[7]

This was more hazardous than it might sound: Greeks were still being summarily executed by roaming Turkish soldiers, and Atatürk had suspended capital punishment for the killing of Christians. On one assignment, while hiding in the grounds of the church in which his parents had been married, he witnessed the blinding and crucifixion of a Greek priest. Bodies lay in the streets, severed heads floated in the harbour and the stench of death was everywhere. Aristotle was literally risking his life every time he left the villa's grounds. One of his uncles had been publicly hanged and others sent to concentration camps.

Once again, his ingenuity came to the rescue. Atatürk had prohibited alcohol for his troops, but Aristotle managed to supply the officers living in his family's home with raki and ouzo and that made him valuable enough to be rewarded with a *laisser-passer*, complete with his photograph and fingerprints, giving him the legal right to move about the city unhampered. Better still, he made contact with the Vice-Consul of the United States, John L Parker — an old family friend — who gave him an entry pass to the US Marine Zone, the area around the partially burned-out US Consulate which was still subject to diplomatic protection. Here, Aristotle was shielded from even the most aggressive Turkish soldiers. With two safe passage documents and his best new suit, he began to look and act like a young official.

As soon as he was able to, he visited his father in prison. Socrates' position was desperate. Every night, Greek prisoners were being 'tried' before kangaroo courts. All were found guilty and immediately executed. With his newfound freedom, Aristotle was able to appeal to his father's many Turkish friends and try to persuade them to intervene. They did as much as they could, even agreeing to march to the prison in protest. Aristotle also managed to open two safes in his father's burned-out offices and recover thousands of Turkish pounds in cash; enough to bribe the prison guards to provide better food and avoid his father's immediate execution. The bulk of the family fortune, however, which had been held in Turkish banks, was permanently lost.

Father and son agreed that Aristotle should take as many members of the family as he could muster (about two dozen in all) to Athens and wait there for Socrates' release. From the safety of the US Marine Zone, he managed to board a ship to Lesbos, where he found his mother and sisters, and from there they travelled to Athens. He was unable, however, to reach his grandmother, Gethsemane, who made her own way to Piraeus, only to be waylaid by bandits outside the port and fatally injured. Aristotle was devastated: after his sister he had loved her more than anyone else. He spent that night praying in a small church and he would pay daily visits to her grave for as long as he remained in Greece.

Years later, he would recall having his fortune told at this low moment, when his circumstances were so wretched, and the future seemed so dismal. 'Western Europeans do it with tea leaves, but the Greeks use coffee grounds. One prediction was that my father would be released in a few weeks. Another was that I would have a dispute and go to the ends of the earth and do well there. Finally, the coffee grounds predicted that I would not marry for a long, long time. Every bit of it came true.'

In addition to his grandmother, the conflict had cost him three uncles and an aunt. With the remaining family safely settled in the Kifizia quarter of Athens, Aristotle took the significant risk of returning to Türkiye to try and secure his father's release, booking his passage on an Egyptian ship to Constantinople. As well as the money he had taken from safes in his father's office, he had been able to transfer the funds that his father had kept in secret bank accounts in London and Geneva. His total resources now came to roughly the equivalent of US $100,000 in today's money, but he was having to support a large extended family of some two dozen people. He took a substantial amount with him to Constantinople in cash, certain that only bribery, on a large scale, could secure his father's release. Using Socrates' connections he contacted the relevant government officials, eventually paying close to US $25,000, a quarter of his family's entire remaining wealth.

Socrates was pardoned and allowed to sail to Greece, arriving at almost the same time that Aristotle returned from Constantinople. We might imagine that the reunion was a happy one, given all that the two men had survived, but we would be wrong. Socrates was furious with Aristotle for having spent so much of the family's remaining fortune. He was convinced that his release was, in any case, imminent, and that Aristotle needed only to have waited. Today, it is difficult for us to be certain which of them was right, but it is also difficult not to sympathise with Aristotle, without whose courage and ingenuity Socrates might well have been executed and would almost certainly have stayed longer in prison. Wherever the truth may have lain, the rift between the two was never entirely healed. Neither fully forgave the other and, while they were never wholly estranged, they would not again be close.

Most men, sooner or later, will think that their father's feet are made of clay and, if only for a year or two, hold them in disdain. In family-owned businesses the transfer of power from one generation to the next is not always smooth, but for Aristotle and Socrates, the fissure was permanent. From that day they communicated as much as filial duty required, but there was little warmth. Sigmund Freud, the father of psychoanalysis, had earlier written, 'You wanted to kill your father in order to be your father yourself. Now you are your father, but a dead father.' Perhaps Socrates felt unmanned by his son's precocity, perhaps Aristotle was reluctant to give up his temporary role as head of the family, or perhaps Socrates had some genuine cause. Whatever the reason, Aristotle realised that he must now make his own future.

Life at home, also, took a turn for the worse. Rather than celebrating their narrow escape from death, the family immersed themselves in bitterness and recriminations. Unlike so many other Greek-speaking Anatolians, they had escaped with their lives and even a small part of their fortune, but they could only see the injustices they had suffered. They endlessly lamented the horrors of Smyrna, daily reducing themselves to anger and tears. Years later, Aristotle would say, '… nothing else, day after day. I was just seventeen and seventeen doesn't nurse its sorrows forever.' [8] Socrates hoped to rebuild his tobacco business in Athens, but Aristotle knew there was no longer a place for him. He began to look for work, but the arrival of 1.5 million refugees in a country whose population had only

THE BURNING OF SMYRNA

been 5 million caused massive unemployment, and Aristotle, anyway, had no professional qualifications.

Young evacuees with no hope of finding work in Greece were trying to emigrate in their tens of thousands. Even if they could afford the fares, the opportunities were limited because most of them were now stateless and without legal passports. Aristotle managed to obtain what was known as a Nansen passport. Named after the Norwegian statesman and polar explorer, Fridtjof Nansen, it was issued to stateless persons by the League of Nations. As a travel document, it was only good for a single journey between two countries, but it was enough to get him to Buenos Aires where, he believed, there would be better opportunities. Argentina, which had remained neutral during the First World War and was now enjoying an economic boom, was one of the few nations prepared to accept stateless Anatolians, and Aristotle decided to try his luck there. Thanks to huge exports of beef and grain, Argentina was then one of the ten wealthiest countries in the world. Throughout the early twentieth century Buenos Aires grew rapidly and absorbed waves of immigration from Italy, Spain, Greece and elsewhere. Today there are as many Italian surnames as there are Spanish and the locals still speak with an accent which has a distinctly Italian lilt.

With only $100, he sailed to Brindisi. The ferry called at Corfu and, for the first time, Aristotle saw and fell in love with the Ionian islands. Ambitious as he was, not even he could have imagined that one day he would own Skorpios, the beautiful island of just seventy-four acres whose green hills he would have seen from a distance as they approached Corfu.[9] From

Brindisi he took a train onwards to Naples, where he spent a few days in a squalid boarding house. Although he was not yet eighteen, he so charmed the landlady and her daughter that they tried to persuade him to stay in Italy. He was tempted, but his heart was now set on Argentina.

When he boarded the 12,000-ton *Tomasso di Savoia*, he found the conditions in steerage to be appalling. More than 1,000 Greek and Italian immigrants lay on pipes and wooden pallets without proper sanitation or even basic washing facilities. Aristotle had to bribe sailors just to be allowed onto the deck where there was an opportunity to wash in seawater. He would always remember the mournful wailing of the Italians as they saw their country's coast for the last time. He paid the ship's purser $5 for the privilege of sleeping in a chain locker on the deck, which was considerably more comfortable and healthier than the hellish conditions below.

He killed time by learning to speak Italian and practised on the Italian crew and some of the wealthier passengers; Aristotle's outgoing charm and affability never deserted him. By the time he landed in Buenos Aires on 23 September 1923, he had just $60 in his pocket. We can only guess at what filled his thoughts during the long sea crossing, but there can be little doubt that the boy who stepped ashore — still only eighteen years old — had formed a clear determination to be as successful, if not more so, than his now detached father. By a combination of inbred talent and intense personal experiences he was perfectly shaped to do so.

Today, we know more about what is known as post-traumatic stress disorder and its residue: flashbacks, nightmares, anxiety and insomnia. Those who've witnessed violent death, especially at a young age, may never entirely shake off its after-effects. Although Aristotle would soon gain an Argentinian passport and a new nationality he would, in all but the legal sense, remain stateless. For the rest of his life he would rove between the old and new worlds without truly settling in either, never trusting governments or officials and treating all of their laws (especially their taxes) with contempt. Seared by an internecine war and having witnessed unimaginable horrors, the lessons of a lifetime had been distilled into a few months. Such experiences rarely produce mediocrity and Ari, anyway, had inherited all his father's acumen and ambition, plus several unique gifts of his own. A turbocharged proto entrepreneur, still only eighteen, had arrived in a country of opportunity. Spectacular success or failure was now, perhaps, inevitable.

Aristotle Onassis experienced appalling conditions sailing to Buenos Aires aboard the 12,000-ton *Tomaso di Savoia*.

CHAPTER THREE

A Bad Omen

In December 1923, just months after Aristotle Onassis had landed in Buenos Aires, Maria Callas was born at the Flower Hospital on Fifth Avenue in Manhattan, New York. Her father had shortened the family surname of Kalogeropoulos to Kalos and eventually to Callas so that Americans could get their tongues around it. She was the third child of Greek immigrants who had arrived in July of that year and settled in the Greek neighbourhood of Astoria in Queens. Their first child, a daughter named Yakinthi (later shortened to Jackie), had been born in Athens in 1917, and a son, Vassilis, had arrived in 1920, but he died of meningitis in 1922.

It was not a happy marriage. Maria's mother, Litsa, was the daughter of a retired general in the Greek army who considered George Kalogeropoulos, a small-town pharmacist, to be beneath his daughter. 'You will never be happy with him. If you marry that man, I will never be able to help you.'[10] Although his parents were poor peasant farmers, George owned his own pharmacy, and the family were moderately well-off; able to afford servants and luxuries. He was, however, a serial philanderer, and the marriage quickly broke down, aggravated by the death of their second child. The decision to emigrate to New York

A BAD OMEN

when Litsa was five-months pregnant had caused a blazing row. Litsa said that only paupers emigrated, but George was determined. Greek-speaking refugees, including the Onassis family, were pouring into Greece from Türkiye and George believed that his son's disease had been brought into the country by immigrants. Litsa, however, thought it was divine retribution for George getting the mayor of Meligalas's daughter pregnant. They arrived in New York to flags at half-mast on the day that President Warren G Harding died. Litsa immediately burst into tears, convinced it was a bad omen.[11]

Litsa was deeply superstitious, and an astrologer had told her that her third child would be Vassilis reincarnated. When a girl arrived, she was bitterly disappointed and refused to even look at the infant for several days. Circumstances at home were deteriorating. George was struggling to learn English and had taken work as a lowly shop assistant in a pharmacy for a salary that barely covered their living expenses. They moved continually from one apartment to another, at ever lower rentals. They finally settled in a working-class Greek neighbourhood where Litsa considered the neighbours to be beneath her and refused to speak to them. She became deeply depressed and even attempted suicide by taking poison. This led to her being briefly committed to a psychiatric hospital. Throughout this period, she completely failed to bond with her new daughter.

From the earliest age Maria would have known that her father was a womaniser who was daily berated by her mother. Her chaotic upbringing meant she was continually moved to new homes and new schools.

She had few friends because her mother reviled the neighbours, and Litsa's frequent mood swings and episodes of mental illness further destabilised the home. When Maria cried or lied, her mother put pepper on her lips to silence her. Her older sister, Jackie, equally unhappy, would attempt suicide at the age of ten. From this improbable background (less promising even than Aristotle's) would emerge *La Divina*, arguably the greatest and certainly the most celebrated soprano of the twentieth century. But then, as with Aristotle, nothing about her was probable, conventional or predictable.

As a young woman she was obese, myopic and awkward. While not conventionally beautiful, her looks were dramatic: she had huge expressive eyes set wide apart, a large protruding nose, an unusually round face and bulbous skull with a wide expressive mouth. But, on stage, with good make-up and lighting, her eyes burned and glittered, while her mouth could express a hundred emotions in a single performance. She would become a great prima donna in every sense: tempestuous and unpopular with colleagues backstage but worshipped by opera-lovers across the world. Audiences of the era had become used to singers whose 'acting' amounted to little more than three or four gestures. Operas had become, in many cases, little more than concerts in costume. Callas, however, could inject a level of sincerity and passion into her performances that left the public believing she had lived every word of the libretto. The film director, Pier Paolo Pasolini would say, 'She is the only actress who can express, even without acting and without saying a word, spiritual catastrophe.'[12]

A BAD OMEN

Her legend has endured to our times. As recently as 2006, *Opera News* wrote: 'Nearly thirty years after her death, she's still the definition of the diva as artist — and still one of classical music's best-selling vocalists.'

Her father found work as a travelling salesman, meaning he was away from home a lot, and that reduced the arguments and removed some of the tension. For all his faults, Maria idolised him. 'I always sided with my father,' she later said. 'I was his favourite when I was a child … or maybe always.'[13]

George managed to borrow enough money to open a pharmacy of his own in Hell's Kitchen, but the Wall Street Crash and subsequent Great Depression forced its closure after only a few months. Maria had begun to show an early aptitude for music: she taught herself arias and sang them well enough to attract a crowd below her window. Before long, a Swedish neighbour had offered to give her free singing lessons. Litsa, sensing that Maria might be genuinely gifted, took her to a local talent contest where she won second prize. From that day, realising that Maria's flair could be an escape from penury, Litsa pressed her daughter into a strict daily regime of voice training, music lessons and contests. Maria deeply resented what she saw as the loss of her childhood, later saying, 'Children should have a wonderful childhood. I had not had it. I wish I could have.'[14]

By 1937, Litsa had taken her daughters to Greece in the hope of enrolling Maria as a student in the Athens Conservatoire. 'In Greece,' she later said, 'I again became Maria Kalogeropoulous.'[15] George raised no objection to his wife and daughters leaving America while he remained in New York. Litsa had almost no money and had to take an unfurnished apartment where the girls slept on the floor. Maria, who was only thirteen, was rejected by the Conservatoire at her first attempt. Her mother added three years to her age and, eventually, persuaded the newer and slightly less prestigious National Conservatory of Athens, to accept Maria. There she was tutored by Maria Trivella, who agreed to coach her for no fee, believing that Callas was not a contralto, as she had been told, but a natural dramatic soprano. As Trivella later recalled, 'The tone of the voice was warm, lyrical, intense; it swirled and flared like a flame ... It was by any standards an amazing phenomenon, or rather it was a great talent that needed control, technical training and strict discipline in order to shine with all its brilliance.'[16] Trivella also discovered that Maria, in addition to her natural talent, had two of the other key ingredients for success: iron discipline and a willingness to work extremely hard. 'She was a model student. Fanatical, uncompromising, dedicated to her studies heart and soul. Her progress was phenomenal. She studied five or six hours a day ... Within six months, she was singing the most difficult arias in the international opera repertoire with the utmost musicality.'[17]

After two years Maria successfully auditioned at the Athens Conservatoire, where she was tutored by Elvira de Hidalgo, who had been a famous soprano herself. De Hidalgo immediately recognised Maria's potential and was, perhaps, the first principal figure in the world of opera to see that she genuinely had the makings of a great singer.

Money remained a pressing problem until Litsa pressurised her other daughter, Jackie, into an affair

A BAD OMEN

with an older, wealthy man. This deeply affected Maria, who accused her mother of literally selling her daughter's virginity. Additionally, just as global events had shaped Aristotle's character from a young age, so they would now touch Maria's. In October 1940, the Italian army invaded Greece through Albania. The Greeks fought back with great tenacity and held the invasion just inside Greek territory. But, by 1941, Germany had intervened on behalf of its Axis ally. The Greek and British forces were overwhelmed, and Greece was occupied by Bulgarian, German and Italian troops.

The Callas family were now cut off with no possibility of returning to America until the end of hostilities. Considered to be non-Greek citizens, they were forbidden to travel outside Athens without a permit. For the first few months Maria continued her lessons at Hidalgo's apartment, receiving distinctions in her exams. Athens suffered the coldest winter for decades and, under occupation, there were soon shortages of almost everything. By 1942 Athenians were starving and 30,000 would die of hunger. Jackie's lover kept the Callas family supplied with occasional packages of black-market food, without which they too might have starved.

Although the family had risked their lives to help escaping British officers, Litsa had an affair with an Italian colonel. She also regularly 'entertained' Italian soldiers at her home, and there seems little doubt that the 'entertainment' included sex. Maria discovered that she could get food from the Italians by simply crying, but there is no evidence she ever did more than cry. She did, however, agree to sing at concerts for

Italian and German soldiers, leading to accusations of fraternisation with the enemy. At this time and, perhaps, because of the 'entertainment', Maria's dislike for her mother turned to loathing and never changed.

In spite of all these trials, by 1942 Maria had taken her first leading role in a professional opera, *Tosca*, followed by Marta in Eugen d'Albert's *Tiefland* at the Olympia Theatre. The reviews were ecstatic and one leading critic wrote: 'Kalogeropoulous is one of those God-given talents that one can only marvel at.' When Greece was liberated, Hidalgo advised to her to go to Italy and build her career from there. Maria, however, who was now twenty-one years old, decided to return to her father in New York, from where she successfully auditioned for the Metropolitan Opera. They were astonished when she turned down both the parts they offered, preferring to appear in a production of *Turandot* which was intended to mark the reopening of the Chicago Opera. The company, however, folded before the first performance.

For two years she hardly worked, but by 1947 she had made her Italian debut as *La Gioconda* at the Arena di Verona under the music director, Maestro Tullio Serafin, the most influential conductor of the twentieth century. She accepted a fee of just $63 for each of three performances with no expenses or travel costs. Lord Harewood, who met her at that time, recalled, 'She was determined, ambitious, and a little uncertain about the way to go about it, and about how one should behave with people who might be able to help her career. I think that was always a part of her. She wasn't an innocent, simple person, I think she had an eye to the main chance.'

A BAD OMEN

Maria Callas with her husband and manager, Giovanni Battista Meneghini.

Further offers of work did not immediately follow, but, while in Verona, she met a wealthy businessman and opera fan named Giovanni Battista Meneghini. Short, round, physically unattractive and with few interests other than opera and women, he was twenty-eight years older than her and had inherited a substantial building business along with several brick factories. Apart from a certain charm with females he was, in almost every other sense, an unprepossessing man and an unlikely partner, but Maria did not hesitate. 'I knew he was *it* five minutes after I met him,' she later recalled.

Girls who are close to their fathers and distant with their mothers sometimes choose older partners, preferring their experience and savoir-faire to youthful looks and vitality. Even so, Meneghini was a startlingly unusual choice for a young and ambitious singer, especially as he was far from overwhelmed by her. He later wrote, 'When she was seated she didn't seem that large, even though she was solid and well set, but when she stood up, I was moved to pity. Her lower extremities were deformed. Her ankles were swollen to the size of calves. She moved awkwardly and with effort.'[18] Maria confided in him that she believed Verona was her last chance for success and that if she failed there, her career in opera would be over.

She was far from the first opera singer he had pursued. What he immediately recognised in Maria, however, was the vehicle by which he could vicariously shake the world of opera. Like her mother, Litsa, he saw that he could create his own destiny through Maria. He sold his businesses and became not only her husband, but also her manager, impresario, financial advisor, mentor and confidant. Over and above those things — and most important of all — he was her security, both emotional and financial: a sheet anchor to steady her following a volatile and unhappy childhood and an investor with enough money to ensure she got the best possible shot at stardom. She showered him with love letters which he kept for the rest of his life, reading them aloud to anyone who doubted her feelings for him. He was a tough and ruthless negotiator and, like Aristotle, a clever manipulator of whatever circumstances he found himself in. Maria, as her tutors had already discovered, had an iron will to succeed and an infinite capacity for hard work. She learnt to speak both Italian and French fluently and her weight fell by half. The change was so dramatic that people joked about

A BAD OMEN

Maria Callas on the opening night of Verdi's *Don Carlos* at La Scala on 12 April 1954.

two post-war miracles: the German economy and the Callas waistline. Meneghini persuaded Tullio Serafin to coach her, and the maestro developed her voice from dramatic soprano to unlimited soprano, making her range almost unique.

As partners, they would strive tirelessly for the next decade with a single purpose: to turn Maria Callas into opera's hottest property. In 1949, she agreed, at only five days' notice, to replace another singer at Venice's La Fenice in the role of Elvira in Bellini's *I puritani*. Serafin coached her day and night to produce a performance which became a triumph and the turning point of her career. She later recalled, 'What I learned from Serafin was that you must serve music because music is so enormous, and can envelop you into such a state of perpetual anxiety and torture, but it is our first and main duty. He always found a reason for something. When one wants to find a gesture, when you want to find how to act on stage, all you have to do is listen to the music with your soul and your ears. The composer has already thought of that.'[19] As her popularity grew, another advantage came into play: she was not managed by a traditional agent. At that time, the established agents cut deals with opera houses: 'If you want this star to perform for you, you must also accept a dozen other singers that we have on our books.' Meneghini only represented Callas; managers no longer had to sign a long list of mediocrities to attract one prima donna.

Later, in that same year, she met Luchino Visconti, who saw her on stage in the role of Kundry in *Parsifal* at the Teatro dell'Opera di Roma. Visconti was a wealthy and good-looking aristocrat who was already building a reputation as a filmmaker. His 1943 movie, *Ossessione*, is credited with being the first Italian neorealist film and by the 1960s Visconti would be lauded as a giant of Italian art and culture. He loved opera and theatre, directed both, and was so taken by Callas that he literally followed her from theatre to theatre. They met for the first time in Serafin's home where she sang for him, and he was immediately captivated. In 1954 he directed her in Spontini's *La Vestale* at La Scala, and five further operas during Callas's golden years; these are still considered to be among her finest performances. She was already a great singer, but it was from him that she learned to become a great actress. His technique with her, as with many of the actresses he worked with, was

A BAD OMEN

seductive and there is little doubt that he and Callas had an affair. She later told friends that there was not much intimacy between her and Meneghini; she had tried to conceive, even taking fertility treatment, but with no result. When rumours surfaced, Meneghini claimed Maria found Visconti vulgar, but, by all other accounts, she adored him.

By 1956, Meneghini and Callas had achieved their dreams. She had been carried shoulder-high by cheering crowds in Genoa, earned solo curtain calls by the score, become the Queen of La Scala, owned the roles of Tosca and Norma, and even conducted a public feud with the other celebrated soprano of the day, Renato Tebaldi, whose voice she compared to Coca-Cola, while likening her own to champagne!

Her backstage quarrels were fabled and Meneghini, who was also petulant and argumentative by nature, often exacerbated her disputes with tantrums of his own. He guided her into unforced errors, involving her in unnecessary squabbles and even legal battles. She would end press interviews at the mildest suggestion that she was temperamental and, more than once, walked out of a performance after the first act, claiming to be unwell.[20] Antonio Ghiringhelli, the general manager of La Scala, loathed her and refused to book her until she became so famous he had no choice. The Metropolitan Opera's Rudolf Bing 'cancelled' her contract — a euphemism for firing her — but when she returned in 1965, fans queued day and night for tickets that instantly sold out. Maria Callas had become not only the most celebrated diva of her age but, arguably, of any age. Henceforth, opera would be divided into two distinct eras — BC and AC — before and after Callas.

CHAPTER FOUR
A Country of Opportunity

In the days following Maria Callas's birth, after a brief stay with an elderly cousin whose lack of hygiene he found intolerable, Aristotle Onassis moved into a cheap boarding house in Buenos Aires and set about learning to speak Spanish. A natural linguist, he quickly mastered it and began to search for work. Initially, he could only find temporary odd jobs as a dishwasher or casual labourer, until he heard that the British United River Plate Telephone Company, a subsidiary of the gigantic International Telephone and Telegraph (today's ITT Inc.), was hiring. He got an interview and his natural charm and nascent Spanish immediately led to an offer. Buenos Aires' telephone system was being modernised and he received three weeks' training as a technician. He learnt quickly and worked hard. With overtime, his salary soon rose to $40 per week, enough to live comfortably and save.

Aristotle was a good oarsman, he'd been a schoolboy champion, and he now widened his social connections by joining L'Aviron, a yachting and rowing club. He also developed a liking and skill for poker which he would sharpen over the years. One of his Greek friends remarked, 'The only time you know what Onassis has got in his hand is when he goes to the can!'

We can be certain that he had resolved, at an early point, not to marry until his status assured a trophy bride, but he was far from celibate. The seduction skills he had acquired so early in life were now honed to perfection. Never good-looking, Aristotle used charm, humour, self-confidence and a preternatural insight into the vulnerabilities of his conquests to deadly effect. He also indulged a taste for the *demi-monde* which would remain with him for life. His first experiences with prostitutes had been in Demiri Yolu, Smyrna's red-light district.[21] Argentina, like Türkiye, had a relaxed attitude towards the sex trade. Until 1936, Buenos Aires had legal, regulated prostitution. 'Prostitutes occupied an important role in national literature and theatre plays; they were part of popular sociability and took centre stage in stories about broken hearts.'[22] This was the city that a few decades earlier had produced the tango, the erotically charged dance which emerged from the brothels and bars combining the influences of Africa, Spain and Latin America. By the early twentieth century it had reached Europe, becoming a craze in London, Paris and Berlin. The nightclubs, bordellos and burlesques of Buenos Aires became regular haunts for Aristotle, who needed little sleep, getting by on as little as three to four hours per night. Prostitutes would always be part of his life. Even in his final years, when meeting his official biographer, Peter Evans, in Parisian restaurants or bars, he would be accompanied by friends including his *aide-de-camp*, Johnny Meyer, and more often than not, one of Madame Claude's call girls.[23]

A less aspiring man might have comfortably settled into the dull but secure routine of an undemanding job; the day-to-day ennui brightened by thoughts of modest promotions and a distant pension. Aristotle, however, boiled with ambition and always had a weather eye on the main chance. It arrived sooner than even he might have imagined: a vacancy appeared for a night time telephone operator at a busy city exchange. Because the hours — 11 pm until 7 am — were deeply unsocial, there were few candidates and Aristotle's application, boosted by his skill in languages, was accepted. Preparation had just collided with opportunity at a crucial moment, and the incipient tycoon was on his way.

At that time, long distance and international telephone calls were booked through the operator. Because the calls were extremely expensive the callers were usually businessmen trying to seal important deals. Aristotle had little to occupy him during the long, uneventful nights and he frequently listened to the conversations. Because he was now fluent in Spanish and five other languages, he rarely had any difficulty understanding them. He soon became the best-informed aspiring young businessman in the city. Today, we would call such eavesdropping 'industrial espionage', but there were no such inhibitions in 1920s Buenos Aires. He began to make small investments on the Buenos Aires Stock Exchange and, with the benefit of inside knowledge, he rarely lost money.

Additionally, the wages he earned from long hours of overtime meant his savings quickly came to more than $1,000: a lot of money at that time. He developed a taste for expensive clothes, and, by day, could pass himself off as substantially more than a mere telephone operator.[24] With a combination of charm, persistence and confidential information, he was soon doing business deals of his own. Unsurprisingly and somewhat cautiously, his first choice was the industry in which his father had already made a fortune and the young Aristotle had been groomed.

Turkish tobacco — a highly aromatic, small-leafed variety — had been cultivated and refined by the Ottomans over centuries. Sun-cured and sweet, it was ideal for cigarette production. Socrates Onassis was one of the most successful exporters, and by the early 1900s, Turkish tobacco was popular in the United States, especially in the hand-rolled Murad cigarettes of the New York-based Greek tobacconist Soterios Anargyros. Aristotle swallowed his pride and asked his father to send him samples. Socrates agreed to bury the hatchet and dispatched the tobacco in the care of two of Aristotle's cousins, Nicolas and Constantine Konialides. Their father had been killed in the 1922 holocaust and both would settle in South America and become his long-term business partners.

He began to call on local tobacco importers. At first, he had no luck, as the buyers would not see an unknown Anatolian refugee with no bona fides; but persistence and unquenchable optimism were among his character traits. He waited for hours outside the offices of Nobleza Piccardo, one of the two biggest Argentinian cigarette manufacturers, until he saw a chance to approach the President, Juan Gaono. Aristotle's natural charm led to an appointment with the chief buyer, and he won his first order, for about $10,000 in today's money.

Within two years Turkish tobacco would account for thirty-five per cent of the Argentinian market.

Aristotle did not, immediately, give up his job as a telephone operator. He no longer needed the money, but the inside information was invaluable. One night he overheard a telephone conversation about a forthcoming movie in which a woman would smoke, on screen, for the first time. In the United States, until the 1920s, it was considered shocking for women to smoke in public and could even lead to a warning from the police. But the First World War had seen females working in factories where smoking was allowed. After the war, American tobacco companies had begun to exploit the burgeoning women's movement by producing new brands labelled 'torches for women'. Aristotle decided to start making cigarettes himself and opened a shop in partnership with his cousin Constantine Konialides. They produced their own brands of hand-rolled cigarettes: Osmans and Primeros. Tipped with rose petals and wrapped in gold foil, these luxury brands were carefully targeted at the emerging female market.

Such a product needs publicising, and few things work better than a celebrity endorsement. The most famous woman in Argentina, at that time, was the Italian soprano, Claudia Muzio, whose regular appearances at the Teatro Colón (then and now a world-renowned opera house), always sold out. Buenos Aires was known as 'the Paris of the South', and the city was passionate about the arts, especially opera and ballet. Muzio's signature role, in which she was thought to be unsurpassed, was Violetta in Verdi's *La Traviata*. Critics, in Europe and North

A COUNTRY OF OPPORTUNITY

America, had hinted that her gestures were a little too theatrical, her pianissimo a shade too energetic, but there were no such reservations in Buenos Aires. Seventeen years older than Aristotle, she was then in her mid-forties; a short and plump woman with looks that were striking rather than beautiful. As a soprano, however, she was in her prime and the porteños loved her, dubbing her 'La Divina Claudia'. [25] [26] [27]

After a performance, Aristotle arrived at her dressing room with an enormous bouquet of red roses. Another businessman might have offered her money and a generous contract, but Aristotle, who was barely half her age, had an altogether different technique: he seduced her and made her his mistress. She agreed to endorse his cigarettes, frequently smoking them in public, and the increase in sales made him a millionaire. He was still only twenty-three years old. Much later in his career he would explain his technique to a journalist: 'I approach every woman as a potential mistress. Beautiful women cannot bear moderation; they need an inexhaustible supply of excess.' [28] Flirting was second nature to him; throughout his life he would call almost any woman either 'honey' or 'my darling', always flattering her, always making her feel that she was the centre of his attention, always showering lavish gifts on the ones who responded. It was the beginning of a lifelong fascination with some of the world's most famous women. Decades later — following his engagement to Jacqueline Kennedy — Aristotle's son, Alexander, would say to his sister, Christina, 'It's a perfect match. Our father loves names and Jackie loves money.'

The majority of entrepreneurs, including the most

successful, work in a field they know and rarely venture out of it. Having done so well from tobacco, Aristotle could, as his father had done, have prudently remained within an industry he understood, but it was never part of his character to be over-cautious. He began to trade in other commodities, in particular cereals, wool, salt and hides. Such was his acumen that he made money from nearly all of them, especially whale oil, which was exceptionally profitable. He had a remarkable eye for detail and was a quick study. If those gifts weren't enough, he also had a near photographic memory and, in an age before calculators, could do complicated mathematical calculations in his head. Later in his career, when his investments were spread across scores of corporations and had become very complex, his accountants would be astonished at how much detail he could accurately recall without notes or reminders.

Since the dawn of civilisation merchants have made money by moving essential commodities from one place to another. The profits can be large but so are the hazards: goods can decompose, devalue or be lost altogether; and delays can easily turn profit into loss. It takes a steady nerve and a deep understanding of the nature of risk to prosper, but Aristotle had both. Among the many attributes required by a successful entrepreneur the most important is, arguably, tolerating greater perils than most of us would be comfortable with. In fact, for the most successful of all, it is probably more than mere acceptance: without chance and fortune they would be unbearably bored. There was no such problem for Aristotle, especially as he had been blessed with one more important attribute: he was a workaholic who needed little sleep and could thrive on a schedule that would have killed most others. Colleagues of his have claimed that he could work for up to forty-eight or even seventy-two hours at a time, and then recover by sleeping for fourteen hours in one stretch. The converse of these phenomenal talents was that he suffered from depression (today, we might say that he was bi-polar) and hypochondria throughout his life. This was a man who knew, from an early age, all the peaks and troughs an adventurous life can offer.

As soon as he became wealthy, he acquired habits that would stay with him for the rest of his life. Rather than buying a house or grand apartment, he moved into a suite at the Plaza, the most luxurious hotel in Buenos Aires, and ate his meals in the finest restaurants. He liked to get drunk and often unleashed his temper, which was volcanic, on unfortunate waiters who had to endure his tirades, sometimes accompanied by smashed crockery. His lifestyle was both sumptuous and transient; he put down no roots and could move on in a moment. Always conscious of his outsider status, he quickly discovered that, despite his new wealth, the *premier rang* of Buenos Aires society remained a closed door. This rejection by the *haut monde* would, throughout his life, be one of the spurs which drove him from one achievement to the next. In those early Buenos Aires years, for example, despite having little genuine interest in the performing arts, he attended all the operas and ballets at Teatro Colón in the hope of widening his social connections. He would later admit to his official biographer, Peter Evans, 'I hate the opera, I must have a tin ear. No matter how hard I concentrate it always sounds like a bunch of Italian chefs screaming risotto recipes at each other.'[29]

When Claudia Muzio returned to Europe, he began a new affair with a dancer from the Anna Pavlova Swan Ballet. Pavlova was then the world's most celebrated prima ballerina and the first to tour the world with her own company. One of her young Russian dancers became so infatuated with Aristotle that she refused to leave Buenos Aires when the company moved on. Pavlova herself went to see Aristotle and told him, 'You're a deeply wicked, wicked young man. You don't know the difference between right and wrong!'

'There is no right and wrong,' he laconically replied, 'there is only what is possible.' The affair lasted a year before he tired of her, but the philosophy remained with Aristotle for the rest of his life.

As Aristotle's wealth grew, he thought more about the vessels which carried his goods and the irksome fact that shipowners often made more money from his trades than he did. For an ethnic Greek, his next venture did not require a huge leap of imagination. Greece has been a maritime nation since classical times. The country — which was at the crossroads of the ancient world — is mountainous with limited farmland, but its long coast and many islands host a myriad of ports and safe anchorages.[30] Greeks have been canny shipowners from the Bronze Age to the present day and in the 1920s their influence was growing. Today, the Greek merchant fleet is still the largest in the world. The Onassis family would always have known that most of the richest people in Greece either owned, or were connected to, fleets of ships.

A COUNTRY OF OPPORTUNITY

Aristotle became friends with the prominent Buenos Aires-based shipowner Alberto Dodero. The son of an Italian immigrant, Dodero had built his father's modest shipping business into the biggest line in South America, becoming fabulously rich in the process. At the end of the First World War he borrowed $10 million to buy 148 war surplus ships from the United States and, as the Argentinian economy boomed, resold them for a spectacular profit. By the beginning of the Second World War he owned a fleet of more than 300 ships and was earning close to $6 million per year, the equivalent of billions in today's money. As well as a lot of specialised knowledge and some useful tips, Aristotle may have acquired some of his later extravagance from his friend. Dodero's spending was legendary: when holidaying on the French Riviera he was estimated to have outlaid upwards of $50,000 per season entertaining his companions, while his gifts to politicians included diamonds and Rolls-Royces. His yacht and aircraft were among the largest to be privately owned at that time and his homes in Buenos Aires, Montevideo, New York, London, Paris and Cannes were little short of palaces. It was Dodero who first nicknamed Aristotle *Ari*, rather than Aristo, as he had been known since childhood, and the name stuck.[31]

Aristotle's first maritime investment was cautious but, potentially, highly profitable. New vessels were still beyond him, but old or broken-down ones were a different matter. He took a short boat trip across the River Plate to Montevideo, to see a small, stricken tanker which lay half-sunk in the harbour. On Dodero's advice, he bought the wreck for a song, intending to quickly re-float and repair her before selling to a new owner at a handsome profit. The renovations took months and went hugely over budget. Worse still, once complete, the vessel promptly sank for the second time. Aristotle lost a lot of money but was undeterred. At the age of twenty-three — only six years after arriving in Argentina as a penniless and stateless refugee — he had become the continent's youngest shipowner; a path from which he would never look back.

The celebrated Italian soprano Claudia Muzio, was one of many famous women to be seduced by Aristotle Onassis.

CHAPTER FIVE
Pater Familias

Although he had built his tobacco importing business with invaluable help from his father, and both had profited from it, Aristotle was now substantially the wealthier of the two and had become, *de facto*, patriarch of a large extended family which he supported financially. As he would later recall, 'By then, they were asking me, *from Athens*, who should marry whom and where the boys should go to school. For my father to live long enough to see that has given me more satisfaction than any other achievement in my whole life.'[32] We can be certain that his satisfaction was, if only in part, a payback for the earlier quarrel. Aristotle well understood that wealth bought stature and power as well as luxury.

In 1929 his father became ill, and Aristotle returned to Greece for the first time since his departure as a teenager. The reunion with his family must have had a vastly different tone to their parting. This voyage, however, was inspired by more than a simple family get-together. Aristotle had crucial business to settle with the Greek government. Greece had imposed stiff import duties on countries with which it had no trade agreement, including Argentina. In the best tradition of trade wars, the Argentinians had responded by imposing eye-watering duties on imports from

Greece and Aristotle's business was now threatened. In the weeks to come he would spend many fruitless hours in the anterooms of Greek ministers and functionaries, unable to penetrate beyond junior or middle-ranking officials. This was not Buenos Aires, where he was already well-connected. In Athens, he was just another businessman, and — for all his Greek heritage — a twenty-three-year-old foreigner and former refugee for whom the corridors of power were firmly closed.

For once, all of Aristotle's charm, cunning and persuasiveness failed him, and it was his father who saved the day. Socrates, who understood the value of networking as well as his son, had tirelessly courted the highest ranks of Greek government from the moment of his arrival, seven years earlier. Among his many acquaintances was Eleftherios Venizelos, the legendary Greek prime minster who had returned to power a year before. As leader of the Liberal Party, he would be prime minster eight times in all, and is still remembered as 'the Maker of Modern Greece', or 'the Ethnarch'. Crucially, he had been instrumental in bringing his country into the First World War on the side of the Allies. Although this brought huge benefits to Greece, following the Allied victory, it also caused a national schism, polarising the nation between Royalists — who had supported the Axis — and Venizelists. In 1929, Venizelos, then sixty-five years old, was set on normalising relations with foreign countries and pushing through economic reforms.

Socrates, by what means we can only guess, connived a meeting between Venizelos and his son, during which Aristotle charmed and coaxed the old

PATER FAMILIAS

statesman, convincing him that if Greece lifted the duties, Argentina would follow suit. As is often the way in politics, the prime minister took no firm decision on the matter, preferring to send a note to his long-time political ally, Andreas Michalakopoulos — then minister of foreign affairs — suggesting a meeting with Aristotle.[33] It was a huge leap forward, but the issue was far from concluded. Michalakopoulos made it clear he would not be easily persuaded, and made Aristotle wait a full two weeks for the meeting. When it finally took place, after the obligatory long interval in an anteroom, he humbled Aristotle by feigning boredom and sat languidly behind his Louis Quinze desk, casually filing his nails as the young businessman pleaded his case.

We only have Aristotle's account of what followed, and that may be fanciful. Towards the end of his life, he would admit to his chosen biographer, Peter Evans, 'I will sometimes lie to you, but Costa will always tell you the truth.'[34][35] At this moment, however, he claims to have lost his temper, jumped up and thundered at the minister, 'I had hoped you would give some practical consideration to a very desperate situation, but you really haven't listened to anything I have talked about. You're more interested in your nails than Greek commerce!' Allegedly, Michalakopoulos asked him to sit down again, offered him a cigar and began to listen attentively. Aristotle would later recall, 'I walked out of that office knowing two things I didn't know when I went in. I knew I had what it takes, and that one day I was going to have a Louis Quinze desk.'[36]

Wherever the truth lies, it is a fact that by the time

Aristotle returned to Argentina he had been made an Envoy Extraordinary of Greece, a rank which enabled him to negotiate a new and much better trade deal between the two countries. By October of that year, he was the Greek Consul General in Buenos Aires. For the rest of his life, he would cleverly and seamlessly combine politics with business, usually profiting hugely from both. From this moment, he would always be more than a simple entrepreneur: he was now a man with real and growing political clout on both sides of the Atlantic.

The importance of his new role as Consul General cannot be overstated. No Greek ship making landfall at Buenos Aires (and there were around a thousand a year) could discharge her passengers or cargo until Aristotle and his assistants had approved the necessary paperwork. Neither could any dispute or strike involving a Greek vessel be resolved without his input. He was not slow to exploit the cornucopia of opportunities his new status presented. The harbour proved to be an infinitely better listening post than the telephone exchange had been. There was little, if anything, that could now move in or out of Argentina without Aristotle knowing every detail. In time, he would appoint one of his cousins as Consul General and persuade the Argentine government to grant him a diplomatic passport. He could now travel anywhere without the need for visas or compliance with any customs or immigration procedures.

While the first rank of society may still have been closed to him, the highest levels of government were not. His new status meant that he was invited to

PATER FAMILIAS

state banquets and other events where he had access to President Hipólito Yrigoyen and his ministers.

Despite working gruellingly long hours, his ability to survive on little sleep meant that he always had time for nightspots. At one of them, he met the man who would become his closest friend, collaborator and confidant: Constantine (Costa) Gratsos. A member of the ship-owning Dracoulis family, Costa had been groomed in the intricacies of maritime trade since birth, was a graduate of the London School of Economics, and had even served at sea. Aristotle now had a business partner who knew a great deal more about ships than he did. It was, perhaps, the last vital piece in an elaborate jigsaw. For the immediate future, tobacco would remain the mainstay of Aristotle's business, but, from this point on, his hopes and dreams lay in ships.[37]

Ship-owning is a very high-risk activity. Freight rates are not, as a rule, fixed or controlled by governments and they can fluctuate wildly in less time than it takes a vessel to sail from one port to another. World events, whether political or natural, can send prices rocketing in one direction or another and in wholly unpredictable ways. The first requirements for any shipowner, are nerves of steel, along with finely tuned commercial and political antennae, and a readiness to make rapid decisions which cannot easily be reversed.

In October 1929, just as Aristotle began to invest in cargo vessels, Wall Street crashed, sparking the longest, deepest and most widespread economic depression of the industrial age. Over the next three years, economic output (Gross Domestic Product) would fall by fifteen per cent, while international trade was cut almost in half.[38] By way of comparison, during the recession of 2008–2009, worldwide GDP fell by less than one per cent.[39] This was the catastrophic state of world affairs in which Aristotle and Costa were trying to build a shipping line. But Aristotle had already survived a bloodbath in Smyrna, and a trade war between his old home and his present one. Once again, his nerve held. Most investors would have taken flight, but he saw only opportunity. The price of cargo ships which had previously been out of his reach would now, he reasoned, fall to fire sale prices. If he bought wisely and waited for freight markets to recover, he would make a fortune.

In 1931 his father, who had been suffering from acute angina for several years, died of a heart attack, and Aristotle made a brief return to Athens for his funeral. From there, he travelled to London where, for the first time, he met many of the other leading shipowners of the day, including Stavros Livanos, André Embiricos, and Manuel Kulukundis. Although they were his fiercest competitors, these men formed a loose fraternity which Aristotle joined. From them, he heard about an opportunity in Montreal.

The Canadian National Steamship Company, like so many other lines, was facing bankruptcy. A fleet of modern medium-sized cargo vessels (8,500–10,000 tons), which had cost more than $1 million each to build, was rusting at its moorings while the company tried to find a buyer. The world, at that moment, was full of ships, but there was precious little cargo. Following engineers' reports, Aristotle focused on six which were still in excellent condition. Experts had valued them at around $100,000 each but Aristotle,

PATER FAMILIAS

Aristotle Onassis at the age of twenty-six.

sensing an opportunity for a killing, offered just $20,000 per ship: their scrap metal value. It was an audacious bid, but he knew they had been on the market for two years without an offer and the owners were now desperate. The directors feigned insult and held out for a day or two, but finally gave in. There were no other offers and both sides knew that a liquidator, if appointed, would take the only money on the table. Aristotle had made a spectacular gamble which could easily have bankrupted him, and nearly did. He had bought the vessels imagining the world had reached the bottom of the Depression and that freight rates would soon recover. In fact, many parts of the global economy would not begin to recover until the advent of the Second World War. He would have to wait a further two years before finding a single consignment for his ships and be forced to sell four of them (at a profit) before he did so. He named the remaining two the SS *Calliroy* and *Antiope*.

The cargo drought was finally broken when the London *Daily Mail* chartered one of his vessels to bring a cargo of newsprint from Canada to London.

In the early 1930s, the newspaper industry was one of the few parts of the British economy to be growing as literacy rates increased and the public became hungrier for news and entertainment. This would, however, be the only time that Aristotle would carry bulk paper.

Slowly, Aristotle's two remaining ships began to find work and make money for him. He travelled the world in search of profitable cargoes and became an enthusiastic passenger of the German Zeppelin airships which could take him across the Atlantic in considerable luxury in as little as forty-three hours, compared to a week by ship. The *Graf Zeppelin* regularly flew from South America to Germany, and he bought a ticket on the ill-fated voyage of the *Hindenburg*, from Frankfurt to New York, only cancelling when business meetings dictated a change of itinerary. The horrendous accident which destroyed her on arrival in New Jersey profoundly disturbed him and he travelled only by surface transport for years afterwards. It also persuaded him that he was fated to survive. He had always been superstitious, frequently resorting to fortune tellers and clairvoyants, but now he convinced himself that God had special plans for him. While he was away, his two cousins, Nicolas and Constantine Konialides, ran his businesses for him from Buenos Aires and Montevideo respectively.

Although Aristotle would remain, always, a commercial magpie investing in virtually anything with the potential for profit, from this point on he would, principally, be a shipowner and ships would provide the bulk of the vast fortune he spent his life building. His skill for adapting his fleet to the needs of the moment was legendary and that, combined with scant regard for the rules, or even the traditions, of the sea, would make him fabulously rich.[40]

By 1936 political events in Greece were, again, threatening Aristotle's business. Ioannis Metaxas, whose appointment as prime minister by the king had provoked a series of strikes, had declared a state of emergency, claiming that the country was threatened by 'communist danger'. He closed parliament and suspended many civil liberties, effectively making himself a dictator. In his own words, Greece was now: '... an anti-Communist State, an antiparliamentary State, a totalitarian State. A State based on its farmers and workers, and so antiplutocratic. There is not, of course, a particular party to govern. This party is all the People, except of the incorrigible communists and the reactionary old parties politicians.'

Declaring himself to be 'the First Peasant', Metaxas, who depended upon the army for his authority, imposed a series of sweeping and, he hoped, popular reforms, many of which had been borrowed from Mussolini's fascist Italy. These included a National Labour Service, an eight-hour workday, mandatory improvements to working conditions, and social insurance. Greece's substantial shipping industry was significantly affected with minimum wages, new safety regulations and compulsory hiring from rotas. Aristotle responded by becoming one of the first Greek shipowners to place his vessels under what came to be known as 'flags of convenience'. To escape prohibition, several American shipowners had moved their registrations to Panama as early as 1922. The Panamanians would allow a foreign ship to be registered for only $500 plus an annual tariff on cargo of ten cents per deadweight ton. Their safety and labour regulations were minimal, or non-existent, and Aristotle was able to pay his sailors paltry wages without recognising trade unions, a practice he continued throughout his career.

Panamanian registration meant he could operate his vessels for nearly half the costs of other European shipping lines. A few businessmen boycotted him, but most were happy to accept the markedly lower freight rates that he offered. Aristotle, who soon discovered that Liberia (a country he never set foot in) was also an attractive tax haven, put it thus: 'As a Greek I belong to the West. As a shipowner I belong to capitalism. Business objectives dictate the details of my operations. My favourite country is the one that grants maximum immunity from taxes, trade restrictions and unreasonable regulations. It is under that country's flags that I prefer to concentrate my profitable activities. I call this "business sense".' He never lost faith in his own unique version of 'business sense'.

There comes a point in the career of a tycoon where momentum and retained wealth become great enough to tide them over the unavoidable intervals of bad luck or unforeseeable setbacks which occasionally beset everyone. From that point, only poor judgement or enemy action can bring them down and Aristotle was, finally, past that point, but he would always be a restless spirit with an unbounded hunger for more. He constantly studied commodities and their place in world markets and was rarely behind the curve as they evolved. In addition, he became one of the

PATER FAMILIAS

first shipowners to grasp that coal would quickly be replaced by oil as the world's primary energy source, and that the future lay in large tankers. His foresight and adaptability would lead to him acquiring, in time, the world's biggest privately owned shipping fleet, and make him one of the world's richest men.

Aristotle Onassis' early recognition that oil would replace coal helped him become owner of the world's largest private shipping fleet and one of the world's richest men.

CHAPTER SIX
A Look of Destiny

In July 1929, as Aristotle returned to Athens for the first time since leaving as a teenager, Jacqueline Lee Bouvier was born in Southampton Hospital, Long Island. She was the first child of Janet Norton Lee and John Vernou Bouvier III, known to his friends as 'Black Jack' because of his darkly attractive features and his reputation as a seducer. The couple had married a year earlier and set up home in Manhattan, spending weekends and summers at their country estate in East Hampton, a resort then known as 'Wall Street by the Sea'. Bouvier was a wealthy stockbroker but, within a few months, the Wall Street Crash had drastically reduced his fortune from $750,000 to less than $100,000. This radical change of circumstances would leave both Jackie, and her younger sister Lee (born four years later) with a lifelong sense of insecurity and permanent fear of poverty. [41]

The Bouvier and Lee families were both wealthy, but the Bouviers looked down on the Lees as second-generation Irish immigrants with 'new money'. They thought that Janet was a social climber and were strongly opposed to her wedding Jack. The marriage ran into difficulties almost immediately. During their honeymoon, while sailing to Europe on the *Aquitania*,

A LOOK OF DESTINY

The young Jackie with her parents, 'Black Jack' Bouvier, and Janet Norton Lee.

Jack seduced the Newport heiress Doris Duke. Later, when they arrived in Biarritz, he lost a fortune in the casino.

Black Jack Bouvier was a relentless womaniser and chronic alcoholic. His behaviour, combined with his change of fortunes, destroyed the marriage and the couple had separated by the time Jackie was seven years old, divorcing four years later. Despite her father's weaknesses, Jackie adored him and, throughout her life, would tend to forgive unfaithful or hard-drinking men. A friend of hers would later recall, 'She told me about the complicated relationship with her father, who she admired and respected because women were crazy about him. For example, if there was Parents' Day … she'd say to him about the mothers of some of her friends, "What about her?" and he'd say, "Yes, I've had her," or he'd say, "No, but I think that's pretty imminent!" She thought that that was the most wonderful thing.'[42]

Jackie loved animals and, like her mother, developed into an expert horsewoman, winning prizes for show jumping. She became her father's favourite, especially when his younger daughter, Lee, showed no talent for riding. Lee would say, 'They were so close and then this horse, *Danseuse*, was the trio in their relationship for a good ten years. My father, the horse and Jackie.' Both girls hated their mother, who had a violent temper, continually criticising and sometimes slapping them. Lee would perpetually walk in her older sister's shadow and, while they could be close, they inevitably became rivals. André Leon Talley, the former editor-at-large for *Vogue*, who would later be a friend of Lee, recalled: 'There's an unspoken rule that if you're friends with Lee you don't talk about her sister at all.'[43]

In 1940, the New York papers broke news of the divorce along with intimate details (probably leaked by Janet's lawyer) of Jack's many affairs. Jackie and Lee, who lived in a community where everyone knew everyone else, were publicly humiliated and the experience marked both girls for life.

Jackie was bright and did well at school but was

mischievous and disruptive, partly because she found the lessons easy and finished them long before the others. She also had a talent for languages, learning French, Spanish and Italian, with a particular flair for French. Whatever pain her parents' divorce may have caused, she masked it well and buried herself in an alternative world of poetry and fiction: traditional refuges for unhappy children. Lee was less talented than her older sister; but she was slimmer, arguably prettier and with better fashion sense: the perfect recipe for a lifelong rivalry. Their half-brother, Jamie Auchincloss, would recall, 'As a young woman, Jackie had a definite look of destiny, as if she was inevitably going to be someone unique. Lee was an attractive girl who seemed like she was struggling to keep up. Whereas Jackie was always sure life would unfold for her with good fortune, Lee had a more pessimistic attitude. Despite this stark difference in their personalities, they truly did love one another. They were constantly whispering to one another conspiratorially as if it was them against the world.'[44]

Following her divorce, Janet traded passion and good looks for stability and a more certain income. There were several suitors, but she never made any secret of her belief that intelligent women always 'marry up', and her second husband was the dull, stuffy, but kind and extremely wealthy Hugh D Auchincloss: heir to the Standard Oil fortune. Lee recalled, 'I remember being totally surprised, because she called up and we were at that moment at my grandfather Lee's house. Jackie took the phone first, and Jackie said, "She's gotten married." And I said, "Who to?" And she said, "Mr Auchincloss." I was expecting two other people instead, so I was really taken aback. Apparently, he had two days' leave because he was in the Navy and so this was her reason as to why we weren't there ...'[45]

Two more children would follow, Janet Jennings Auchincloss in 1945 and James Lee Auchincloss in 1947. The Bouvier sisters now moved between two sumptuous estates, one in McLean, Virginia, and another in Newport, Rhode Island, but still visited Black Jack's homes in Manhattan and Long Island. While Jackie always remained closest to her father, she also warmed to her stepfather, who gave her a stable home while pampering her lavishly. By nature, Hugh was unassertive, and Janet firmly ruled the household. When she exploded into one of her periodic rages, Hugh would disappear behind a newspaper and say nothing. The social circles that the Auchincloss family moved in, however, were largely protestant. As Catholics and daughters of a divorcee, the sisters always felt a sense of alienation.

Jackie graduated from school at the top of her class with a distinction in literature. Her own preference would have been Sara Lawrence College, but her parents insisted on the more exclusive, and more isolated, Vassar. She was a good student but took little part in college social life, preferring to return to Manhattan every weekend, where she was unofficially dubbed 'Debutante of the Year'.

One year of her degree course would be spent in France at the Universities of Grenoble and Sorbonne on an exchange programme. While in Paris, Jackie was deflowered in a hotel lift by John P Marquand Jr, the son of the writer John P Marquand.[46] She confided in Lee, swearing her to secrecy, but her sister betrayed

A LOOK OF DESTINY

Jackie Bouvier was a good student with a flair for languages.

the tryst to their mother during a transatlantic phone call. When they next met, Janet slapped Jackie in the face, twice — not for her promiscuity, but because Marquand Jr was penniless: 'Writers are always poor as church mice.'

On her return to America, she studied French Literature at George Washington University and worked as a photojournalist on the *Washington Times-Herald*. Her celebrated beauty and dress sense would only be fully developed later; in those early years, she was still considered a little awkward and gangling. Her socialite friend Cissy Patterson would recall, 'Her looks at that point were not up to the prevailing standard … She seemed tall and gawky, with the puppyish charm of feet and hands too big. Her face seemed spotty — not pimples but just a sort of uneven, tweedy look, a little "ridden hard and put away wet". She mocked her looks and complained of those wide-set eyes, saying the oculist could not find frames wide enough to go over the bridge of her nose …'[47]

According to, Truman Capote, who became a friend of both Jackie and Lee, 'Virginity was something Jackie wanted to get rid of as soon as possible. If my calculations are correct, she went to bed with at least five guys before Jack sampled the honeypot'.[48] She briefly became engaged to a young stockbroker but called it off after a few months. At the age of twenty-three, she would soon be considered too old for marriage within the social circles her family moved in. To wed outside those circles, however, would have been unthinkable for her mother and stepfather, and the list of potential suitors was further shortened by her Catholicism.

She would always have known the Irish American Kennedy clan, whose patriarch, Joe Kennedy, was one of the richest men in America, and she would also have known that his oldest surviving son, Congressman John (Jack) Kennedy, had to marry soon if he was going to take a serious shot at the Senate, never mind the presidency.[49] At thirty-five, Jack's long bachelorhood and reputation as a womaniser needed to be squared off by a suitable marriage; ideally one followed by children. In 1952, Jackie and Lee Bouvier were invited to stay with Jack Kennedy, his brother Bobby and sister Eunice at the Kennedys' Palm Beach home. The visit was engineered by a mutual friend,

A LOOK OF DESTINY

Charlie Bartlett, who followed it up with a dinner invitation to the Bartletts' Cape Cod home. It was suggested that Jackie bring Jack Kennedy to dinner with her, and, from that date, the courtship became public knowledge.[50]

Jackie would certainly have heard of Jack's reputation, as well as that of his father, Joe, who openly conducted affairs in front of his family, regularly bringing his mistresses into the home. Joe had a three-year affair with the movie star Gloria Swanson, which ended when she discovered that a gift from him had been charged to her account, and a nine-year affair with his secretary who was nearly forty years younger than him. He even slept with the pals of his children. When Pamela Digby — a childhood friend of Kathleen 'Kick' Kennedy — stayed overnight at the Kennedy home, Joe slipped into her bedroom during the night and seduced her.[51] She later remembered how, over breakfast the next morning, he was insouciant and behaved as if nothing had happened. In 1938, while the Kennedy family were holidaying at the Hôtel du Cap in the south of France, Joe openly began an affair with Marlene Dietrich. In 1963, on a visit to the White House, Dietrich (then sixty) also slept with his son. After an 'ecstatic three to six minutes', Jack fell asleep.[52] Jack's mother, Rose Kennedy, responded to Joe's behaviour by a combination of denial and retail therapy, punishing his infidelities with extravagant shopping trips. Jackie would later adopt the same tactic herself.

Despite the cold calculations that both families must, inevitably, have made, Jackie may genuinely have been in love with the congressman for the eleventh district of Massachusetts. As well as being extremely rich, Jack Kennedy was tall, witty, good-looking, ambitious and charming. Despite poor health and constant pain from Addison's Disease — along with a host of other serious complaints — he had a vigorous, almost athletic appearance. Only close friends and family knew of his lengthy stays in hospital and reliance on pain killers and other medication.[53] Like Jackie, he was very well-read, possibly the result of childhood illnesses which had kept him bed-bound. He was also an independent thinker who had written a successful book: *Why England Slept* (W Funk 1940).[54] Jackie enjoyed the company of thoughtful, articulate men who could hold their own in debate.

There is less evidence, however, that Jack was in love with Jackie. His Senate campaign meant a lot of travelling and he continued to see other women throughout their courtship. He showed little sign of wanting to propose, even when Jackie's younger sister, Lee, became engaged in 1952. In fact, he procrastinated long after Lee's wedding, waiting until May 1953 before finally putting the question. Jackie, in turn, made him wait for an answer, sailing to Britain with friends who were attending the coronation of Queen Elizabeth II. Jack was waiting at the airport on her return to Boston, and the engagement was finally announced in June 1953. A few weeks later he took his last bachelor holiday with a male friend in the south of France. While there, he seduced a beautiful Swedish girl, Gunilla von Post, who recalled that he 'looked and sounded stricken' when he told her that he was going back to the States to get married.[55] Shortly before his death, Kennedy was asked by his friend

A LOOK OF DESTINY

Chiquita Astor whether he had ever been in love, to which he replied, 'No, but I've been very interested once or twice.'[56]

The lavish wedding, attended by 1,300 guests, took place in Newport, Rhode Island, in September 1953 and was considered 'the' society marriage of that year. Jackie's mother, Janet, forbade her father, Black Jack, to attend the reception; plunging him into an alcoholic depression. The ceremony was conducted by the Kennedys' friend Archbishop Cushing of Boston, who read out a special blessing from Pope Pius XII before the nuptial Mass.[57]

There was a clear and visible distinction between the bride's family and friends, and the groom's. Despite their huge wealth, the Irish American, *arriviste* Kennedys were still looked down upon by much of the WASP establishment. Cecilia Parker Geyelin later recalled, 'I remember on the dance floor all the Kennedy friends, political friends, seemed to have bright blue suits on and they all seemed florid and beefy and they kind of arrived on the scene and swamped the place. There definitely was the air of Newport people curling their lips a bit.'

The early years of their marriage were challenging. 'I was alone almost every weekend,' Jackie recalled. 'It was all wrong. Politics was sort of my enemy and we had no home life whatsoever.' Jack complained that she spent money like water and redecorated their various residences too often.[58] In 1954, Jack almost died during an operation on his back. In 1955, Jackie miscarried and, in 1956, she gave birth to a stillborn daughter, Arabella. Her problems with childbearing were almost certainly caused by the chlamydia she had contracted from Jack, itself the outcome of a dose of gonorrhoea he had caught while at university in 1940. It would be 1957 before a healthy child, Caroline, was born, followed by John Junior in 1960.[59]

By 1957 it was clear that Jack would run for the presidency in 1960. On 2 December, *Time* wrote, 'In his unannounced but unabashed run for the Democratic Party's nomination in 1960, Jack Kennedy has left panting politicians and swooning women across a large spread of the US.'[60] From this point, his need for the appearance of a happy marriage was essential, 'Jackie had learned the power game in family relationships a long time ago and in that sense their marriage was a trade-off.' [61]

Jackie Bouvier married John F Kennedy at Newport, Rhode Island, in September 1953. It was the society wedding of the year.

CHAPTER SEVEN
A Shipboard Romance

In 1934, Ingeborg Dedichen was returning to France following a year-long expedition to Antarctica. She was travelling with a group of family and friends who sailed from Buenos Aires to Genoa aboard the packet steamer *Augustus*. Their mission had been to visit the Douglas Islands — then claimed by Britain — and assert the rights of Norwegian fishermen. When they found, due to chart errors, nothing but empty sea at the coordinates they had been given, they reported that the fishing was, in fact, unrestricted, and counted the exercise as a success.[62]

Ingeborg was the daughter of Ingevald Martin Bryde; one of the first Norwegians to recognise the potential of steam-powered factory ships and their ability to spend months in the Antarctic capturing and processing colossal numbers of whales. The Bryde family, who were one of the richest ship-owning dynasties in Scandinavia, had connections to royalty and the aristocracy. Ingeborg had grown up in a château surrounded by a vast park in Sandefjord, on the coast south of Oslo, where her parents entertained the great and good of fashionable society. Her mother was known for her flawless taste, and her father for his clairvoyant ability to predict the vicissitudes of maritime trade.

Educated at private schools in Norway and Switzerland, she was an accomplished horsewoman, skier, and tennis player, as well as a polyglot who spoke seven languages fluently. She had studied music in Paris, counting some of the world's most renowned soloists among her friends, and she was a confidante of Maud of Wales, the daughter of King Edward VII and Queen Alexandra. As the wife of King Haakon VII, Maud was Queen of Norway and Ingeborg was a regular guest at court.

Tall and slim with sculpted features, naturally blond hair and bright blue eyes, Ingeborg was also a celebrated beauty. At the age of thirty-six, she was enmeshed in a messy divorce from her second husband, Hermann Dedichen, a well-known international bridge player, who had squandered most of her fortune. Still grieving for her recently deceased father, she was at a low point in her life as she returned to her marital home in Paris and was unwilling to burden her seriously ill mother with her problems. Two failed marriages and Hermann's fecklessness had greatly reduced her inheritance, leaving her close to penniless.

On a journey of several weeks, first-class passengers cannot avoid each other, and Ingeborg's group soon became aware of a saturnine young man, expensively dressed and travelling alone, who drank little but endlessly stared at her from across the public rooms of the ship.[63] One of her Norwegian companions asked her, 'Why does that dark little man stare at you incessantly? He follows you everywhere; it's as if he wants to eat you alive.' For days he said nothing, to the point where her companions thought the 'little Levantine' might be dumb, or unable to speak any of the fifteen languages that they, between them, understood.

Aristotle remained silent until they met one morning, at the swimming pool, where Ingeborg was being instructed by a Spanish couple in the subtleties of the crawl. Aristotle, who was an excellent swimmer, dived into the water and emerged, like a seal, beside her, saying, 'That isn't the way to crawl. You will never learn from your Spanish friend.' Having made his introduction, he relentlessly courted her for the rest of the voyage.

Although he was a habitual and accomplished seducer, for the duration of the crossing he was unable to progress much beyond polite conversation which, given his personality, probably inflamed his appetite. For all his intelligence, charm and persuasiveness, he had never shaken off his middle-class, eastern Mediterranean roots, and remained — in the judgement of some Europeans — unsophisticated to the point of boorishness. The ship's crew had told him who the Norwegians were, and he completely understood that, for all his wealth, the first rank of society was still out of his reach; part of the reason, no doubt, that he was struck dumb in their presence.

Travelling in Ingeborg's group was Lars Christensen, also a prominent Norwegian shipowner. He too was cautious of Aristotle at first, but eventually found some common ground with him and the two became friends. In time, all of Ingeborg's group began to attend the lavish parties Aristotle held every day and they eventually fell under his spell. It was Lars who would later introduce him to the Swedish shipwrights Götaverken, whose yard in Hisingen, Gothenburg, was then the largest in the world.⁶⁴ Here, Aristotle discovered that Scandinavian shipbuilders required only a twenty-five per cent deposit and the balance could be repaid over ten years. This would enable him to replace many of his older, second-hand ships with brand new vessels which were vastly more efficient and much kinder to his cash flow.

When the *Augustus* docked in Genoa, Aristotle, who well knew he was punching above his weight, searched for a pretext to stay in Ingeborg's company. She would later recall, 'We had an instant affinity for each other. Although he was not in the least what you would call "well-bred", you could sense his acute intelligence behind those dark, impish eyes, and when he smiled, he could charm mountains. He was all at once funny, tender and brutal, and his voice, his warm sweet voice, ironic and tender, was as expressive as his southern hands, always arguing in counterpoint to his conversation. He had great magnetism.'⁶⁵

While Ingeborg had kept a certain distance at sea, once on land and away from her companions she did accept Aristotle's offer of a lift. 'My car is waiting on the quayside,' he pleaded, 'I am going to Marseille. If you like, you can come with me. From Marseille you can easily take the train to Paris.' Ingeborg accepted, sending her luggage ahead to Paris and joining Aristotle in his Cadillac. On the outskirts of Genoa, he stopped the car and said, 'Are you really in such a hurry to return to Paris? I can easily delay my trip to Marseille. Why don't we spend a few days together in Venice?' She demurred for as long as etiquette required, and then agreed.

Since the *Hindenburg* disaster, he had avoided

flying, preferring to drive long distances across Europe. It would have taken the couple more than a day to cover the 400 kilometres across northern Italy, and they must have stopped en route, but Aristotle made no attempt to seduce her until they booked into Venice's most luxurious hotel. We know exactly what happened there because Ingeborg, uniquely among Aristotle's lovers, later recorded the details in a memoir.

'There was a gentle sound as my bedroom door slid ajar. In the darkened room I could see the silhouette of a figure, dressed in blue silk pyjamas, who moved silently towards me and sat upon the counterpane. In the semi-darkness I could just make out the letters ASO, embroidered over the heart of my seducer, in an elegant monogram.

'Aristotle Socrates Onassis began to banter, and laugh, clearly relieved that his gambit had not been repulsed. We had known each other for fifteen days and were occupying adjoining rooms in the Hotel Danieli in Venice. Foolishly, I had forgotten to bolt my door.

'My travelling companion now brought all of his charm into play, regaling me with his unique humour and enchanting, multi-faceted personality. He gently brought my hand to his lips and lightly kissed my wrist. Then he found the courage to entwine me in his arms and our mouths met in an interminable embrace. In that moment, we became lovers. It was the most intense sexual pleasure I ever knew. We did not sleep until the dawn.' [66]

Within a month, Aristotle had proposed marriage, but she was not yet divorced from her second husband.

The affair would last for twelve years, and Ingeborg became the only woman in Aristotle's life to succeed in fundamentally changing him. He installed her in a vast, splendid Parisian apartment at 88 avenue Foch — then and now one of the most expensive addresses in the world — and allowed her to spend a fortune redecorating it. More importantly, she set about reforming him. As she told society columnist Lloyd Shearer, 'He was very unsure of himself socially. His manners were not the best. He knew little about food, wines, clothes, culture, but he was industrious and intelligent, and he learned fast.'

Aristotle Onassis bought a vast apartment at 88 avenue Foch, one of the most prestigious addresses in Paris, which he shared with his lover, Ingeborg Dedichen.

A SHIPBOARD ROMANCE

It was Ingeborg, seven years older than Aristotle, who began to smooth over the rough corners and crude habits of the young tycoon. By day she took him to galleries and museums, teaching him enough about fine art to become a collector. By night, she took him to the most expensive restaurants in Paris, especially Maxims in the rue Royale, where she gently coached him in the conventions of fine dining: how to order dishes which complement each other and are in season and how to choose the right wine for each; which utensils to use, how to deal with waiters and, above all, how to tip, essential if you want a good table and attentive service on your next visit. Aristotle was delighted to learn that such an exclusive institution had, originally, been made chic by Irma de Montigny, an upscale nineteenth-century courtesan who used it to regale her most fashionable clients. Maxims became his favourite restaurant in the world, and he would entertain friends, mistresses and business associates there until his final days.

Just as importantly, having Ingeborg on his arm meant, for the first time, the salons, soirées and homes of Europe's *haut monde* were, at last, open to him. He was not slow to benefit from his new social circle. Scandinavia would, from now on, play an important role in the growth of his shipping line. In order to get government finance, he would form a Swedish company which would operate Swedish-built ships. At that time, coal still provided seventy-five per cent of the world's energy needs. Aristotle was one of the first major shipowners to divine that, within the near future, oil would largely replace coal and there would be a growing need for large vessels to carry it. He also knew that oil tankers, once in port, could be turned around in far less time than dry cargo vessels as they needed only pipes rather than stevedores to discharge their oil. Not only did this save him money, but it also reduced the chances of delays caused by industrial disputes.

In 1937, Ernst Haden, the General Manager of the Götaverken shipyard in Sweden, was told by his secretary that Aristotle Onassis wished to speak to him. 'Put him through,' he replied, imagining that this was a telephone call from Paris or Buenos Aires. To his surprise, Aristotle walked into his office, sat down, and began to bargain with him for the construction of a 15,000-ton oil tanker, a colossal size for the day. Haden was a shrewd and seasoned businessman who was rarely outmanoeuvred in negotiations but, as he later admitted, Aristotle got the better of him, persuading him to accept terms far superior to those he would have offered to anyone else. He later described the young tycoon as a 'sorcerer'. When the ship was unveiled, a year later, Aristotle — who never forgot his heritage — christened her *Ariston*, after the Greek philosopher. She was launched in June 1938, just as the economic effects of the Depression were beginning to dissipate and freight rates were rising.

His oil tankers would, in time, grow into the world's biggest fleet of large crude carriers and make him one of the world's richest shipowners, but he was not content. Always, he kept a weather eye open for new opportunities. Through his new connections he met Norwegian shipowner Andres Jhare, who had recently bought a thirty-year-old American collier, in poor condition, with the intention of refitting her as a whaling vessel. Aristotle, who had learnt a lot about buying second-hand ships, believed Andres had paid far too much but, because he knew that Ingeborg's family fortune had come from whaling, he was keen to dip a toe into the water, and he agreed to take a small stake in the vessel. The advantage was that because she was US registered, she could hunt in American waters which were then rich in whales. In the meantime, he ordered two more large tankers: the *Aristophanes* and the *Buenos Aires*. Uniquely, for oil tankers, he had them equipped with sumptuous private quarters for himself and his entourage, allowing Ingeborg a free hand in the interior design and choice of furnishings which even included a grand piano! As a condition of the government loan that he had used to finance the *Ariston*, he was obliged to register her in Sweden so, for once, he proudly flew Sweden's blue and white flag from her stern. He registered the *Aristophanes* in Greece and the *Buenos Aires* in Argentina.

As would happen throughout Aristotle's career, global geopolitics were about to reshape the world. By the late 1930s a second global war was fermenting in Europe. Its immediate short-term effect was to send freight rates rocketing upwards. Perhaps because of his searing, near-death experiences as a boy in Smyrna, he did not have the least compunction about profiting from the rise of fascism. Although Greek shipowners were not expected to carry cargoes, especially military material, to Spain, Italy or Germany, he did so and profited hugely.

When the *Ariston* was complete, Aristotle, along with Ingeborg, his sisters Artemis and Merope and their husbands, joined her for the maiden voyage as if it was a pleasure cruise. Merope and Nicolas

Konialides were newly married, and this would be their honeymoon. They crossed the Atlantic and then entered the Pacific from the Panama Canal. A temporary swimming pool had been rigged on the deck, Ingeborg played piano in the evenings and the voyagers were spoiled with every conceivable luxury.

When they arrived in San Francisco the *Ariston* undertook her first commercial work: a year-long contract to carry oil to Japan for the Mitsui Steel company on behalf of one of John Paul Getty's companies. The profit was $600,000, which almost paid the vessel's entire construction cost. Aristotle and his entourage stayed in the United States for several months, completing a grand tour from coast to coast and visiting many of America's major cities. The gamble to invest in oil tankers had paid off spectacularly and Aristotle had transitioned from rich to super rich. The oncoming war was continually pushing up freight rates and there was no longer any shortage of cargoes. They were halcyon days but, for all that, momentous political events were, once again, unfolding in ways he had not predicted.

At first, Aristotle appeared to be safe as all three of his tankers were registered in neutral countries (Sweden, Greece and Argentina) and his diplomatic passport allowed him to travel freely across borders which were officially closed. But that ended in the spring of 1940 when Germany invaded Norway and Denmark. Sweden remained neutral but had little choice but to accept humiliating demands from the Germans, including permission for German troops and military equipment to be transported on Swedish railways. A further German demand was that all ships in Swedish ports be confined there until hostilities ceased. As luck would have it, all three of Aristotle's oil tankers were in Göteborg at the time. He had other ships and other business interests across the globe, but the sequestering of his large tankers would lose him millions. Reluctantly, he returned to Buenos Aires and set about remodelling his tobacco companies.

Turkish tobacco was no longer available; he now had to import from Cuba and Brazil. The war, however, had created a global tobacco shortage and prices soared, as did freight rates. Even the most dilapidated ship could now make money for its owner if it could avoid the torpedoes of German U-boats and, even if it couldn't, the insurance money was usually enough to pay for a new ship. Aristotle's smaller tankers were now profitably employed taking oil from the west coast of the United States to Canada. In 1940, he moved his centre of operations from Buenos Aires to New York, a city he had fallen in love with during his earlier visit in 1938–1939. Prior to the war, most of the significant Greek shipowners had based themselves in London but, as the Nazis advanced across the Continent, they moved their headquarters to the safety of New York. The war had created an insatiable global appetite for cargo vessels of any kind or size — irrespective of their age or state of seaworthiness — and they were all making a great deal of money. They were among the so-called 'new men' of shipping — Greek, Norwegian, Danish, American, Japanese or Hong Kong owners — who were replacing the British families who had dominated merchant shipping for generations.[67]

Ingeborg had stayed in France until the Germans invaded, and only with some difficulty — and a lot of help from Aristotle and his American friends — managed to get a United States visa from the American Consul in Marseille, arriving in New York in November 1940. While they still publicly declared their undying love for each other, both had periodic affairs with others. They took a cottage on Long Island where they entertained lavishly, and Ingeborg became known as a popular hostess. When in Manhattan, Aristotle, who had always loved nightclubs, could be found on most evenings at either the Copacabana, the Stork Club, the Monte Carlo, 21, Versailles on East Fiftieth Street or his favourite: El Morocco (known to its habitués as *Elmo's*). The Greek journalist and writer, Taki Theodoracopulos, recalls meeting him there: 'I was twenty years old and in the company of a beautiful blonde socialite. Onassis sent over Costa Gratsos to ask us to join them. I did and Onassis began to flirt outrageously with my date.'[68]

The oil shipments meant frequent trips to Los Angeles, where Aristotle stayed at the fabled Beverley Hills Hotel. His oldest and most trusted friend, Costa Gratsos — now the Greek Maritime Consul — would travel down from San Francisco and the two men became regulars on the Hollywood party scene where Aristotle's flamboyance quickly became a legend. Another old friend, the Greek shipowner Spyros Skouras, was now the President of Twentieth Century-Fox and he introduced Aristotle to many celebrities including Otto Preminger, Simone Simon, and the Greek actress Katina Paxinu.[69] At parties, Aristotle would invariably give the hostess a diamond bracelet while the host would receive a silver cigarette box containing his own specially rolled brand of Turkish cigarettes. His flamboyance and extravagance, even by Hollywood standards, quickly became a legend.

One of the many actresses with whom he had affairs was Gloria Swanson. By the 1940s, her career was waning, but she had been a major star during the silent era, and had previously been the mistress of Joe Kennedy, the banker and erstwhile film producer who had serious political ambitions for his sons.[70] Another actress and sugar heiress, Geraldine Spreckels, was captivated by Aristotle but refused to sleep with him. He promptly began an affair with Veronica Lake, and when Lake became very drunk, he took her to Spreckels' beach apartment and deposited her in the bed. Forty years later, Spreckels would recall, 'He thought it was funny, but it was also to show me that he could always get another pretty girl … he used to make me so mad.' Aristotle was briefly betrothed to Spreckels, but she called off the engagement shortly before the wedding and quickly married her cousin, divorcing him only a few months later.[71]

Aristotle never forgot that the fortune of Ingeborg Dedichen's family had been founded on whaling. This was a time when the industry was so dominated by Scandinavians that, according to legend, no other nationality could successfully operate a whaling fleet. He and Costa found a little-used whaling station in Eureka, in northern California, and they bought an elderly whaling vessel for just $15,000. A Swedish gunner was hired, and thirty-five whales were successfully harpooned in the first year. The profits were not great to begin with, but the two men persevered.

CHAPTER EIGHT
A Marriage of Convenience

Much as Aristotle enjoyed his trips to California, he spent most of his time on the east coast. New York had become the city of choice for many of the world's major shipowners, Greek and non-Greek alike, and Aristotle could now count, among his neighbours, not only Spyros Skouras, but also his old pal Alberto Dodero, along with Stavros Livanos and Stavros Niarchos. The great shipping families of that era behaved rather as royal families had done for centuries. They fought each other relentlessly on the high seas, but married into each other's families and maintained informal friendships, playing poker and frequently entertaining each other at their homes on Long Island.

His love for Ingeborg was waning. He still showered her with lavish gifts and public displays of affection, but she had to endure his vicious temper and periodic violence. On one occasion, when the couple visited his arch-rival, Stavros Niarchos, at his home at Lloyd Neck, Aristotle objected to the green-striped trousers which she wore. Nothing was said in front of Niarchos and his family, but when they were back in their own home he beat her black and blue. On another occasion he beat her so badly that the servants had to be laid off for a week so that they would not see the bruises. Friends tried to persuade her to leave him, but she remained loyal. Aristotle was unrepentant and would repeatedly say: 'All Greek men beat their women. He who loves well beats well.' Aristotle's predilection for beatings, and Ingeborg's acceptance of them, suggest there was a sado-masochistic element to their relationship. Aristotle had boasted to her that, with previous mistresses, he had enjoyed the best sex following a beating.

For the first time in his life, he was making money so easily that he no longer had to work hard. Many of his ships were on charter to the US government. This, alone, netted him more than $250,000 per year and, by the end of the war, his fortune was estimated to be in the region of $30 million. Rumours began to circulate about Aristotle's extraordinary luck during the war. Unlike most owners, he had not lost a single ship or sailor to enemy action, and he was also known to have conducted an affair with Maria Constantinesco, who was later convicted as a German spy. The FBI had, anyway, been suspicious of his close relationship with the officially neutral but unofficially pro-Axis Argentinian government, and they began surveillance on him, but no incriminating evidence was ever found. The US Office of Naval Intelligence, however, wrote to the FBI in 1943 with details of a commercial fraud. In Genoa, a consignment of tobacco had been sprayed with brine in order that Aristotle could collect from the insurance company. An employee gave the game away and one of Aristotle's cousins, Nicolas Konialides, who worked for him in Buenos Aires but happened to be in Genoa at the time, went to jail.

As soon as the hostilities ended, Aristotle brought his family to New York and his three large tankers were released. He was now close to forty years old and had begun to think seriously about marriage. Like many self-made men, he wanted a dynasty and a son who would, one day, take over from him. He had proposed to Ingeborg several times over the years they had been together, pleaded with her to have his child and, on one occasion, had even sent another cousin — Michael Dologlou — to offer her a million dollars if she would accept him (Onassis would always treat his marriage proposals as if they were business transactions) but she had always declined. By 1946 their affair was over, although she would remain a friend and confidante for many years and Onassis would continue to telephone her several times per week to ask her advice. It was, after all, Ingeborg who had fine-tuned his transformation from an uncouth and unsophisticated tobacco salesman into an international businessman and diplomat who rubbed shoulders with presidents and kings.

There is a tradition in Greek families that a man does not marry until his sisters have found husbands, and all three of Aristotle's sisters were now married. Additionally, there was another custom among Greek ship-owning families of intermarrying, in other words, 'keep your friends close but your enemies closer'.[72] That convention probably influenced Aristotle more than any other. While he could now be counted among the world's major shipowners, he was by no means the richest. That title belonged to Stavros G Livanos, whose shipping empire eclipsed Aristotle's several times over. Livanos was a third-generation Greek shipowner who had profited enormously from the First World War and managed his investments shrewdly after it. He and his family lived mainly in London but spent the war years in their home near Oyster Bay on Long Island, New York. His father had sent him to sea, first as a deck hand, later as a captain, and few shipowners knew more about the technicalities of the business than Livanos. He had two daughters: Athina — better known as Tina — aged seventeen, and Eugenia who was nineteen. Both had been privately educated in England and Switzerland and both were multilingual, intelligent, sophisticated and charming. Tina, however, was the prettier and more vivacious of the two. Aristotle had first met Tina when she was only fourteen and appears to have secretly fallen in love with her at first sight.

Although their backgrounds and personalities were very different, Livanos liked Aristotle and they would spend many hours together playing poker and talking endlessly about shipping and the sea. His daughters liked him too, despite him being more than twice their age, and often went swimming, boating or water-skiing with him. The meetings were always chaperoned, but it soon became clear that Livanos would not object to Aristotle becoming his son-in-law and may even have suggested it to him.

It was around this time that the affair with Ingeborg finally ended, making Aristotle one of the most eligible bachelors in the world. The support of Livanos would quickly dissipate, however, when Aristotle wrote to him asking for the hand of not Eugenia, but Tina, the younger of the two. Livanos saw this as an affront. He felt he would be humiliated among other Greeks if, against tradition, his younger daughter married first.

He forbade the couple to speak to each other and a year went by before the ice began to thaw. He only finally relented when it became clear that another Greek shipowner, Stavros Niarchos, was thinking of divorcing his second wife and marrying Eugenia, whom he'd been seeing secretly.[73] That meant that the two marriages would unite three great shipping families and he finally removed his objection to Aristotle marrying Tina, although Tina would later claim that she only agreed to the marriage because of pressure from her mother.

They were wed in a Greek Orthodox ceremony in New York by Father Euthimion, who had been Aristotle's theology teacher at school and was also a refugee from Smyrna. After the ceremony, Gratsos whispered to him, 'You've got your revenge now, Ari.' But Aristotle knew that many of the wedding guests, behind his back, called him the 'parachutist' because he had dropped in on them out of the blue. He replied to Gratsos, 'It's not enough, Costa. I'm looking to beat the shit out of these sons of bitches. I'm at war with these gorillas.'[74] Stavros Livanos's wedding present to the couple was a ship and the honeymoon was spent at Key West, Palm Beach and Buenos Aires.

While on the private yacht of Alberto Dodero, Aristotle was reintroduced to Eva Perón, the wife of President Juan Perón, who had just become Argentina's First Lady. Dodero had assiduously courted the Peróns, showering them with gifts including jewellery and even Rolls-Royces. The former actress's influence on her husband was known to be huge and she ran at least two government departments herself: labour and health. Dodero's shipping empire was

A MARRIAGE OF CONVENIANCE

The Livanos sisters. Eugenia (right) married Stavros Niarchos, but she died in mysterious circumstances in 1970. Tina first married Aristotle Onassis, then the Marquess of Blandford, and finally became the fifth wife of her sister's widower, Stavros Niarchos.

waning and, strongly supported by Eva, who offered featherbed terms from the government, he tried to persuade Aristotle to buy it. The negotiations went on over several days and long into the nights but, despite the newly married Aristotle sleeping with Perón (as Dodero had expected), he finally judged the investment to be too risky, and declined. Subsequent events would prove that he had been wise: a few years later the Argentinian government nationalised Dodero's ships at fire sale prices, paying him a fraction of their true value. Aristotle had shrewdly avoided a devastating loss and Dodero would later say, 'The president did to me what I fixed for Onassis to do to his wife!'[75]

On their return to New York Tina's father bought the couple a four-storey townhouse at 16 Sutton Square for $460,000 and Aristotle refurbished it at a cost of millions. Within a few months Tina's older sister, Eugenia, had married Stavros Niarchos. There is another long-standing Greek tradition by which men who marry sisters are expected to become brothers, but this was a custom that neither man subscribed to: throughout their lives they would be bitter rivals in both business and love. Both were successful shipowners, but that was where all similarity ended; in every other way, they were fundamentally different. Stavros was born into wealth and privilege having been educated at the finest private schools on both sides of the Atlantic, followed by law studies at the University of Athens. His parents were Greek, but they had business interests in America, where Stavros spent part of his childhood. He had film star good looks, an athletic figure and was always immaculately dressed. If that weren't enough, he had also acquired a level of self-confidence, savoir-faire and charm which meant he was at ease in any social situation. In the days before Ingeborg had smoothed out Aristotle's rough edges, Stavros was welcomed in the highest echelons of European and American society, but they still shunned the dark, Anatolian refugee.

Whereas Aristotle could win women's hearts by flattery and persistence, Stavros found that they simply fell into his arms without him making any perceptible effort. On the other hand, although Stavros was undoubtedly a good businessman, his acumen didn't entirely match that of Aristotle, and he resented the fact that he rarely managed to make quite as much money as his rival. The two men disliked each other from their first meeting and when it became clear that his wife, Tina, enjoyed Stavros' company, Aristotle's dislike turned to loathing. He even went as far as forbidding her to attend her sister Eugenia's wedding, which led to a lifelong feud between the two families. A former employee in London observed that Aristotle '… considered forgiveness a weakness and détente a defeat. He needed adversaries. He would have been lost without an enemy to hate … sometimes the enemy had to be drawn from the closest circle of his own family.'[76]

By 1948, Tina had presented Aristotle with a child, Alexander, named after an uncle who had been executed in Smyrna. He now had the solitary son and heir that he had always wanted and forbade Tina to have any more children. As a fatalist, he did not entertain the thought that he might need an 'heir and spare': God had granted him a son and would not take him away. Tina's next two pregnancies were ended by medical abortions, but when she fell pregnant again in 1950, her doctors warned her against further terminations. Aristotle was furious and — using his normal tactic when any woman in his life displeased him — repeatedly beat her, but Tina would not give in and a healthy daughter, Christina, was born. She closely resembled Aristotle, inheriting most of his physical features (even shadowy bags under her eyes) and none of Tina's svelte beauty. While she was always an embarrassment to her mother, Aristotle would now dote on the child he had never wanted, calling her *Chryso mou*, Greek for 'my golden one' and later naming his yacht after her. His dotage, however, did not extend to spending very much time with her.[77]

As well as their home in New York they now had a house in Montevideo, a permanent suite in the Plaza in Buenos Aires, a beachfront villa in Athens, a house in Paris and the forty-two-room Château de la Croë, set in 215 acres in Cap d'Antibes.[78] When Stavros Niarchos took another vast château a little further up the coast, Aristotle responded, 'I think Stavros suffers from an identity crisis. He hates me because he has no original ideas of his own.' The combining, by marriage, of the world's three largest ship-owning families might have created a redoubtable powerhouse of maritime trade with no serious rival, but the antipathy between Aristotle and Stavros ensured that there was little cooperation.

Before long, Aristotle was operating alone and eyeing up the substantial fleet of Liberty ships that the United States government was keen to sell. Thousands of these simple, graceless but cheap freighters had

A MARRIAGE OF CONVENIANCE

been built during the war and those which had survived were now rusting at anchor in river estuaries and harbours across the continent. American buyers showed little interest and the law prohibited their sale to non-Americans. Acting independently of each other, Aristotle and Stavros both formed corporations in which American citizens held the majority of the shares, but the two Greeks financed and controlled the companies. The Liberty ships were then bought cheaply, but, unlike their other vessels, were registered in the United States and operated with American crews. The profits were huge but voices in Congress soon began to complain of 'foreign' ownership of American assets and profiteering at the expense of the US taxpayer.

Committee hearings began to investigate the sales and the staggering profits that had been achieved. In one investment alone, Stavros Niarchos had made $3.75 million on two ships which he had originally purchased for just $101,000. By 1953, a Federal Grand Jury had drawn up indictments against thirty-two people including Stavros Niarchos and Aristotle Onassis. For the first time in their lives both were at serious risk of going to jail. The two men, however, reacted in very different ways. Stavros took flight, decamped to London and remained there until the crisis was resolved. Aristotle, on the other hand, sent a cable to the US Attorney General:

> I WISH TO INFORM YOU THAT HAVING ARRIVED FROM EUROPE ON MONDAY NIGHT, I PLACE MYSELF AT YOUR DISPOSAL DURING MY VISIT IN THIS COUNTRY FOR ANY INFORMATION YOU OR YOUR DEPARTMENT MIGHT CARE TO HAVE.

Aristotle Onassis with his first wife, Tina.

When this drew no response he barged, uninvited, into the Attorney General's office and confronted him directly. This led to Aristotle becoming, at the time, the richest person ever to be arrested in the United States, and he had to pay bail of $10,000 to gain his freedom. He and eight other defendants were, eventually, charged with a range of offences, mostly revolving around false statements of assets and citizenship. Stavros Niarchos escaped prosecution by returning some of the Liberty ships, placing orders to build new ships in American shipyards and paying multiple fines. Aristotle was outraged that Niarchos had given in to the American authorities. He may have been partly justified in his anger because, in time, all the charges against the other defendants were dropped, aided by the fact that Aristotle had placed orders worth $50 million with US shipyards.

The Liberty ships were, mostly, dry cargo vessels and there was plenty of work for them, but the most profitable part of Aristotle's business was his growing fleet of oil tankers. In the years following the Second

A MARRIAGE OF CONVENIENCE

World War — just as Aristotle had predicted — oil was rapidly replacing coal as the world's primary energy source and Saudi Arabia had emerged as the world's largest producer of crude. Included in the Liberty ships were five T2 tankers which Aristotle bought with loans he had raised from American banks and insurance companies. He told an English friend, 'Five tankers — and the only time I had to put my hand in my pocket was to scratch my balls.' [79]

Stavros Niarchos with his third wife, Eugenia.

As Germany began to recover from the war, Aristotle, encouraged by Costa Gratsos, saw the German shipyards as a cheaper alternative to the United States. The 1945 Potsdam agreement forbade the Germans from building anything over 5,000 tons, a size which Aristotle dismissed as 'God damned toys'. His business antennae, however, sensed the potential energy which could be released by German economic revival: 'We've got to find a way around that goddam agreement because these people are willing to break their balls to give us a job.' Gratsos discovered that there was no size limit on conversions, and thereby revived Aristotle's interest in whaling. Long meetings took place in Hamburg's Ehmke's restaurant and the Tarantella nightclub (Aristotle always eschewed meetings in conventional offices). Before long, they had contracted for one of their 18,000-ton tankers to be converted into a whaling factory ship, the *Olympic Challenger*, and registered her in Panama to avoid the quotas which were applied to American and European ships. With a German crew, a Norwegian harpoonist, a fleet of smaller 'catcher' ships (all flying Honduran or Panamanian flags) and a helicopter (then, an innovation) she was soon plundering the Pacific and Antarctic Oceans for whales and making the two men a great deal of money.

Aristotle saw the whale hunts, which literally turned the ocean red with blood, as an entertainment, inviting his guests — many of them oil executives or financiers — to take turns with the whale gun. 'I think he simply wanted them to feel the blood on their hands and share in the guilt,' Gratsos later said. Practically all the regulations and conventions of whaling, including the close season and embargoes on immature whales, were ignored. As Aristotle would frequently say, 'The only rules are that there are no rules.' Friends of the couple believed that Aristotle and his wife were at their closest during these pursuits. One would later comment, 'For Tina, I'm sure that the hunt evoked a pleasurable psychic high.'[80]

By 1951 all the restrictions on German shipyards were lifted (as Gratsos had predicted) and Aristotle organised a $100 million loan to build eighteen giant tankers in Hamburg. He was now on his way, closely pursued by Stavros Niarchos, to becoming the world's largest shipowner. As his wealth and power grew so Aristotle — who had always been an itinerant businessman, roving from state to state and continent to continent — started to look for a new home for his many investments; preferably one which had the fewest possible taxes and restrictive rules. His focus soon narrowed on Monaco, the tiny principality between Nice and Menton which had remained for centuries a sovereign city and microstate on the French Riviera. The taxes and financial oversight were negligible, it had a fine climate and its Mediterranean location made it ideal. If all that were not enough, Tina had many friends among the principality's residents and liked spending time there.

He discovered that a third of Monaco's 375 acres, including the Yacht Club, Monte-Carlo Casino, Opéra de Monte-Carlo, and the Hôtel de Paris, all belonged to a company with the eccentric name of the 'Société Anonyme des Bains de Mer et du Cercle des Étrangers à Monaco', known locally as SBM. Aristotle first tried to rent their premises but, when the board turned him down as an 'unsuitable person', he began to acquire their shares. By 1953 he had taken control and moved his staff into the Old Sporting Club on the avenue d'Ostende. From the balcony, practically everything to be seen now belonged to him. It was exactly thirty years since, as a penniless refugee, he had first seen Monaco from the decks of the *Tomaso di Savoia*, en route to Buenos Aires.

Prince Rainier, the hereditary ruler of Monaco, was unperturbed and welcomed the new money that Onassis would bring. Rainier knew, anyway, that he retained the right to veto any SBM decision, so he saw little risk in Aristotle's control. The United States, however, was less sanguine and began to take a renewed interest in Aristotle's affairs. J Edgar Hoover wrote to the Assistant Attorney General, 'Onassis's agent, one Charles Simon, was elected General Manager of the Société on June 29, 1953, and Onassis, therefore, except for the Prince of Monaco, whom the French regard as an inconsequential person whose only interest is in a reliable source of funds for his pleasures, may be regarded as the real ruler of Monaco.'

Aristotle, in marked contrast to his father-in-law, Stavros Livanos, loved publicity and actively courted the media who, by now, had dubbed him 'the Golden Greek' and the 'King of Monaco'. Taking over the SBM assured him the worldwide fame that he had long sought. People now asked him for his autograph in the street and waiters treated him as if he were royalty. He employed full-time PR people who daily read him his press cuttings and he basked in his newfound celebrity. He was not yet fifty years old.

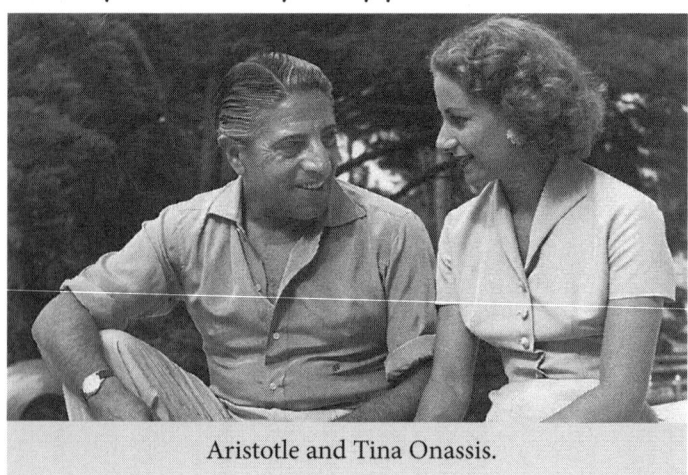

Aristotle and Tina Onassis.

CHAPTER NINE
Richer Than Croesus

Aristotle was rich beyond the dreams of avarice, but heavily indebted, and he knew that even small fluctuations in freight markets could have a have a devastating effect on his business. His loans were based on an assumption that the global demand for oil would continue to grow at around eight per cent per annum, but the actual growth was now less. Consequently, several of his tankers were laid up with the prospect of more becoming idle. He conceived the idea of doing a deal with the Saudi government through which he would get first option on shipping the huge quantities of crude oil which sailed, every day, from Saudi ports.

The oil conglomerate ARAMCO, which was controlled by the big four US companies (Standard, Mobil, Exxon and Texaco), already had a treaty with the Saudis which gave them exclusive rights, not only to exploration and production, but also to transportation; the treaty had been signed in 1933 and ran until 2000.[81] Although he knew this, Aristotle was undaunted, believing that the deal could be unpicked, and he began mediations, using intermediaries who were close to the Saudi royal family. He was an unsurpassed negotiator who loved nothing more than sealing a contract, but he dubbed this one 'the biggest dry-throat deal of my life'. The stress aggravated his natural hypochondria, and he was plagued with insomnia, headaches and bleeding gums.

Aristotle decided to offer the Saudis something that ARAMCO had never considered: their own Saudi-based shipping line which could ship Saudi oil to the world. ARAMCO carried oil on their own vessels and when they lacked sufficient capacity, as frequently happened, they chartered ships from Onassis, Niarchos and others. A new shipping line, the Saudi Arabian Maritime Company (SAMCO), would be established. Aristotle would provide 500,000 tons of shipping but the company would be headquartered in Jeddah, the ships would fly the Saudi flag and a Saudi maritime college would be established to provide future officers. The new line would have first option on all Saudi oil exports and would be guaranteed ten per cent (or a minimum of four million tons) of the annual oil output. From now on, Aristotle would have a stranglehold on the transport of more than forty-five million tons of Saudi oil per year. He was about to become not only the richest man on earth but, also, one of the most powerful. On his forty-eighth birthday the Saudis entertained Aristotle and Tina at a lavish banquet, and the king presented him with two Arab ponies and a pair of gold scimitars.

This was, potentially, the biggest and most significant business deal of the twentieth century, and it had massive implications, not least for the government of the United States. Energy security had long been a worry for America: her own domestic oil supplies only met a small fraction of her needs. Aristotle's new deal would mean that delivery of essential crude oil would now be in the hands of a non-American, nonresident tycoon whom they had long distrusted and even tried to imprison. For all Aristotle's acumen, it was politically naïve of him to think the United States would stand idly by. The first to react, however, was Aristotle's long-time nemesis, Stavros Niarchos, who paid Robert Mahue — a private detective — $5,000 to sabotage the deal by fair means or foul.

Mahue was a former FBI agent with links to the CIA who had a reputation for successful 'black' operations. He began by leaking details of the Saudi deal to a Rome-based newspaper. This led to immediate pressure on the Saudis from ARAMCO, and widespread condemnation across the world. He next placed bugs in Aristotle's New York offices and his Paris home. Finally, he managed to contact Richard Nixon, who was then President Eisenhower's Vice President, and convinced him that the Onassis deal would undermine American influence in the Middle East. Nixon had sat on the Senate subcommittee which examined Aristotle's Liberty ship purchases and he had already formed a low opinion of Onassis. He was close to the head of the CIA, Allen Dulles, whose older brother was John Foster Dulles, arguably, the most forceful personality to hold the office of Secretary of State, and Nixon convinced both men that the Onassis deal had to be scuttled.

Mahue, and an associate, John Gerritty, were briefed personally by Nixon to carry out a 'Mission Impossible'-style dirty tricks campaign against Aristotle Onassis. While Nixon warned them that the government would deny all responsibility if they were caught, he made it clear that he wanted Onassis to be smeared to the point where the deal would be bound to fall through.[82] Nixon even went as far as telling Mahue, 'If you have to kill this son of a bitch, don't do it on American shores.'[83] Mahue, using his contacts in the CIA, was able to organise a strike at the Hamburg shipyard where Onassis was building a tanker named after the Saudi king. The pressure on Onassis soon gained momentum and in April 1954 he returned to Jeddah for a personal audience with King Saud. The agreement was amended, and a clause added which read: 'A.S. Onassis shall have the right to combine the company whose head office will be in Saudi Arabia with one or more of the companies a majority of whose shares are directly owned by himself or by members of his family of Greek origin, provided that Jews have no direct or indirect interest in any of these companies and the company shall not deal with Israel.' There is no evidence that Aristotle baulked at this clause.

By May, the deal had been formally ratified, which put it to the top of the agenda in Washington. The addition of anti-Semitic clauses to the contract, once made public, had enraged opinion and America's ambassador in Saudi Arabia was dispatched to King Saud to deliver a strongly worded communiqué. The State Department was now openly playing hardball and threatening dire consequences if the Saudis went ahead. They knew there was a danger that Saudi Arabia might respond by simply nationalising all ARAMCO's assets in the kingdom, and they countered this by reminding King Saud that when Iran nationalised its oil industry in 1953 their prime minister, Mohammad Mosaddegh, was toppled in a CIA/MI6-assisted coup and replaced by the young Shah Muhammad Reza Pahlevi.

RICHER THAN CROESUS

At the same time, another Greek businessman, Spyridon Catapodis, who had helped fix the deal with the Saudis, was claiming that Aristotle had hoodwinked him by signing an agreement in disappearing ink and cheating him out of millions of dollars. Catapodis deposited an affidavit at the British Consulate in Nice which detailed the many substantial bribes Aristotle had paid to a wide range of influencers in Saudi Arabia. By October, Aristotle had been summoned back to Riyadh to be told by the king that the deal must now go to arbitration. The game was up, in the end ARAMCO yielded practically nothing and Washington's ambassador in Riyadh was able to cable: 'Onassis, when finally pinned down ... has weaselled and outsmarted himself.' Aristotle was more phlegmatic: 'I played for high stakes, and I lost.'

America had won but that did not mean they felt any magnanimity towards Aristotle. The CIA knew that his whaling fleet, operating off the coast of Peru, was largely illegal and they put pressure on the Peruvian government to act. In 1947, Peru had extended its territorial waters to 200 miles and Peruvian newspapers were now campaigning against 'Onassis the whaling pirate'. Before long, Aristotle's vessels were being arrested at sea and forcibly taken to Peruvian ports. His factory ship, the *Olympic Challenger,* was strafed and bombed by Peruvian fighter jets before her German captain would capitulate.[84] Aristotle seemed unperturbed, he had shrewdly insured his ships against all possible losses, even military action or seizure by another state. The massive fines levied by the Peruvians were paid from the money he collected from Lloyds of London, and the ships were released. A Lloyds underwriter later admitted, 'It was a very bad misjudgement by us and a very good one by Mr Onassis.'

Aristotle took his family back to the Mediterranean to spend Christmas aboard his newly launched yacht, the *Christina*, which he had named after his daughter. Following the Second World War, he had bought numerous war-surplus ships for negligible sums. One of them was a former Canadian frigate named HMCS *Stormont*, for which he paid just $34,000, her scrap metal value. At a time when German shipyards were severely restricted in what they could build new, Aristotle knew that there were no restrictions on what they could convert, and he conceived the idea of turning *Stormont* into a yacht that would put those of his rivals, especially Stavros Niarchos, into the shade. It was a novel concept at a time when private yachts tended to be sailing vessels with limited deck and cabin space. The frigate, at 325 feet and 1,450 tons, had a vast hull and very powerful engines; she could cruise at eighteen knots and manage twenty-two in an emergency. He would spend more than $4 million — an astounding sum at a time of post-war austerity — to create a floating palace that even the jaded King Farouk would describe as, 'the last word in opulence'. *The New York Times*, not often given to hyperbole, would enthuse, 'Here are such teak decks, flawless varnished woodwork and polished brass as have been rarely seen since the passing of J P Morgan.'

Her on-board equipment included a forty-two-line telephone and telex system, air-conditioning (rare at the time), an operating theatre with an X-ray machine, an amphibious aircraft which could carry five passengers and their luggage, and a heated swimming pool which could be raised to deck level and covered to form a dance floor. His own suite comprised four rooms on the bridge deck and there were nine luxurious state rooms for guests. Priceless paintings were hung in her public rooms, but Aristotle was not above displaying a few fakes. When experts declared two of his El Grecos to be of 'dubious' origin (*Boy Lighting a Candle* and *Madonna Supported by an Angel*) Aristotle merely shrugged and said, 'If people wish to believe them to be genuine, why spoil their pleasure?' The *Christina* was stocked with eight varieties of caviar, a priceless wine cellar, and sixty crew including two hairdressers, three chefs, a Swedish masseuse and an orchestra for those who wished to dance. Marble, gold and hand-painted frescos were everywhere, but her sleek white hull and streamlined funnel made her a graceful sight when she rode at anchor or steamed slowly along the Mediterranean coast.

The actor, Richard Burton, would later say, 'I don't think there is a man or woman on earth who would not be seduced by the sheer shameless narcissism of this boat.' That was precisely what Aristotle had intended. Networking and schmoozing had always been a part of his business strategy, but he could now entertain the great and good in a style that left even them speechless. Because the bar stools were covered with the foreskins of whales, Aristotle was able to tell Greta Garbo, 'Madam, you are now sitting on the largest penis in the world.' Garbo was nonplussed but Cary Grant's wife, Betsy Drake, laughed and retorted, 'Oh, so that's Moby's Dick!'

Aristotle had long eschewed conventional offices, preferring to do business in nightclubs, restaurants and even bordellos. But the Louis Quinze desk he had long promised himself was now installed on the *Christina* and she became a floating headquarters for his many businesses. The ship's captain was a war-hardened German and Onassis kept a substantial armoury aboard, should the vessel ever be threatened. Alan Brien recalls Aristotle showing him dozens of modern weapons, from rifles to machine guns and bazookas, concealed behind a secret panel. Since becoming a refugee at seventeen, he had never truly settled anywhere and despite holding several passports he was still, spiritually, a stateless person and a nomad. Those who have once been refugees, especially when young, never entirely lose the terror of having to flee, wherever they settle. The idea of a moveable home on the open sea clearly made him feel more secure and, from the day of her maiden voyage, he would spend far more time aboard the *Christina* than in his many houses ashore. While Monaco was her home port, and the *Christina* displayed the initials of the Yacht Club of Monaco on her hull, she flew the flag of Liberia from her stern staff, and her lifebuoys showed the port of Monrovia. As with most of Aristotle's investments, her true home was opaque.

He was happiest when at sea, and he would give her captain orders to sail on the least whim and at a moment's notice. Mostly, he cruised the Mediterranean, Ionian and Aegean Seas, often calling at Venice, the city where he had first seduced Ingeborg Dedichen. On one occasion, Ingeborg happened also to be in Venice and saw the *Christina*

RICHER THAN CROESUS

Tina Onassis aboard the *Christina* with her son, Alexander, and below, sitting by the gold-plated poolside.

at anchor with Aristotle strolling on the deck. She sent a note to him but received no reply. In her diary she wrote, '*Christina* passed in! Ari walked up deck — could have called — feeling awful — wrote letter — depressed, dined and returned — ah! ah! ah!' A guest on the yacht remembered the surprise when they immediately and inexplicably sailed away, 'We were to spend four or five days in Venice, but we left early and very suddenly.' Ingeborg would never see him again.[85]

With the Saudi deal in tatters, and his whaling fleet under new restrictions, his thoughts now turned to his investment in SBM. He announced to the world that he would 'turn that sorry-ass town into something very tasty'. This would bring him into bitter conflict with Prince Rainier who, quite apart from being mortified by the term 'sorry-ass town', had quite different ideas for his kingdom. Rainier had long wanted to develop Monaco into a Las Vegas-style holiday resort with gambling, entertainment and multiple hotels to encourage high-volume tourism. Aristotle, on the other hand, wanted Monaco to remain a lightly taxed and lightly regulated home for a handful of very rich people.

Rainier, however, had pressing financial problems. Although he was, technically, lord and master of the tiny principality (less than a square mile), the purse strings were held by a committee of eighteen wealthy citizens and bankers who were elected by 600 male residents. The joke among the Monégasques was that Rainier was the 'throne behind the power'. Thanks to some poor investments, both Rainier and Monaco were virtually bankrupt. At the same time, France's

General de Gaulle, who deeply disliked the presence of a tax haven on France's borders, was threatening sanctions. If that were not enough, Rainier also lacked an heir. Now in his early thirties, he seemed to be showing little interest in marrying, preferring to live with a divorced French actress, Gisèle Pascal, whose parents had once run a vegetable stall in the marketplace in Nice. This was beginning to unnerve the wealthier residents because, legally, if Rainier failed to produce a legitimate male heir the principality reverted to France and that would mean French laws and taxes.

Aristotle, who wanted to encourage American gamblers to come to his casino, seriously suggested that the prince should marry Marilyn Monroe, who had just divorced her second husband, the baseball player, Joe diMaggio. Monroe had recently dated Marlon Brando and was now living with Arthur Miller (she would marry the playwright a year later). Aristotle even went as far as persuading Gardner Cowles, the publisher of *Look* magazine, to broach it with her. Cowles invited her to his farm in Connecticut, and later recalled her response: 'She listened very carefully and said, "Is he rich? Is he handsome?" Those were the only questions she asked. I don't think she even knew where Monaco was. But she agreed that we should go ahead and arrange a meeting.

'As an afterthought I said to her, "Do you think that the prince will want to marry you?"

'Her eyes were full of light. "Give me two days alone with him and of course he'll want to marry me."'

Aristotle's plans, however, were soon overtaken by events. In 1955 Grace Kelly travelled to the Cannes

Film Festival to promote *The Country Girl*. While on a train journey with her friend Oliva de Havilland, a meeting with Rainier in Monaco was suggested. Within a year Kelly had wed the prince in one of the most publicised marriages of the twentieth century.[86] Aristotle's private aircraft dropped thousands of red and white carnations over Monaco as Kelly arrived and the festivities went on for days.

When the Rainiers returned from their honeymoon, however, the relationship with Aristotle was markedly cooler. In one conversation, Rainier said, 'Mr Onassis, you were badly brought up. Your money has bought you everything except an education.'[87] This new condescension may, in part, have been triggered because Rainier knew — following the failure of the Saudi deal — that Aristotle's companies were haemorrhaging money. On the other hand, it may also have been because the guests being entertained aboard the *Christina* often outshone those being entertained at the Grimaldi Palace. The prince and princess of Monaco were generally seen as social minnows by the *haut monde* (Queen Elizabeth II and her family had stayed away from the wedding, sending only a middle-ranking diplomat). Aristotle, on the other hand, could now boast a lengthening list of glitterati as his shipmates, including Sir Winston Churchill.

Friendship with the elder statesman had followed a long, hard climb up the social ladder. The suspicion and gossip remained that Aristotle was a 'shady character': a low-born Levantine who 'collected' famous guests aboard his lavish but vulgar yacht. Society, on both sides of the Atlantic, has always made a clear distinction between old and new money. Even Princess Grace was derided in some circles because her father was a self-made millionaire who had once been a humble bricklayer. Aristotle had first befriended Churchill's only son, Randolph. The bibulous and gossipy former MP was happy to accept Aristotle's lavish hospitality, and the two became drinking companions. Not only did Aristotle benefit from Randolph's social connections, but he also proved to be a reliable source of information on the worsening political situation in Egypt, resulting in Aristotle becoming the best-prepared shipowner during the Suez crisis.

After six years in the political wilderness, Churchill had been returned to Downing Street with a narrow majority following the 1951 General Election. At the age of seventy-seven, however, his health was declining following two strokes. Privately, colleagues were urging him to stand down in favour of his deputy, Anthony Eden. King George VI agreed but died himself before he could persuade Churchill to go. His heir, Queen Elizabeth II, developed a close friendship with her prime minister and was reluctant to force him out of office, but, in 1953, Churchill suffered a major stroke which left him paralysed down one side. Eden also had serious health issues, and, for a while, Britain was effectively leaderless, although that fact was kept secret from the public. Churchill did not finally retire until April 1955, having reached the age of eighty.

Although famously born in a palace, the departing prime minister had little money of his own other than royalties from his books. He was a direct descendant of the Duke of Marlborough, but his father had been the third son, inheriting only a courtesy title with little property or money. In 1946, a group of businessmen had bought Churchill's home, Chartwell, for the nation, with the proviso that the couple could remain in it for life. This enabled them to pay off their debts, but they remained far from wealthy. Winston had never believed in living frugally and, during his twilight years, he liked to spend the summer months in the south of France, where he could paint, swim and enjoy hospitality at the villas of moneyed friends. In the 1950s, before the advent of cheap air travel, the Côte d'Azur was still an exclusive resort for rich Americans and Europeans who vied with each other to entertain the world's most famous living statesman.

Aristotle's first meeting with Winston Churchill had not been a success. Through Randolph's friend and Churchill's literary agent, Emery Reeves, he had obtained an invitation to dinner with Churchill and his entourage at Reeves' villa, La Pausa.[88] Reeves' fiancée, Wendy Russell, later recalled, 'Onassis looked absolutely dreadful, in an ill-fitting suit, clutching a bouquet of long-stemmed roses almost as big as himself.'[89] [90] Aristotle behaved obsequiously at first, wanting to kiss Winston's hand while praising him in grandiloquent terms. Churchill, who disliked sycophants, brushed him aside irritably. The atmosphere did not improve when the dinner conversation turned to Cyprus. Aristotle sympathised with Archbishop Makarios, who wanted the island to be unified with Greece, whereas Churchill — who saw Cyprus as a vital military asset — was outraged by the deaths of British soldiers. Aristotle, realising he'd committed a series of *faux pas*, apologised to his hostess when he left, and was pleasantly surprised when she suggested inviting the whole party onto his yacht. 'Would you come?' he asked.

'It would be the gravest of ill manners not to,' she replied.[91] Aristotle solemnly promised there would be no media and promptly broke his word by tipping them off.

The next day, surrounded by many paparazzi, Churchill — with some assistance from his attendants — ponderously mounted the gangplank of the *Christina*. The two men could hardly have been more different and yet, paradoxically, they became friends. With his other guests, Aristotle would often become an enchanting imp, regaling them with his humour and horseplay. Dressed casually in slacks and an open-necked shirt — and usually with a cigarette or cigar in the corner of his mouth — he was a warm if profane host, although some guests would witness his volcanic tantrums. When Churchill was onboard, however, he literally sat at his feet, sometimes spoon-feeding him when the old man's hands shook too much to eat properly. The two men discussed everything from politics to history while being served limitless quantities of Dom Perignon and caviar. They played card games and sang songs together. Churchill was already suffering from dementia, but he still had lucid periods when all his old sharpness and wit returned. 'I like your boat,' he frequently told his host. His wife, Clementine, however, disliked both the boat and Aristotle.

The *Christina* sailed to whatever port took Churchill's fancy. If the weather was rough when

Winston Churchill took pride of place among the many celebrities entertained by Aristotle Onassis.

Churchill retired, Aristotle would stand on the bridge, directing the helmsman to turn this way and that to avoid the biggest waves. On shore, he would personally drive Churchill around the town in a curious kind of buggy that the *Christina* carried in her hold.

Randolph Churchill often travelled with his father on the *Christina,* knowing that his drunkenness and occasional outbursts would be tolerated because, without him, Aristotle might have lost his most glamorous guest. The relationship between father and son was a complex one. Randolph worshipped his father but was crushed by the impossibility of equalling him in any walk of life, least of all politics. In 1940, after three failed attempts, he gained a Conservative parliamentary seat in an unopposed by-election but lost it during the Labour landslide of 1945.

Following the war, he was notionally a journalist, employed mainly by his father's friends, Lords Beaverbrook and Rothermere, but he wrote little. Like many a disappointing son, he developed a big personality. He was good-looking, witty and occasionally charming but, when drunk, prone to competitive and extreme behaviour. Churchill's wartime secretary, Jock Colville wrote, 'I thought Randolph one of the most objectionable people I had ever met: noisy, self-assertive, whining and frankly unpleasant. He did not strike me as intelligent. At dinner he was anything but kind to Winston, who adores him.'[92] Randolph always felt compelled to be the loudest, rudest and funniest man in the room. Consequently, he drank, gambled, and fornicated more than any of his friends.[93]

Randolph's love life was chaotic. While serving in the army at the outbreak of war, he had been in love with the socialite Laura Charteris, but despite being estranged from her husband, she did not reciprocate. At the same time, he was conducting an affair with (among others) the American actress Claire Luce, but decided he had to marry quickly prior to going overseas on active service. He was rejected by eight different women in the course of two weeks, but finally succeeded with the young socialite, Pamela Digby. She was notoriously promiscuous and, during the marriage, would conduct affairs with, among others, Edward R Murrow, John Hay 'Jock' Whitney and Averell Harriman (Harriman would become her third husband in 1971). The journalist and historian, Max Hastings noted, 'She was … described as having become "a world expert on rich men's bedroom ceilings".' [94]

Harriman was Franklin D Roosevelt's Special Envoy in London, co-ordinating the vital Lend-Lease programme, without which Britain's war effort might well have failed. Pamela would later recall, 'If anything, Winston made it easier for the two of us to see each other outside London by inviting both of us to Chequers nearly every weekend.' Posted to Cairo, Randolph was conducting affairs of his own, drinking wildly and turning up at hotels in the company of prostitutes. When Harriman toured Egypt on a fact-finding mission, the two men became friends and Randolph confided his infidelities. Harriman, however, was by nature more discreet and did not reciprocate. On returning to London and hearing the gossip about his wife, Randolph would be bitterly angry with his father, convinced he must have known about the liaison and may even have encouraged it.

RICHER THAN CROESUS

Randolph and Pamela Churchill.

One evening, at dinner aboard the *Christina*, Randolph's long-held grudge exploded into a bitter rant, and he accused his father of literally 'pimping out' Pamela during the war. He became so angry, actually screaming at his father, that Winston's secretary, Anthony Montague Browne, took him back to his cabin, fearing that he might suffer another stroke. Aristotle, who was no stranger to tantrums (or, for that matter, extra-marital affairs), said nothing. The following day no one mentioned the quarrel, and all behaved as if nothing had happened.

Churchill hated the attention of journalists, but

Aristotle revelled in it and, with the old statesman at his side, he became the world's most photographed and recognised businessman: exactly what he had always wanted. Even the other guests were often those suggested by Churchill, including the up-and-coming politicians who, Churchill thought, were potential leaders. One such was the newly married Senator for Massachusetts, Jack Kennedy, who visited with his wife, Jackie. Churchill had disliked Jack's father, Joe, because while United States ambassador to Britain in the late 1930s, he had opposed American involvement in the war claiming that Britain had no hope of defeating the Nazis. In spite of that, Churchill had heard encouraging things about Joe's son and said to Aristotle, 'They tell me he is presidential timber; I should like to meet this presidential timber.'[95] Churchill was not the only one to believe that Kennedy was marked for stardom: one of his biographers later wrote, 'Jack's election to the Senate opened the way to a romance between Jack Kennedy and millions of Americans. It would be one of the great American love affairs, and in his election day grin, it was just possible to imagine that Jack himself knew the match had been made.'[96]

Aristotle was not immediately impressed when Jack Kennedy came aboard, telling him dryly, 'I must ask you to leave by seven-thirty. Sir Winston dines sharp at eight-fifteen.' He was, however, fascinated by Jackie. Years later, he could even remember how she was dressed at that first meeting: a simple white skirt cut just above the knee in the 'trapeze line' made fashionable by Yves Saint Laurent. She wore no hat, and her short brown hair was gently ruffled by the breeze. Quiet, without being shy, she spoke excellent

French to his French guests, was obviously intelligent, but hid it and deferred to her husband's opinions in a way that Aristotle approved of. Winston Churchill — in one of his periodic 'gaga' bouts of dementia — was uncommunicative and Jackie later joked to her husband, 'Maybe he thought you were a waiter.' Once

The *Christina* was then the world's most sumptuously appointed private vessel.

the Kennedys had left, Aristotle exchanged confidences with his close friend and business partner, Costa Gratsos. 'There's something damned wilful about her,' he said, 'there's something provocative about that lady, she's got a carnal soul.' Costa warned, 'She's too young for you.'⁹⁷ But, she was only four months younger than his wife, Tina.

What Aristotle would probably not have known was that the Kennedys' marriage was then in crisis. After the meeting on the *Christina*, Jackie had left for Paris and Jack sailed to Capri. He was still seeing Gunilla von Post and even tried to persuade her to join him there. From Capri he travelled to Poland and from there telephoned Gunilla again, saying that he loved her, and he would tell his father that he wanted a divorce from Jackie. Joe Kennedy, however — who liked Jackie and knew that she liked him — would hear nothing of it. 'He yelled at me, "You're out of your mind. You're going to be President someday. This would ruin everything. Divorce is impossible. Look at what happened with me and Gloria Swanson!"'⁹⁸

Aristotle was not immediately impressed by his first meeting with John Kennedy.

CHAPTER TEN
A Turn of Providence

Throughout his career, Aristotle would win and lose fortunes by responding to geopolitical events. Usually, he won, but the failure of the Saudi deal cost him dear and — had fortune not turned once more in his favour — he might have lost everything. Events in Egypt, however — which few could have predicted — would now make him the richest man in the world.[99]

In the middle of the nineteenth century a French diplomat, Ferdinand de Lesseps, formed a company to build a canal through Egypt and connect the Mediterranean to the Red Sea. The Suez Canal opened in 1869 and reduced the sailing distance between the two oceans by over 5,000 miles. For most vessels of that era, the journey time was reduced by more than two weeks. The effect on trade between Europe and the East was spectacular and, for the next century, almost all deep-sea vessels were built to 'Panamax' dimensions, i.e., the maximum size that could navigate the Suez and (slightly narrower) Panama Canals.[100]

The Suez Canal never, as is sometimes claimed, 'belonged' to France and Britain (it had always belonged to Egypt) but the company which ran it belonged primarily to British and French shareholders. In 1952, the Egyptian monarchy was overthrown in a military coup led by Lieutenant Colonel Gamal Abdel Nasser, who became President in 1954 and introduced widespread reforms. By 1956, he had nationalised Egypt's most valuable asset, the Suez Canal, prompting Israel to invade the Egyptian Sinai. Within days, Britain and France had landed paratroopers with the clear aim of seizing control of the canal and deposing Nasser. The Egyptians promptly blocked the canal by sinking forty ships in it, forcing vessels to take the much longer Cape of Good Hope route to Europe and America.

Aristotle, who had been prewarned by Randolph Churchill of a possible canal closure, was the only major shipowner whose fleet was ideally positioned and largely available. The spot market for chartering oil tankers rocketed by 1,000 per cent, and Aristotle began to make money on a scale that not even he could previously have imagined. On one voyage alone, from the Persian Gulf to Europe, a 65,000-ton tanker netted him a profit of more than six million dollars, and in less than six months he made eighty million dollars. In an irony that he hugely enjoyed, the principal charterers were the same ARAMCO companies who had conspired to force him out of Saudi Arabia. When Costa Gratsos warned him of a post-Suez slump, he replied, 'I'm hot, I'm in front of the parade, I've got the touch, why the hell should we crap out now?'[101] Nevertheless, by the time the canal reopened in 1957, he had accepted the counsel of the more cautious Gratsos, who saved him from losing millions.

Even when the Suez Canal had fully reopened, however, the ocean charter business would never be quite the same. Shipowners, including Onassis and Niarchos, now knew that sailing around the African Cape was not as troublesome as they had once feared. No longer limited by the width of a canal, they could now build the largest mobile manmade structures the world had ever seen. By 1958, shipyards were producing 'super-tankers' with capacities over 100,000 deadweight tons, bigger than even the largest aircraft carriers, freighters or cruise ships. By 1979, the largest crude carrying vessels afloat had capacities in excess of 550,000 deadweight tons. Too big to enter most ports, they loaded their cargoes at offshore platforms and discharged to smaller tankers at lightering points off-coast.

In Greece, the 1956 elections had been won by Constantine Karamanlis and his right-wing National Radical Union Party. The new government wanted to harness the wealth and expertise of the country's many expatriate businessmen, and they encouraged Aristotle to take over Greece's small, struggling national airline, TAE, allowing him to buy it for only $2 million. No one knew better than he how to exploit such a windfall and he ran rings around Karamanlis and his advisors in the negotiations which followed. He coaxed and cajoled the government into granting him concession after concession, including some previously unheard-of benefits for a private company. These included compensation for unofficial strikes, subsidies for loss-making routes, tax rebates, restrictions on foreign competitors and low-interest loans from the government. If all that weren't enough, he was also given an exclusive concession to handle and refuel all the foreign airlines which landed in Greece.

The company, which he renamed Olympic Airways, should have been a licence to print money but, in truth, Olympic would always be a troubled organisation. The airline business turned out to be nothing like the ocean freight business in which he'd made his fortune. On the high seas a shipping line (especially one sailing under flags of convenience) can raise or lower its rates at a moment's notice without needing anyone's permission. Vessels can sail to any port where they can find a profitable cargo, turn around in mid-ocean or be laid up until better times arrive. Airlines, however, are tightly bound by laws and regulations. Profits, even in good times, are wafer-thin and unforeseeable events can plunge even the best operation into deep losses overnight. Scheduled air services, in particular, must be painstakingly built up over many years and the air transport business is heavily unionised, making it prone to strikes and unrest. On top of these inherent problems, Aristotle's erratic rule meant that Olympic was plagued by frequent management changes. Donald McGregor, a British pilot who joined Olympic Airways when he retired from BOAC, recalled, 'I used to go around saying "morning sir" to everyone; I didn't know who the hell was going to be my boss the next day.' Aristotle made little money from Olympic but revelled in his status as the world's only private owner of a national airline. Like the *Christina*, Olympic Airways brought him benefits in different ways. As he put it, 'The planes are the leaves of the tree. The roots are the ships.' [102]

By 1959 Aristotle had lost control of SBM. Rainier forced his appointee off the board by the simple technique of issuing new shares (which Monaco law allowed), thereby eliminating Aristotle's majority. Increasingly, he lived abord the *Christina*, which was never short of glamorous guests, Winston Churchill and Greta Garbo topped the bill of an ever-changing cast of actors, entertainers, businessmen and politicians. Garbo, who was fifty years old when she met Aristotle, had never married and was notoriously reclusive, but enjoyed the privacy and luxury of life aboard the *Christina*. Sexually, she preferred women to men and her friendship with Aristotle may well have been platonic.

Ava Gardner — who was introduced to Aristotle by Grace Kelly with the caveat that he was a 'forceful lover' — made a telling observation which helps explain Aristotle's appeal to some women. What struck her was that, although ugly, he looked like a satyr: a lustful, drunken, priapic, woodland god. 'If he hadn't had a dollar, he could have snapped a lady's garter anytime he liked. He was a primitive with a yacht. For some ladies, that's an irresistible combination.'[103] In spite of these assets, Gardner refused his advances.

Tina Onassis, however, preferred to live ashore, especially in Paris and London. She had been educated in England, spoke English with a 'cut glass' accent and was accepted by European society in a way that Aristotle had never entirely achieved. In England, accents counted: George Bernard Shaw once noted, 'It is impossible for an Englishman to open his mouth without making some other Englishman hate or despise him.'[104] She enjoyed the summer events which the English call the 'social season', a string of sporting fixtures, horse races, regattas and concerts which are *de rigueur* for the great and good. Aristotle's nomadic life aboard the *Christina* was less to her taste but, in public, she still fiercely defended him.

Some of Churchill's older friends, especially the newspaper baron Lord Beaverbrook, resented his new closeness to Aristotle. Sam White, the Paris correspondent of Beaverbrook's *Evening Standard*, was regularly running negative stories, reporting that Aristotle's loss of SBM had followed an acrimonious row between him and Rainier, and that Tina Onassis had suffered a nervous breakdown. Both these claims were true, but had not previously been widely known, and Tina reacted angrily, writing to Beaverbrook and pleading with him to rein in White. Beaverbrook's disingenuous reply is worth repeating in full:

> Dear Madame Onassis,
> I am very distressed by your letter. The *Evening Standard* will always present you in a favourable light. And indeed it would be impossible for the paper to take any other course.
> I am far from London for ten months of the year. The papers are not really under my control. I still have the right to vote the majority of the shares and to that extent I am responsible. But my son is conducting the business now and I am sending him a copy of your letter and my reply.
> And with all good wishes and great admiration.
> I am,
> Yours ever,
> Max Beaverbrook

Aristotle's response to Tina was, 'Barony bullshit — he promises nothing, admits nothing. His newspapers will go on crucifying me and this Canadian son of a bitch will go on washing his hands of the whole business.' He knew this was Beaverbrook's revenge for his friendship with Churchill and sent him a letter of his own following a protracted newspaper strike: 'Together with Lady Churchill and Sir Winston we all send our heartiest congratulations and greetings. We all hope now the strike is over you could fly to Athens, and our plane will bring you on board.' Beaverbrook declined, claiming to be '… tied and bound and fenced in by duties'.

Neither Aristotle nor Tina had been faithful during their marriage. Tina, influenced by her friends and upbringing, may have accepted the long-standing upper-class convention that once a wife has provided an heir (if not a spare), she is free to have affairs, the provisos being that she is discreet and does not publicly embarrass her husband, nor question him too closely on his own private life. For both the nobility, and the shipping royalty that she came from, marriages were usually strategic partnerships rather than love matches, and her own marriage to Aristotle would never have been permitted had it not suited her father's business interests and her mother's dynastic ambitions. Nevertheless, there can be no doubt that the couple loved each other when they married, and that their love endured for a long time. By the mid-1950s, however, it was waning. At a dinner party, Tina confided in a friend, 'I think it's beastly that we still sleep together, it makes me feel soiled.'[105]

In 1957, Tina returned to the Château de la Croë to find Aristotle in bed with a mutual friend, the American socialite Jeanne Rhinelander. The subsequent row led to the château being sold (no sooner did it come on the market, than it was bought by Stavros Niarchos for his wife, Tina's sister, Eugenia). It was not the first time Tina had either suspected, or known for certain, that he had been unfaithful, but this humiliation was the beginning of the end of the marriage. Tina began to complain openly to her friends that Aristotle had never recognised her contribution to his life: 'Like Mark Anthony, Ari is a colossal child, capable of conquering the world, incapable of resisting a pleasure.' Tina also, however, was not especially good at resisting temptation. A friend later observed, 'Her susceptibility to handsome men, was second only to her susceptibility to extremely handsome men.'

As with his relationship with Ingeborg Dedichen, there was a sado-masochistic component to their bond, which may be the clue to other relationships. Aristotle made no secret of the fact that he beat the women in his life, often claiming that 'all Greek men beat their women: He who loves well beats well'. We can reasonably assume this included his father, and that the young Aristotle grew up in a house where his mother and stepmother were beaten.

In 1954, the British journalist, Alan Brien, was a guest of the Onassis family at the Château de la Croë. Randolph Churchill had arranged for him to write an article on Aristotle for *Illustrated* magazine. Unlike other tycoons, Aristotle actively courted publicity and regularly invited journalists into his home and aboard the *Christina*. In conversation with Peter Evans, Aristotle's official biographer, Brien later recalled witnessing a violent argument between Aristotle and Tina. Unable to sleep on the second night, he went down to the library to find a book to read and heard sounds of a physical fight coming from another room. Aristotle was screaming 'You whore! you whore!' while raining blows onto Tina, who sobbed uncontrollably. Through the half-open door, Brien could see 'the shadows of a man hitting out and a woman covering up. I knew I was going to have to stop it. I was about to enter — I'd decided to go in and say, "You can throw me out of your house tonight if you like, but I cannot stand by and allow you to beat up a woman," when they threw their arms around each other and began kissing passionately. They moved into the bedroom, and clearly they went off to bed to fuck. I've never forgotten that scene. The menacing shadows ... it was like an Orson Welles movie; even the château could have been modelled after Kane's Xanadu.'

In 1957, Aristotle attended a ball in Venice organised by Elsa Maxwell, the American gossip columnist and professional hostess. Since the early 1920s, Maxwell had been paid to attract stars — including Cole Porter, Tallulah Bankhead, Noël Coward and Fanny Brice — to Venice's Lido. Maxwell and Porter were lifelong friends, and he mentioned her in several of his songs.[106] Her parties were fabled, and she invented the 'Treasure Hunt' party game which remains popular to this day.[107] Although Maxwell publicly condemned same-sex relationships, in private she was the lover of the Scottish singer Dorothy Fellowes-Gordon. The two met in 1912 and remained together until Maxwell's death in 1963.[108] She professed to be celibate but was the twentieth century's most celebrated matchmaker. Her couplings included Rita Hayworth, whom she introduced to Prince Aly Khan; and Marilyn Monroe, whom she introduced to Arthur Miller.[109] By the late 1950s, Maxwell had fallen obsessively in love with Maria Callas, showering the soprano with *billets-doux*.[110] Maria, who was forty years younger than Maxwell, declined an affair but accepted some of the social invitations. At the 1957 Venice ball, Maxwell introduced her to Aristotle Onassis. The following morning, Maria and her husband were given breakfast aboard the *Christina*, anchored in a lagoon close to the Grand Canal.

As with Aristotle's first meeting with Jackie Kennedy, Maria made an intense impression on him, but there was no immediate *coup de foudre*, and more than a year would pass before the two met again. By then, Maria Callas was at the very peak of her fame. The most celebrated diva of the twentieth century was thronged by journalists, photographers and admirers wherever she went. Along with Marilyn Monroe and Brigitte Bardot, she filled column inches everywhere and everything she did or said was news. Her 1958 Paris debut was attended by the President of France, the former King Edward VIII, Charlie Chaplin, the Rothschilds, Jean Cocteau and practically every other mover and shaker of the era. Throughout the day enormous bouquets of flowers arrived every hour at her dressing room, each with an unsigned card written in Greek. Only the final one was signed by Aristotle. Her husband, Meneghini, was furious, especially when Maria remained unperturbed by what was clearly the beginning of a courtship.

It had become common knowledge that Aristotle's marriage to Tina was breaking down and she was now being openly photographed with the Venezuelan millionaire, Renaldito Herrera. When she flew to New York to be with her sister, Eugenia, for the birth of her first child, Aristotle was angered by Tina's renewed closeness with 'the Niarchos Woman'. The Onassis family remained apart for Christmas and Aristotle explained the separation to journalists by claiming he had been unavoidably detained by business in Monaco. Tina, however, told friends she now found the principality, 'paralysingly vulgar'.

There was, perhaps, an inevitability to Aristotle's interest in Maria. Even his sister, Artemis — always one of his closest confidantes — would later say, 'All his life my brother loved meeting and making love to famous women. The more important or well-known the woman, the more he loved to love her. Maria was the most famous Greek woman of our time. It was inevitable he would love her.'[111] In the spring of 1959, they would all be brought together at the annual ball of Contessa Castelbarco in her palazzo in Venice. Aristotle openly flirted with Maria who did nothing to discourage him, while Meneghini visibly fumed. It was obvious to all the guests that she was thrilled by Aristotle's attention and rumours began to circulate. Tina, in a gown designed by Jean Desses (he dressed all Aristotle's women) and wearing priceless jewels, was nearly six years younger than the soprano and considered a greater beauty, but she, like Meneghini, was powerless to stop what was plainly unfolding before everyone's eyes. As Aristotle danced with Maria, Meneghini took Tina aside and whispered to her, 'What kind of man is your husband?'

'He requires space in the world,' she replied, 'without space he wreaks damage on things and people.' Aristotle — usually the last to leave and always wanting to 'go on somewhere' in the small hours after a party — invited Maria back to the *Christina*, anchored nearby, for an early champagne breakfast. Meneghini, however, insisted that they had to leave promptly the next day for Madrid and the invitation was declined. Aristotle countered with an invitation to join his family on the *Christina* for a summer cruise. This time, Maria neither declined nor accepted, saying that she had a busy schedule but would be thinking of them when she opened in *Medea*, at Covent Garden, in June. Aristotle interpreted this as a green light and, from that moment, the seduction of Maria Callas became a priority for him. He approached his love affairs in the same way that he approached his major business deals. Once the target had been identified he was relentless and unstoppable; nothing was left to chance, irrespective of cost or effort.

By June, Aristotle had bought more than fifty tickets on the black market, enabling him to fill the best seats at Covent Garden with his own guests. He had also arranged a lavish 170-guest afterparty at the Dorchester with an all-star VIP list including Gary Cooper, the Churchill family (minus Winston) and royalty. Johnny Meyer, one of Aristotle's fixers who'd formerly been Howard Hughes' right-hand man, warned him that Meneghini was threatening to boycott the party: 'He's pissed off with the way you're climbing on Maria's bandwagon.' Aristotle's reply was characteristically pithy: 'I hear Meneghini likes a little spare pussy now and then. Anyway, he's not servicing the account, so what the hell.'[112]

Tina quickly sensed that her husband was taking

A TURN OF PROVIDENCE

Onassis and Meneghini each hold the fur coat of Maria Callas following a party at London's Dorchester.

Maria a lot more seriously than his other dalliances. 'He talked about her too much; he never talked about the others.' She told a friend that Maria Callas, who was born in New York, was the only woman who could make her (born in London) feel less than European.[113] The first night of *Medea* was rapturously received by the audience and Maria took a dozen curtain calls. The reviews were ecstatic: 'Fury hot and fury cold,' from the *Saturday Review* and 'Burning passion and intensity,' from *Opera*. She made her entrance to the afterparty tantalisingly late, at one o'clock, and received a long and loud ovation from the guests. Aristotle, who must have been a little unnerved by her late appearance, did not leave her side from the moment she entered the ballroom. When she said it was a pity that no one danced the tango any more, he ordered the Hungarian orchestra to play nothing else, severely taxing their repertoire. For Tina it was a public humiliation and another nail in the coffin of her marriage. Watching her husband enjoy dance after dance with Maria, she dolefully told a society columnist, 'I wish we could stay in one place and have the opera come to us, instead of us having to go to the opera.' If there was anyone in the room who had not previously heard the rumour of Aristotle's new obsession, they would certainly have known by three am when the party ended. As they left, photographers snapped Aristotle, Meneghini and Maria in the foyer. In one photograph, Aristotle grins and hugs Maria's fur coat but Meneghini, who also hugs the coat, has a slightly less convincing smile. Aristotle recalled, 'I will never forget the warm smell of her furs as we kissed goodnight.'

Kensington and Knightsbridge are threaded with tiny streets of mews houses. These former stables became fashionable homes when cars replaced horses in the early twentieth century. Their narrow, cobbled passageways — often *cul de sacs* — are rarely accessed by vehicles, making them far more discreet than the larger houses in surrounding streets. A mews house played a key role in the Profumo scandal which shook the British establishment in 1961. More recently, a London mews house has featured in allegations against Ghislaine Maxwell and Prince Andrew.

A TURN OF PROVIDENCE

Onassis owned a vast mansion in Grosvenor Square, but he could not take Maria there while Tina was in London, so he rented a mews cottage, and it was there that Maria slept with him for the first time. He would also boast of her performing fellatio on him as his Rolls-Royce was driven down Park Lane. If Maria held out on him, it could not have been for long: her role in *Medea* ended in late June, after which she had concerts in Amsterdam and Brussels. Her surrender appears to have been quick and total, reinforced by the discovery that her husband had made advances to her Dutch secretary, Elle Schotte. While they were staying at a hotel, he entered Schotte's room through a connecting door and put his hand up her skirt. 'How would you like to become the chief secretary of my secretaries in Italy?' he asked. Schotte recoiled, and later told Maria what had happened.[114]

For Maria it was the last straw. She wrote to the manager of the Holland festival: 'Don't book the money over to my agent. Don't get fooled by Meneghini. I will need that money myself in the near future. Big things are about to happen in my life. All my instincts tell me so. You'll hear many things … Please stay my friend.'[115] This was a major departure, for until that date Meneghini had rigidly controlled all her finances, banking her earnings in a Swiss bank account which she had no access to. Since selling his businesses he had no money of his own and lived entirely on her earnings.

When the Meneghinis returned to Italy, Aristotle showered them with invitations to join him for a cruise on the *Christina*, telephoning several times. Maria kept him waiting for an answer, but in Milan she spent a fortune on her new found taste in lingerie and what appeared to be a trousseau. In his autobiography, Meneghini claimed that it was he who finally persuaded his wife to accept: 'They say the Greek's yacht is very comfortable. Let's give it a try.'[116] Whether or not this was true, the Meneghinis arrived in Monaco on 21 July and dined the same evening with Aristotle, Tina and Elsa Maxwell at the Hôtel de Paris.

Maxwell was offended that she had not been invited to join the cruise. Having brought the couple together in the first place, she thought it was her due. Before the dinner she sent Maria a note urging her to 'Take everything ... and give all that you can bring yourself to give.' Over dinner she made her feelings clear. 'Rich husbands,' she announced, 'always roam,' looking squarely at Aristotle. When the meal was over, Tina kissed Maxwell on the cheek and issued a thoughtful putdown: 'You know, Elsa my dear, there really isn't a lot of difference between being married to a moderately rich man and a very rich man ... if only you could understand that, you'd be a much smarter person.'[117]

At midnight the following day, the *Christina* steamed majestically out of the harbour. On board were Sir Winston and Lady Churchill, plus their canary, Toby. Other guests included Churchill's daughter, Diana Sandys and her daughter, Celia, along with Churchill's doctor, Lord Moran; Churchill's private secretary, Anthony Montague Browne, and his wife Nonie; Aristotle's sister Artemis and her husband Dr Theodore Garofalides; and Umberto Agnelli of the Fiat dynasty. Garofalides had come medically equipped because Aristotle feared that Lord Moran was almost as senile

A TURN OF PROVIDENCE

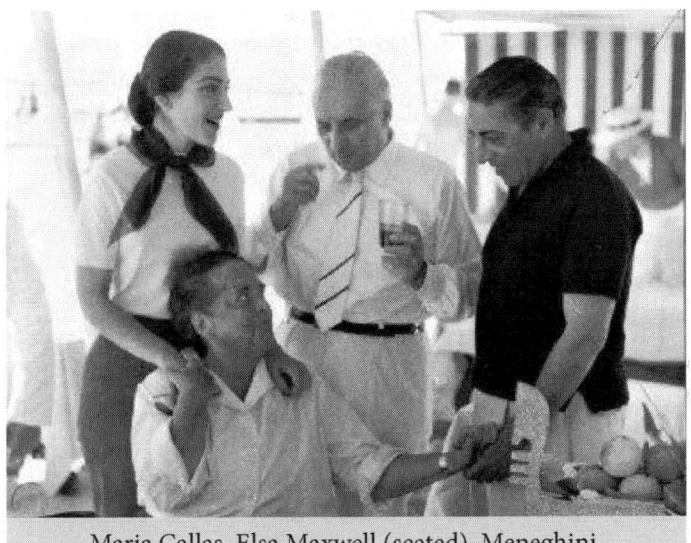

Maria Callas, Elsa Maxwell (seated), Meneghini and Onassis.

as Winston. The last two guests, who boarded moments before they sailed, had been the Meneghinis. For Tina Onassis and Giovanni Meneghini it must have been an uncomfortable departure as each clearly knew what Aristotle had in mind.

As they headed for the Italian coast, the first few days were uneventful. Meneghini spoke nothing but Italian and, with the conversation mostly in English, French and Greek (Maria was fluent in all three), he understood only what he could glean from body language. He consoled himself with unsuccessful attempts to play footsie under the table with Nonie. Almost all the guests took a dislike to him and nicknamed him 'meningitis'. Montague Browne recalled, '... he seemed to epitomise the very worst traits of a greedy and selfish Milanese bourgeois'. Of Maria, he observed, 'She seemed almost to be trying to parody a stereotypical prima donna in her behaviour.'[118] When they docked in Portofino, Aristotle, as usual, took his male guests on a tour of the nightspots, but Meneghini stayed behind. When they reached Capri, Meneghini, who had been suffering from seasickness, wanted to leave the ship, but Maria insisted it would be bad manners for them to depart so soon. Before they left the island, Gracie Fields, who lived there with her husband, was invited aboard to sing Sir Winston's favourite songs. As usual, Aristotle fawned over Churchill. During one party game the old statesman was asked what animal he would like to be reincarnated as; 'a tiger,' he replied before putting the same question to Aristotle, who said that he would like to be Toby, Winston's canary.

By day, Tina sunbathed on deck wearing a bikini, a clear reminder to Maria that she was younger and had a better figure. Whatever misgivings Tina may have felt, she remained a sparkling hostess, constantly amusing and entertaining their guests. Nonie Montague Browne, who became friends with both Tina and Maria, wrote in her diary, '... one was aware of the well-controlled tension — I seemed to be the pig in the middle.' Nonie and Maria shared a taste for practical jokes: they made apple-pie beds for everyone (except the Churchills) but the joke did not go down well. Churchill's family thought Maria was being laughably self-aggrandising when she said, 'I like travelling with Winston Churchill. It relieves me of some of the burden of my popularity.' In Nafplio the locals had prepared a floral tribute. 'Flowers for me, how kind,' said Maria. 'They are not for you,' came Diana's cool reply, 'they are for papa.'

A TURN OF PROVIDENCE

Maria Callas aboard the *Christina* with the Churchills in the background.

As they sailed along the Amalfi coast, Meneghini was confined to his cabin with seasickness, and Maria could now spend more time with Aristotle. When they were alone, he confided that his marriage was effectively over, and that Tina already had a younger lover. He also explained, disingenuously, that the original marriage, when Tina was just seventeen, had been purely a business arrangement. Had this been true he would have married the older sister, Eugenia, rather than Tina but, by now, Maria was clearly in love. With Meneghini out of the way she was constantly at Aristotle's side; even when he made long business telephone calls in languages she could not understand, she was happy to just be in his ambit, to hear his voice.

The following evening, after sunset, they sailed passed the island of Stromboli, one of Italy's three active volcanoes. Aristotle, clowning as usual, sounded the ship's horn and challenged the mountain, 'Come on! Show us your face!' At that very moment Stromboli erupted and molten lava poured into the sea. Superstitious and fatalistic, both Aristotle and Maria were thunderstruck, and Maria crossed herself in fear. Fortunately, she also believed in the powers of Greek deities, and when they called at Delphi, she convinced herself that Pythia — the High Priestess and Oracle — had foreseen good fortune for her. [119]

As the cruise progressed Aristotle began to take dinner with Maria in his state rooms while the other guests dined together in the saloon. Knowing that they were being gossiped about, he asked Nonie to accompany them as a kind of chaperone while they dined, walked on deck, or swam. Having become close to Maria, however, Nonie was prepared to turn a blind eye when they kissed.

Maria's background was dramatically different from those of most of the other women Aristotle had pursued. Like him, she had known poverty, danger, and turmoil during her childhood. Like him, she had made her fortune by hard work and talent; and like him she had moved backwards and forwards between the old and new worlds, never feeling entirely settled in either. Between them they understood things that those born into wealth, security and privilege, including Tina and most of the other passengers, could never imagine. It formed a bond and Aristotle began to talk of the childhood he had once tried to conceal. Uniquely, on this cruise, they called at Smyrna (now İzmir), a town he had not visited since fleeing as a teenager.

Aristotle loathed being called a Turk and, in the past, had even tried to reinvent himself as a native Greek, claiming to have been born in Greece's second city, Salonika (today's Thessaloniki). Now, and perhaps because of Maria, he embraced his roots and took his guests on a tour of his birthplace, pointing out the Onassis villa in Karataş, along with what remained of his father's offices and warehouses, and even his mother's grave. By day he controlled his emotions, speaking to his guests in English but making no secret of the horrors he had witnessed as a boy. At night, however, when the others had returned to the *Christina*, he took Maria and her husband to Demiri Yolu, the city's red-light district. Here he became very drunk, reminiscing about prostitutes he had known and claiming they had taught him 'wisdom about sex'. One of the pearls he shared was 'One way or another, sweets, all ladies do it for money.'[120] Meneghini would later recall, 'We made merry all night in the company of dealers, prostitutes and assorted sinister characters.'[121] They did not return to the *Christina* until five in the morning. Once alone with Maria, Meneghini was jubilant, convinced that Aristotle had revealed too much, and that Maria would now turn away from him. Peter Evans, Aristotle's official biographer, believed it may have been one of the last truly happy moments in his life.[122]

But Meneghini was not happy for long. Maria had fallen deeply in love with Aristotle, and it was too late for her to turn back now. Perhaps the final straw had been the unconcealed contempt of the other guests for her anthropomorphic husband: she had even seen the marks his white deck shoes had left on the shins of Nonie as she tried to avoid his clumsy advances. There was a blazing row and Maria stormed out of the cabin. On deck, she found Aristotle leaning over the stern rail and gazing out to sea. He began to talk of his mother, whom he'd lost at the age of six, and wondered if he would have been a different man if she had lived. Maria also talked of her childhood and the sense of rootlessness that she shared with him.

The next morning, Aristotle apologised to Maria and her husband in English, and then quoted an old proverb in Greek, knowing that Meneghini would not understand. 'When dealing with the wicked, the gods first deprive them of their senses.'[123]

'Are you wicked?' Maria asked, also in Greek.

'Most men are knaves,' he replied.

Sailing north, the *Christina* passed by the shore of Mount Athos, taking care to go no nearer than 500 metres: the closest that any female — even an animal — could come to the sacred mountain. The Virgin Mary is believed to have visited the site and prayed that it would always remain her own. The Orthodox monks who have lived there since ancient times still tolerate no women. When they dropped anchor in the Bosporus, Athenagoras I, the Ecumenical Patriarch and Archbishop of Constantinople, was brought aboard for an audience with Churchill. Before meeting him, Aristotle and Maria knelt to receive the Patriarch's blessing.[124] Calling them 'the world's greatest singer and the greatest mariner of the modern world, the new Ulysses', he offered prayers for the honours they had brought to Greece. Maria, who had a deep faith in God, began to weep and was profoundly affected. Before lunch, all the non-Greeks — with the sole exception of Winston Churchill — were sent ashore. For the rest of her life Maria would keep a statue of the Virgin Mary at her bedside.

That night, at a party in the Istanbul Hilton, Aristotle and Maria danced until the small hours of the morning. Back on board the *Christina*, she finally told Meneghini what everyone else (with the possible exception of Churchill) already knew: that she was in love with Aristotle. The tension that had been building for days was now tangible and only Churchill seemed ignorant of it. Enjoying lunchtime singsongs and games of bezique, his lucidity varied from day to day, but there were still flashes of the old statesman. When the conversation turned to Eisenhower and Sherman Adams, Churchill said: 'You must either wallop a man or vindicate him.'[125] Aristotle went further: 'You must let your nearest and dearest go to hell when they are no longer any use to you.'

Raging quarrels between Maria and her husband could now be heard in nearby cabins. One of the stewards opened a book offering odds of five to two against their finishing the cruise together. On the night of 12 August, while walking on deck, Tina looked through the saloon windows and saw Aristotle, beneath his fake El Greco, making love to a naked

Maria. She found Meneghini and told him what she'd seen: 'He has taken her away from you, Battista. Poor Maria, she'll learn soon enough what sort of man he is: a brutal drunk.' Meneghini, however, was still clinging to the hope that the affair would blow over.[126]

Onassis and Callas leave the *Christina*.

CHAPTER ELEVEN
A Man with a Compulsion

When the *Christina* returned to her home port of Monaco, Tina's father, Stavros Livanos, was waiting on the quayside to see Aristotle and he demanded an explanation. By then, the secret was out: right across Europe newspapers were openly speculating about the affair. Livanos did not get a sympathetic response from his son-in-law. 'I'm fifty-four years old, I'm richer than you are, and I have never been this happy in my life. Don't tell me how to run my affairs.' The next day, the *Christina* sailed for Venice with only Tina and her children aboard.

When the Meneghinis returned to Italy, Maria told her husband she wanted a divorce, asking him to move into their Lake Garda villa while she remained in their Milan townhouse. Aristotle joined her there as soon as her husband had gone and demanded that she separate from him permanently. Maria then asked Meneghini to return to Milan so that the three of them could work out an agreement.

Aristotle, as always, approached the negotiations as if this were a business deal. Meneghini would later recall, 'He talked like a man with a compulsion. As if afraid that if he let up for even a minute everything would crumble.' The talks went on long into the night, with frequent interruptions while Aristotle made lengthy business telephone calls. Meneghini noticed how Maria never took her eyes off him, apparently transfixed by his presence. They talked until four in the morning but agreed nothing and Meneghini returned to Lake Garda in the early morning. By then, however, the paparazzi knew the couple were in Milan and followed them everywhere. When they went, hand in hand, into the Hotel Principe e Savoia, journalists were quick to point out that it was too late for dinner and too early for breakfast. At the same time, they were printing photographs of Tina dancing cheek to cheek with Count Brando d'Adda in Venice. Aristotle was jocular, telling reporters, 'I am a sailor, and these are things which sometimes happen to a sailor.'

Another meeting took place at the Meneghinis' lakeside villa in Sirmione, but Aristotle and Maria arrived late and drunk. There is a fine line between heavy drinking and alcoholism. Few of Aristotle's biographers have accused him of being physically addicted to alcohol, but he drank prodigiously and became both garrulous and aggressive when drunk. One witness to a party aboard the *Christina* recalled, 'Onassis drank everything. And when he couldn't drink any more, he would go to the side of the boat and empty his stomach in the sea and drink some more.' [127] When taken on a tour of the villa he sniped at Meneghini saying, 'You have a nerve confining a woman like Maria to the edge of a puddle like the lake of Sirmione.'[128] [129]

Over dinner, Aristotle drank continually and began to goad Meneghini in Italian, the only language they shared. 'I am bad people but I am richer than you will ever be and a better lover than you ever were. I do what I want and I take what I want.' As before, he talked as if this were a business deal: 'What do you want? Five million dollars? You've got it. Ten? Just don't bother us.'[130] Meneghini confided in friends that, at this point, he told Aristotle to 'stick his money up his Greek ass'. In his memoirs however, he gives a more nuanced version: 'I replied, "You are a poor drunk and you turn my stomach. I would like to smash your face in, but I won't touch you because you can't even manage to stand up."'[131] Maria became hysterical and accused her husband of denying her 'this last chance of happiness'. Meneghini remained vindictive: 'For what you have done to me you will pay over and over again for the rest of your days. You will never know happiness; I pity you because you both will pay in hell for this.'

If that were not enough, Maria's mother turned the knife further when she told an Italian newspaper, 'It's painful, because Maria is always unhappy. She carries bad luck inside her, in her inability to love. She's condemned to that. Also, I feel bad for her husband, because he's old and dared to marry her. He dared to touch the Goddess, to walk on her altar. Everything in her has been sacrificed to art.'[132]

On 8 September Maria made an official announcement that she was seeking a divorce from her husband and that her lawyers would work out the details of a settlement. Over the telephone, she screamed at her husband, 'I will come to Sirmione with a gun and kill you!'

'I'll be waiting to machine-gun you down,' came the reply.[133] The Meneghini marriage was ending as dramatically as one of the operas in which Maria had starred. Aristotle, however, meeting reporters in Venice's Harry's Bar, was insouciant: 'How could I help but be flattered if a woman with the class of Maria Callas falls in love with someone like me?' Class would always be one of his preoccupations.

In Paris, Tina was learning that divorce divides friends as well as spouses, and it hurt her to see so many of their mutual acquaintances flocking to Aristotle and deserting her. She refused to meet him and returned a gold bracelet engraved 'Saturday, April 17, 1943, 7 p.m. T.I.L.Y.'

In Milan, Maria spent seven days recording *La Gioconda* at La Scala. In the short time that Meneghini had ceased to be her manager, she was already experiencing a rapprochement from leading figures in the world of opera. Antonio Ghiringhelli, who had once found her impossible, now became a friend. Even Rudolf Bing, who had actually fired her from the Metropolitan Opera, was prepared to bury the hatchet: 'Naturally, I want you back and, if you feel that you would like to reappear in New York … I would certainly be very willing to make an effort,' he said.[134]

At that time, divorce was not legal in Italy, so Meneghini could only file for a legal separation on the grounds that his wife's behaviour was 'incompatible with elementary decency'. Maria was given the Milan townhouse, most of her jewellery and the royalties from all her recordings. Meneghini kept the villa and some other real estate, they even agreed to separate their dogs, but this did not prevent Meneghini from trying to get Maria arrested for adultery, then a criminal offence in Italy. Because she was an American citizen, nothing happened, except to further enflame their mutual hatred.

A few days later, Tina filed for divorce and custody of her children in New York on the grounds of adultery, the only grounds then recognised by New York courts. Her attorney read out an agreed statement for the press:

'It is almost thirteen years since Mr Onassis and I were married in New York City. Since then he has become one of the world's richest men, but his great wealth has not brought me happiness with him, nor, as the world knows, has it brought him happiness with me. After we parted this summer in Venice, I had hoped that Mr Onassis loved our children enough and respected our privacy sufficiently to meet with me — or, through lawyers, with my lawyers — to straighten out our problems. But that was not to be.

'Mr Onassis knows positively that I want none of his wealth and that I am solely concerned with the welfare of our children.

'I deeply regret that Mr Onassis leaves me no alternative other than a New York suit for divorce.

'For my part I will always wish Mr Onassis well, and I expect that after this action is concluded he will continue to enjoy the kind of life which he apparently desires to live, but in which I have played no real part. I shall have nothing more to say and I hope I shall be left with my children in peace.'

Aristotle was back aboard the *Christina* when Costa Gratsos telephoned to read him the statement, having first warned him, 'This stuff's been written by lawyers and scored for Jascha Heifetz.'[135]

On the advice of his PR people, Aristotle moved Maria from the *Christina* to the Hermitage Hotel, but it made little difference to the paparazzi who surrounded both of them. When the divorce papers were served, Tina had not cited Maria, but her old friend Jeanne Rhinelander, as having committed adultery with her husband 'by land and sea in the United States, France, Monte Carlo, Greece and Turkey from 1957 up to the present time'. She told friends, 'I won't give that canary the satisfaction of being named the other woman.' There may also have been a more practical motive: pre-dating the adultery by several years made it harder for Aristotle to claim a countersuit on the grounds that Tina had also been unfaithful.

Aristotle was surprised and alarmed by the naming of Jeanne Rhinelander, especially when she threatened to sue Tina for slander. He told friends that he had invited her onto the *Christina* to help her '... overcome emotional and drug problems ... [but] put her on the witness stand and she's likely to say anything.' He drove to Grasse and spent several hours with her, following which she issued a statement: 'I am an old friend of Mr and Mrs Onassis. I am astonished that after so many years of friendship of which everybody knew, here and in the United States, Mrs Onassis should try to use it as an excuse to obtain her freedom ... I repeat that I know Mr Onassis and that I remain a devoted friend.'[136]

Aristotle's own statement to the press was even more equivocal: 'I have just heard that my wife has begun divorce proceedings. I am not surprised; the situation has been moving rapidly. But I was not warned. Obviously, I shall have to do what she wants and make suitable arrangements.'¹³⁷ In the background he was telephoning Tina and pleading with her not to divorce him. After one lengthy call, made from the Claridge's suite of his old friend Spyros Skouras, he sobbed like a child. When press photographs appeared of him dining with Tina, he encouraged journalists to think there might still be a reconciliation. It was to no avail, for Tina's mind was firmly made up, but her father, who feared bad publicity for his family and his business, persuade her to drop the adultery suit in New York. She was finally granted an uncontested 'quickie' divorce in Alabama on the grounds of mental cruelty. If Maria was expecting a public declaration of his love for her, she would be disappointed and would remain disappointed for the next eight years.

In Bilbao, Maria had a foretaste of things to come. A local priest, Father Joaquim de Dios Liserna, publicly denounced her, saying, 'One must not forget she is still a wife and, therefore, now a sinner.'¹³⁸ She responded by calling the concert 'a silly little engagement', and that led to further criticism. In Britain, even *The Stage* sniped at her, 'Who is Maria Callas? We don't mean the opera singer, we mean the woman who insults her public when it suits her.'¹³⁹ Her performance before the Bilbao audience drew little applause and no curtain calls. Backstage she raged at her own people, 'How was this fantastic? You made me believe I was alright. You lied to me!'¹⁴⁰

In London, for a concert at the Festival Hall, she snubbed more than fifty reporters by missing a scheduled press conference. The London audience, however, were enthusiastic, giving her twelve minutes of applause and ten curtain calls. But, when a violinist appeared to block her exit from the stage, the *Evening News* wrote, 'And the tigress went out like a lamb.' At the same time, Greek newspapers were reporting that, in Athens, Aristotle had got drunk in a taverna with the Greek actress Melina Mercouri, telling reporters, 'Callas is a sister to me, and that is all.'

Aristotle had always been drawn to fame as irresistibly as iron to a magnet. If he and Maria Callas were the two most famous Greeks, then Mercouri came a close third. Her role in *Never on Sunday* had won her an Academy Award nomination, and Best Actress at that year's Cannes Film Festival. She was not, however, taken in by him. Years later, when asked what kind of man Aristotle was, she replied simply, 'He is a pirate.'

On her return to Milan, Maria found that many of her old friends were now shunning her. Even her former champion, Elsa Maxwell — who was now trying to curry favour with Tina — had written, 'I have not been able to defend her or explain her as a person since August 1959'. Aristotle's sister Artemis was one of the few to publicly defend her: 'A woman who is adored by her fans but mistreated by her husband will never be secure.'

A tour in the United States followed but — possibly because of the emotional pressure — her voice began to fail her. In Dallas, she was unable to reach E flat in the mad scene of *Lucia di Lammermoor*. The *Dallas Morning News* wrote that her high notes were 'badly aimed attacks which she barely covered by roulades downward into the more comfortable register'. Afterwards, she said, 'I gambled my career tonight,

A MAN WITH A COMPULSION

my career ends here.' In her hotel room, she sobbed until three o'clock in the morning.[141] Other health issues followed: she began suffering from a hernia, inflammation of the jaw and fluid in her nasal cavity. 'I was like a deaf man shouting,' she said.[142] With Aristotle tied up by business in London and Monaco, she spent her thirty-sixth birthday, and Christmas of that year, alone.

Aristotle's long absences, along with his refusal to make any public statement about his feelings for her, should have been an early warning of his fickle nature. But Maria was, undoubtedly, deeply in love. Aristotle had aroused feelings in her she had not previously known, just as he had done decades earlier with Ingeborg Dedichen, and many others. Her marriage had been a business arrangement: loveless and largely sexless. She had slept with few other men, and Aristotle, who had had slept with hundreds of women, made her feel, possibly for the first time, a sexually fulfilled woman. For years she would live with the hope that he would marry her, failing to see that for him the chase and conquest were everything. His affairs were like his shipping deals: once the profits had been banked, his appetite quickly moved on to the next opportunity. It is always difficult to know precisely where such a mindset springs from, but it is possible, as he himself suspected, that losing his mother at an early age crushed his ability to commit to any woman for very long.

Another factor may have been his children, both of whom loathed Maria. Alexander and Christina had been raised with every conceivable luxury but largely absent parents. Their father — always a nomad —

Alexander Onassis.

had put business, and his personal whims, ahead of family contact, while their mother liked to follow the social calendar of Europe and America. The children were reared largely by nannies and servants, getting little more from their parents than briefly scribbled cards bearing the postmarks of far-flung cities. When they did spend time with them, it was often against the surreal backdrop of the *Christina*, where they would be presented to VIP guests and allowed to sit with them at dinner. 'One lunch with Sir Winston,' Aristotle told his son, 'will teach you more than three years at Oxford.' Alexander would later remark that even when they did meet their offspring they were '... so absorbed in themselves that they might just as well have not been there'. As often happens with children who are given everything but their parents' attention, it took a psychological toll. On one occasion, Alexander smashed every window in the massive Château de la Croë, costing his father thousands in repairs.[143]

The journalist, Alan Brien, recalled meeting Alexander at six years old: 'A ghastly little creature, very brattish.' When Aristotle was showing him around the Château he took him to see Alexander's private apartment. 'He opened one wardrobe. There must have been fifty suits in there. Military uniforms, sailor suits, yachting outfits. He said, "What do you think? Do I spoil the boy?" I said I thought he did. I said it must be terrible to have so much so young. To be denied the excitement of expectation.' To Brien's surprise, Aristotle agreed. But, when Brien complained of narrowly avoiding injury as Alexander raced towards him in a miniature petrol-driven racing car, Aristotle breezily dismissed the near-accident by saying, 'It's only a toy.'

The boy never went to school, had no friends of his own age and showed little interest in anything beyond boats, cars and planes. Aristotle indulged his every whim, even giving him a powerful Chris-Craft speedboat on his tenth birthday. Unlike his sister, however, he was not especially shy or withdrawn.

Christina was so introverted that, for a while, she stopped speaking altogether. A psychiatrist told her mother it was an attention-seeking device. Christina would later say, 'I became a woman at nine years old,' the age she had reached when her parents divorced.

Tina announced that she would, henceforth, be known as Tina Livanos; a reminder to Aristotle that her surname was still grander than his. In a further humiliation for Maria Callas, Aristotle said that he had no thoughts of remarrying, and that, 'There was never any romance between Callas and myself.' Maria responded by saying, 'I don't want to sing anymore, I want to live just like a normal person, with a family, a home, and a dog.' She cancelled a concert in Belgium amid speculation by critics that her career was over. Secretly, Aristotle continued to have affairs, including a two-year relationship with Agnetta Castallanos, the Vice President of his airline, Olympic Airways.[144]

In the summer of 1960, however — once it became certain that Tina would never take him back — Aristotle renewed his interest in Maria. The courtship again became a public affair with the two regularly being photographed in the Maona nightclub in Monaco, which Aristotle owned. In London, the William Hickey column of the Beaverbrook-owned *Daily Express* waspishly reported: 'It is impossible for them to dance cheek-to-cheek as Miss Callas is slightly taller than Mr Onassis. But as they dance she has lowered her head to nibble his ear and he has smiled rapturously.'[145] There was soon speculation of a marriage proposal but, when Tina broke her leg skiing, Aristotle rushed to her bedside. Gossip of a rapprochement would continue until 1961, when Tina

A MAN WITH A COMPULSION

Christina Onassis.

announced her engagement to John Spencer-Churchill, who would become the eleventh Duke of Marlborough. Known to his friends as 'Sunny' Blandford, he was the heir to Blenheim Palace, the birthplace of Winston Churchill and Britain's grandest stately home. 'Sunny' (his courtesy title was Earl of Sunderland) was something of a misnomer as he had a famous temper, having once thrown a vicar out of his parish, and later calling his son's wife a 'dirty little scrubber' because her photograph had appeared in *Tatler*.[146]

The contrast could hardly have been greater: Tina had divorced a once-stateless refugee and married into the first rank of the nobility. She would now be a marchioness, as well as a future duchess and chatelaine of a glittering palace which eclipsed even the Château de la Croë.[147] George III had once lamented, 'We [the royal family] have nothing to equal this [Blenheim].' It was even rumoured that the Luftwaffe had avoided bombing Blenheim because Hitler had earmarked it for himself. In marrying an heiress, Sunny was following in the steps of his grandfather, who had rescued the family fortunes when he wed the American railroad heiress Consuelo Vanderbilt. Tina well knew that she was rubbing salt into the wounds of Aristotle, who had always felt rejected and spurned by the highest echelons of society. His brother-in-law and eternal rival, Stavros Niarchos, turned the knife further by lending the newlyweds his private aircraft for their honeymoon.

The wedding ceremony, which took place in Paris, was chaotic with more journalists attending than guests. Friends of the couple felt they were obviously unsuited and had little in common. Sunny was lonely, vulnerable and on the rebound (he had divorced his first wife when he discovered she was having an affair with a stockbroker), while Tina was status-conscious and liked the idea of becoming a duchess. They quickly grew apart and Tina eventually moved to Paris taking her servants and art collection with her.[148] Ironically, one of the few people who approved of the marriage was Aristotle who, once he'd overcome his initial bitterness, boasted that he was now related to Winston Churchill.

A MAN WITH A COMPULSION

Johnny Meyer would later recall, 'The plain fact was that the kids hated her [Maria Callas]. If it hadn't been for the kids, he'd have got it sealed the moment Tina did the Mendelssohn march with the marquess.' Both children blamed Maria for their parents' divorce, and both still hoped they would get back together. Unlike Aristotle, Maria did not get on with children and lacked the ability to communicate with them. Alexander always referred to her as 'the Singer', just as he would later call Jackie Kennedy 'the Widow'. When Alexander spoke to Maria, it was usually in a slightly mocking tone and Christina tried not to speak to her at all. Maria responded by avoiding her, telling Aristotle, 'She has the look of a child marked for the nunnery.'

In public, Maria made denials: 'There is no love interest in my life at present.'[149] But she told *France-Soir*, 'I want to have a baby; I'm thirty-six-years-old, with no one in my life, and I do not even know if I am capable of giving [birth] to a being.' This was a bold statement at a time when illegitimacy was still considered to be scandalous. Italian tabloids had been printing rumours of her pregnancy ever since it became known that she was leaving Meneghini.[150] Maria threatened to sue the papers for libel, but by early 1960 it was true: she had conceived a child by Aristotle. He was determined to have no further children and demanded that she have an abortion, offering her any amount of money if she did so. Worse still, for Maria, when Meneghini found out she was pregnant, he used it as a weapon against her, knowing that under Italian law, he would have rights to her child, irrespective of paternity. If that were not enough, her mother published a ghost-written autobiography with a highly subjective account of Maria's childhood. It was badly reviewed and sold few copies, but it still wounded her at a point when she was already vulnerable.

Just as all these crises were blowing up into a perfect storm, Aristotle decided to leave on a month-long cruise with Winston Churchill, and Maria was not invited. He claimed that her presence 'would embarrass Winston', who had been fond of Tina. Maria returned to Greece to sing *Norma* at the Epidaurus Theatre, where she had another great success. Aristotle was not in the audience; he enjoyed the publicity, but rarely listened to opera.

He hoped Maria would give up the stage and become a movie star and went to great lengths to persuade Carl Foreman to cast her opposite Anthony Quinn in *The Guns of Navarone*. At the last moment, she changed her mind, turning down the role, which ultimately went to Irene Papas. Aristotle was livid. 'I get up every day of my life to win!' he shouted, 'I don't know why you bother to get up at all.'

Aristotle continually tried to mould her, persuading her to change her clothes, hair and appearance. Sometimes she complied and sometimes she fought him. They were both hot-tempered and their fights were as spectacular as the eruption of Stromboli they had once witnessed from the decks of the *Christina*. He had always been a heavy drinker but was now also addicted to the barbiturate Nembutal (Yellow Jackets), which he took for insomnia. At the same time, he was injecting amphetamines, steroids and testosterone, which — mixed with alcohol — formed a cocktail that did nothing to pacify his erratic behaviour. Maria became accustomed not only to his mood swings but also to his violence. Along with his ex-wife and other mistresses, she too was regularly and severely beaten. 'He knew where to hit you till it hurt and it wouldn't show in the morning.'[151] During one hiding she had literally feared for her life, telling him, 'You can kill me … but you can't break me.'[152] He had also introduced her to Mandrax (methaqualone) which he believed to be an aphrodisiac. She became addicted and her dependence was a factor in her early death. Between quarrels, Aristotle returned to his favourite bars in Athens to get drunk on ouzo and metaxa, dance to the bouzouki and smash plates. One of his friends, Professor Yanni Georgakis, recalled, 'In Greece he behaved like a Greek, in England like an Englishman. He had this facility for adaptation. In Greece among Greeks he adopted the conduct of the marketplace.'

Maria had stopped the daily practice an opera singer needs to maintain their voice. She was coming to the end of her career and critics increasingly noticed the decline. Suffering from several conditions which may have been related to stress, she finally lost her child. Her part-time secretary, Giovanna Lomazzi recalled: 'During the period of 1960, I was in almost daily contact with Maria … During this time, [she] went to a clinic in Milan, under a false name and had an abortion. What is not known is whether this was a natural abortion [treatment following a miscarriage] or was planned.'[153] Abortion was then illegal in Italy, but some gynaecologists — especially those with wealthy clients — performed them in the guise of dilation and curettage procedures following a miscarriage. After Maria's death her friend, Edith Gorlinsky, would confirm that the child was aborted at the insistence of Aristotle: 'He would end their friendship if she had the child, so it had to be finished.' Maria would never conceive again.

Their love affair would last for more than a decade, always ebbing and flowing like a spring tide. Aristotle, fickle as always, would, at times, be a passionate and attentive lover, at other times an absent and disinterested businessman and, occasionally, a violent bully. He was repeatedly unfaithful to her, sometimes clandestinely and sometimes openly. While they were a dinner party together, a guest recalled that Puccini once described himself as a passionate seeker of beautiful women and good libretti. Aristotle banged his fist on the table in delight: 'Son of a bitch, just like me! Only I don't give a damn about the libretti.' It was a deliberate snub to Maria, who, although she must have come to understand the true character of the man she had taken as a lover, clung to the hope that he would, one day, marry her. There can be little doubt, however, that once the initial infatuation had passed, he never had any serious intention of doing so. Friends continually urged her to leave him, but she replied, 'When slight has followed slight, and insult has been added to insult, the love which remains is often illogical, but it is also indestructible. It's a kind of madness and nobody chooses to be mad.' The greatest soprano of the twentieth century had built her reputation by playing women who died for love, and now her own chaotic love life seemed to be slowly killing her.

For Aristotle, whatever torments Maria may

A MAN WITH A COMPULSION

have lived through, the affair provided him with an abundance of the single commodity (after money) that he most valued. For as long as he publicly courted Maria, he would remain the world's most photographed, written about and gossiped about businessman. Column inches were the benchmark by which he judged himself and, with Maria at his side, he was rarely short of them.

Maria Callas surrounded by press and photographers.

CHAPTER TWELVE

Dukes, Princes and Kings

Aristotle continued to gather VIP guests aboard the *Christina* and by the early 1960s there were few who declined his invitations. He loved fame and worshipped power, relentlessly wooing those who held it, or were close to it. One such was Prince Stanisław Albrecht 'Stas' Radziwiłł, an expatriate Polish businessman. The title 'Prince' was something of an exaggeration. Although Stanislas's family had technically been princes of the Holy Roman Empire since the sixteenth century, Poland had abolished all such titles in 1921 and the Holy Roman Empire was, anyway, dissolved in 1806. Additionally, Stanislas had agreed to give up all foreign titles on becoming a naturalised British citizen. Aristotle, however, would have taken little interest in a minor aristocrat had his wife not been the sister-in-law of the most powerful man in the world.

Jackie and Lee Bouvier had always been urged by their mother, Janet, to marry money. Lee's first fiancé, John Husted, had been encouraged, until Janet's enquiries proved his income to be only $17,000 a year, at which point he was immediately dropped. When Jackie showed concerns about Husted's feelings, Janet snapped, 'Why care about him when, in a week, he won't be in our lives? We won't even remember his name.'[154]

Jackie's sister, Lee Radziwill, with her second husband, 'Prince' Stas Radziwill.

Two years later Janet was equally unenthusiastic about Lee's next suitor, Michael Canfield, who had a private income but no fortune. This time, however, Lee dug her heels in — possibly to escape her overbearing mother and possibly to beat Jackie to the altar — and they married in 1953. Unlike Janet, Jackie liked Canfield, who worked in publishing, the same industry that Jackie herself would join — decades later — as an editor. When Lee threw her wedding bouquet, it was Jackie who caught it, but Lee's marriage quickly ran into the sand.

Canfield was believed to have been the son of Prince George, Duke of Kent, and his mistress, the American heiress Alice 'Kiki' Gwynne Preston. George was the fourth son of King George V and Queen Mary and two of his older brothers became kings: Edward VIII and George VI. He was a bisexual drug addict who had affairs with, among others, Jessie Mathews, Cecil Roberts and Noël Coward. His most notorious affair was with Canfield's mother, Kiki Preston, whose appetite for drugs was so prodigious that she was known as the 'girl with the silver syringe'. He even enjoyed a *ménage à trois* with Preston and José Uriburu, the bisexual son of the Argentinian ambassador to Britain. George died in an air crash in 1942 and, although Michael Canfield's paternity was never officially acknowledged, many contemporaries, including his older brother the Duke of Windsor, believed he was Prince George's son.

Michael had been adopted as an infant by Cass Canfield, head of the New York publishers, Harper & Brothers, and his wife Katharine Emmet. Unlike Jackie or his adoptive father, Canfield had no interest in books and hated the publishing business. Once married he began to drink heavily and talked of opening a small antique shop; hardly likely to provide the kind of income that Lee expected. As sometimes happens to unhappy people, Lee concluded that their fortunes would change if they lived in another country. Through his father, Canfield got a job in the London office of Harper & Brothers, and the couple moved to Britain.

When the change of location failed to raise Lee's spirits, Canfield turned to his sister-in-law, Jackie, for help. 'Can you give me any advice as to how I can make your sister happier?'

'Well, Michael,' she replied, after considering for a moment. 'I think the best thing is for you to get her some real money.'

'But listen, kiddo, I make a perfectly good living.

I've got a certain amount of money of my own and Harpers pay me well.'

Jackie shook her head. 'I mean real money, Michael. *Real* money!'[155]

Canfield had connections to Britain's royal family so — having rented a house in fashionable Belgravia — the couple were able to move in the highest echelons of British society: 'Men liked her for her exquisite looks, her taste and her wit. Women, for whom she never made an effort, did not.' Lady Antonia Fraser recalled, '… here [Jackie] was someone who was very nice to me, unlike Lee. As far as I know, Lee never spoke a civil word to a female under eighty in her life.'[156] *Tatler* was soon featuring Lee on its cover with the by-line, 'An American Hostess in London.'

The publishing job was abandoned when Lee persuaded Winthrop Aldrich, America's ambassador in London, to hire Canfield as his social secretary. Lois Aldrich, also a social secretary at the time, recalled, 'Michael's job was to basically squire around the ambassador's visitors and make sure they got into the best restaurants and nightclubs. He was given entrée to the best places in London, the most select private clubs, which worked out well for Lee. So, even though this was nothing more than a secretarial job for Michael, he seemed to enjoy it. I'm not sure that Lee had much respect for it, though. There was definitely growing tension between them.'[157]

Canfield's drinking continued and Lee began an affair with David Somerset, the eleventh Duke of Beaufort. During a dinner party in their home, the Canfield's started to argue in front of their guests, with Lee taunting her husband: 'David is perfectly lovely. Not only is he rich, but unlike some others I know, he is a true royal.'[158] The dalliance ended during a spectacular row in a crowded football stadium. 'And don't you ever call me,' she railed, walking away. 'Don't worry, I seldom do,' Somerset responded, at which she strode back and slapped his face. 'He is such a small measure of a man,' she told friends, but the public spat had sent London's rumour mill into overdrive.

In 1956, Jackie Kennedy suffered a still birth, having had a miscarriage the year before. Her husband, Senator Jack Kennedy, who was cruising around Elba with a group of friends including unattached girls, saw no reason to return home and Jackie became depressed. Although she felt isolated, she may have been more tolerant of Jack's behaviour than appearances suggested. In his memoirs, her friend and relative Gore Vidal revealed, 'She and Jack both loved gossip and could go on talking endlessly about other people's sex lives, but I always got the distinct impression that she was very interested in sex the same way that Jack was very interested in sex. It was a game for them, and they both played it.'

She flew to London to recuperate with her sister, Lee, who was shocked to discover that Jackie was seriously contemplating divorce because of Jack's absences and infidelities. 'Daddy did it to Mummy and it all worked out fine,' she told Jackie, forgetting that their parents' marriage had ended in a bitter divorce.

During her stay, Jackie joined the Canfields for a weekend shooting party at the Northumberland country estate of Lord and Lady Lambton. Among the other guests were Stas Radziwill and his second wife Grace. Although Lee claimed she found Stas

Jackie and her sister Lee.

frightening, it was plain to the others that there was an instant rapport between the two, and the Radziwills soon became regular guests at the Canfields' London home. Stas was twenty-nine years older than Lee, but, despite the dubious title, he was rich, and charming. Short and rotund with a lumbering gait, few would have considered him good-looking, but he overcame this with a mixture of natural charisma and persuasiveness.

By the time that Jackie returned to America the relationship with her sister was becoming strained. In December, the Canfields flew to the United States to spend Christmas with the Auchinclosses' extended family at their Merrywood estate in Virginia. It was to be a chilly yuletide for all, despite Janet having flown in a chef from Paris to regale them with a new gastronomic creation every evening. By this time the Canfields weren't speaking at all, while Jackie and Lee were now cool and defensive in each other's company.

When the Canfields returned to London, Michael found Lee's open flirting with Stas intolerable, leading to a row that finally made divorce inevitable. Terrance and Betty Landow, close friends of the Canfields, witnessed the disintegration of the marriage from close quarters. On one occasion they were at Heathrow Airport with Michael, seeing off Lee, who was on her way to Paris. When she leant forward to kiss her husband he turned away. 'My God, Michael, when will you learn to kiss me like a man? Why must you insist on humiliating me?' When she was gone, Michael said to Terrance, 'That bitch. Who would want to kiss her? Not me! Kiss like a man? Fuck her. Who does she think she is?'

The final showdown came one evening when the six of them were at the Canfields' home and Lee was telling Stas, disingenuously, that she had 'always' wanted to visit Poland: 'Michael just shook his head and rolled his eyes. "That's it. I'm done with you now," he told Lee before taking off. [We] then watched Lee and Stas and wondered how long it would take before we'd hear that they were together. It was just in the air. Everyone knew it. Stas's wife knew it, you could tell by looking at her. It was as if we were all playing a bizarre parlour game, which was, "Let's act as if this thing we all know full well is about to happen is not about to happen."'[159]

Stas's wealth, like his title, was less princely than London society might have imagined. In fact, it originated from his first wife, Rose de Monléon. The Radziwills had once been very rich, but the family fortune was largely gone by the twentieth century, and entirely lost following the 1939 Soviet occupation of Poland. Stas escaped to Switzerland but — as a penniless refugee — had to survive in shelters as he lacked the money for a hotel or even a cheap apartment. According to his friend, Michael Tree, 'Stas lived in soup kitchens for about three weeks in Switzerland and then he "met woman" — he always talked that way, "I met woman" — who had money, who was Swiss, who he married. He always said, "Much best wife I ever had, first."'[160] This marriage lasted only five years, but he divorced Rose with enough of her wealth in his pocket to be able to marry his second wife, the shipping heiress Grace Kolin, with whom he moved to London. There he started a property business, eventually teaming up with the developer, Felix Fenston. A shrewd investor, Fenston well knew how to exploit Radziwill's title, aristocratic charm and contacts. They benefited from changes in the law which coincided with a series of property booms in London that made both men multi-millionaires. His success was considered by some to be extraordinary: '... because he practically couldn't write, no one could understand a word he said.'[161]

By 1958 the Canfields had divorced and in June of

1960 Michael became the third husband of Frances Laura Charteris. Her first husband had made her a viscountess and her second a countess. Following Canfield's death from heart failure in 1969, she would marry for the fourth time to John Spencer-Churchill, (the tenth Duke of Marlborough and the father of Tina Livanos's second husband), who would make her a duchess. When Laura took her new husband to lunch with the Duke and Duchess of Windsor she saw that, 'The Duke never stopped staring at Michael. So much so that I asked: "Is anything the matter?" The Duke quietly replied: "Yes. I am certain your husband is my brother's son."' [162] Canfield was bitter after his divorce from Lee, and he remained a tormented and unhappy figure for the rest of his short life. The heart failure which killed him at the early age of forty-three was probably brought on by the drugs and alcohol he was chronically addicted to.

Canfield was happy to share his contempt for Lee with anyone who would listen, and he revealed to the author, Gore Vidal, that among Lee's conquests was Jack Kennedy, Jackie's husband. She had slept with him in 1957 at the Kennedys' home where Jackie was recuperating from the birth of Caroline, her first surviving child. Gore's sister, Nini, later confirmed that Lee had told her the same thing and added that she'd left the bedroom door open so that Canfield, in the next room, would be able to hear them. The tale was widely repeated, and, at some point, Jackie too must have heard it.

Before Lee could marry Stas each hoped to get their former marriages annulled by the Catholic Church. Both would — according to Canon law — be 'living in sin' if they married without the church's approval. The Catholic church can be slow to process annulments and the matter became urgent when Lee fell pregnant with Stas's child. It was easier for Stas because he only needed an annulment from his first marriage; the church did not recognise his second. Grace obligingly agreed to a quick legal divorce, upon repayment of her money, freeing him to remarry without difficulty. Lee consulted Joe Kennedy, who introduced her to Cardinal Spellman, and he helped her to begin the process, which would be decided by a tribunal in London. In the event, the pregnancy decided matters and they were married in a civil ceremony in Virginia. On hearing this, the London tribunal described it as an 'indignity' and refused the annulment with no right of appeal. The only person who could overturn that decision was the Pope himself. The child, Anna Christina, was born five months later in Lausanne and the couple explained the discrepancy in dates by claiming she was several months premature. In truth, she *was* premature, weighing only three pounds and having some breathing difficulties, but not as premature as her parents had claimed.

In July, Jack Kennedy won the Democratic nomination for the presidential race of 1960. From this day forward the Senator for Massachusetts and his wife would be the most photographed, filmed and written-about couple on the planet. A new Camelot was in view and, as the flashbulbs popped, Jackie announced that she was pregnant with her second child. Stas and Lee travelled to America, where Stas agreed to help Kennedy secure the Polish vote. He proved to be an effective campaigner and the two men became firm friends. Stas had always understood the value of contacts, and joining the Kennedy clan would, in time, make him one of the best-connected men on earth. He was not slow to exploit the myriad of opportunities now in his line of sight.

The 1960s, the decade that changed everything, had begun. The economic boom which followed the Second World War had created previously undreamt-of prosperity in the developed world, and a growing middle class had more disposable income than any previous generation. The demands of the war had also created new technologies including satellites, jet engines, plastics and transistors which, along with new manufacturing techniques, were making luxuries such as cars, refrigerators, TVs and telephones affordable to the common man. The strict censorship of books, plays and films which had characterised the 1950s was being swept away and there was a wave of experimentation and taboo-breaking in all the arts. The contraceptive pill meant that, for the first time, women were in control of their own fertility, and the post-war baby-boom generation looked forward to a brave new world in which technology would continue to deliver seemingly unalloyed benefits. Social distinctions were blurring too, with working-class musicians, writers, actors and artists redefining our tastes and aspirations. Into this maelstrom came a new, young, attractive president with a glamorous and beautiful wife. All things seemed possible as the Kennedy family entered the White House.

In the London home of the Radziwills, however, problems were emerging. Lee, who had returned to England leaving her baby in an incubator in a

New York hospital, was suffering from depression following the birth and the realisation that she had now been comprehensively upstaged by her sister. Matters worsened when she discovered that Stas was having an affair, which he readily confessed to. Lee was devastated but saw no irony in the fact that she herself had been unfaithful to Canfield many times and had often defended her father's infidelities. Stas was still under pressure, especially from his father, to get Lee's earlier marriage to Michael Canfield annulled by the Catholic Church. Only Pope John XXIII could reverse the decision of the London tribunal, but, with the support of the Kennedys, even that became a possibility. Jack's younger brother, Bobby Kennedy, who would later be controversially appointed Attorney General, despite having never appeared in any state or federal court, took charge of the matter. 'You supply the prayers', he told Lee, 'we'll provide the pressure, and God will deliver the miracle.'[163] In 1962 the annulment was finally granted.

In Washington, Jackie was in her pomp. Parents named their daughters after her, and women copied her hairstyle, hats, and shoes. Within living memory there had not been a First Lady as beautiful or glamorous as Jackie Kennedy and only one, Frances Folsom, had been younger. Eleanor Roosevelt had been widely respected and admired, as had been Mamie Eisenhower, but neither was beautiful or especially stylish. Jackie, however, who was often dressed by leading Paris and Milan couturiers, was more than beautiful. On television and in magazines she seemed to exude charm and confidence. From the get-go, the media of America and the world devoted page after page to her, with endless photographs and descriptions of her clothes, her hair, her accessories, and the careworn White House that she was now refurbishing. For her husband, who had been elected by a margin so small it could barely be measured, she was an invaluable public relations asset.

In May 1962, Marilyn Monroe sang for Jack while he celebrated his forty-fifth birthday at a party at Maddison Square Garden. *Time* recorded, 'It was Marilyn who was the hit of the evening, Kennedy plainly meant it when he said, "I can now retire from politics after having had *Happy Birthday* sung to me in such a sweet, wholesome way."' Jack had been introduced to Monroe by the actor Peter Lawford, who was married to his younger sister Pat Kennedy. Monroe's masseur, Ralph Roberts, would later confirm that Jack had slept with Monroe at Bing Crosby's house a few months earlier. In a confidential memo the FBI warned Bobby that a forthcoming book might accuse both him and Jack of having affairs with the actress. The book was never published but, within three months, Monroe had died from an overdose of barbiturates.[164] Following her death, Lawford 'cleaned up' Monroe's apartment to ensure nothing was found that incriminated the Kennedys.[165]

Aboard the *Christina*, Aristotle watched Jackie Kennedy on newsreels and ruefully remembered that her husband was 'the guy I *didn't* ask to stay to dinner'. He had already met the Radziwills, but now he began to take more interest in them, especially Lee, then twenty-nine years old and known to be drifting away from her husband. The Radziwills had previously entertained Aristotle and Maria at their home and

DUKES, PRINCES AND KINGS

For President Kennedy, who had been elected by a margin so small it could barely be measured, his wife, Jackie, was an invaluable public relations asset.

at Claridge's. Aristotle treated every woman he met as a potential mistress and Lee received the same flattery that he had extended to so many others. She would later recall, 'Onassis was an outstanding man, not only as a financier but also as a person. He was active, with great vitality, brilliant and up to date on everything. He was amusing to be with. And he had charm, a fascinating way with women. He surrounded them with attention. He made sure they felt admired and desired. He took note of their slightest whim. He interested himself in them — exclusively and profoundly.'[166]

Early in 1962, Aristotle began to take Lee to dinner at Claridge's and Maxims. He approached her as he had always approached women he was attracted to, by indulging their every impulse and making them feel that their happiness was the only thing that concerned him. In Lee, he found a willing recipient. Perhaps her lack of confidence appealed to him given that Maria was unshakably self-assured. He even encouraged one of his other mistresses, Agnetta Castallanos, to become Lee's friend and protector. 'It didn't take long before Lee was completely swept off her feet by him,' Castallanos recalled. 'I was with Onassis as a lover just before Lee came into the picture. We ended it because the business we shared [Olympic Airways] complicated things. He talked a lot about Lee. He was crazy about her. I told him I felt jealous, the way women do when they're being replaced. He wanted me to befriend her, telling me she was a sad and lonely little creature. "Ari, I tend to shy away from charity work," I told him. But I called her anyway and invited her to dinner.'

'So, what's it like to have a sister who is the most famous woman in the world?' Castallanos asked Lee over their meal at Claridge's.

'I make it a policy to never talk about her,' Lee replied.

'That's probably wise.'

Then Lee responded with a searching question of her own. 'So, what's it like being with one of the wealthiest men in the world?'

'I make it a policy to never talk about him.'

'That's probably wise,' came the reply and both women laughed.

'We became instant friends after that night,' Castallanos said. 'I thought she was fabulous. I saw what Ari saw. At first, she seemed like a winsome little thing, but once you got to know her, you saw the inner resolve. The stories she told about her mother! Eventually, after a couple weeks, she opened up about Ari to me. She said they had a deep connection. "It is not insignificant," she told me. "It's profound." I said, "Lee, I think you're falling in love with this man." She said, "I know. It was love at first sight, I admit it. But I also love my husband." However, I believe Stas had come to represent sadness in her life — her postpartum depression, an affair he'd apparently had. I don't think she fully trusted him. Being with Ari was just better for her. She asked me if I thought a woman could love two men at the same time. I said I didn't know.'[167]

As the relationship intensified, Aristotle continued to see Maria Callas who did not, immediately, see the threat. Lee too was simultaneously having an affair with Panagiotis 'Taki' Theodoracopulos, the son of a Greek shipping magnate. He recalled, 'I was twenty-four and impressed with her because, well, she was beautiful, she was the sister-in-law of the President of the United States, and she was flirting with me, all of which was a lethal combination. When I saw that she had a rather loose marriage, I started pursuing her. Two years of on-again off-again romantic behaviour then began. I had mixed emotions about Lee. On one hand, she was a magical creature who, when we were alone together, was romantic, charming, and lovely. However, when we were out in public, she would change. I never understood why. She would become bitchy, critical. She would say dreadful things about me, be very condescending. I would have to wonder, who in her life spoke to her like that, giving her license to then think she could speak to others the same way? Looking back, I think she just wasn't happy. She wanted love and acceptance so badly, it was crippling for her. The more time I spent with her, the more I knew she wasn't the one for me, nor was I the one for her. That said, for a little sliver of time there, I was crazy about her.'[168]

Aristotle's sister Artemis had a villa in the fashionable Greek coastal resort of Glyfada which she made available to Lee, meaning that when Aristotle was in Greece, the couple could spend time together discreetly. Aristotle owned the next-door villa, which was connected via the garden, so she could inconspicuously slip from one to the other. Stas did not object to these trips and was not, initially, suspicious. For Aristotle, however, discretion could never be maintained for long. Flamboyance was second nature to him: he loved to be noticed, admired and, above all, envied. By the summer of 1962 he no longer saw any reason to hide his latest trophy mistress and he invited Lee to join his summer cruise aboard the *Christina*. Only when she came aboard would she discover who the other guests were. To her astonishment they included not only Winston, Clementine and Randolph Churchill, but also Maria Callas. Just as Tina Onassis had once been humiliated by her husband's public seduction of Maria, so Maria would now be expected to witness his public seduction of Lee. It was an imperative for Aristotle not merely to seduce, but also to be *seen* to seduce. His character had been shaped by two of the most patriarchal societies on earth: Türkiye and Argentina.

In both, the open acknowledgement of not only mistresses but also of courtesans, and even common prostitutes, was considered normal. For Aristotle, it was part of the reason he maintained the *Christina* at such expense: she was the showcase not only for his success in business, but also in influence, and in love.

As with the seduction of Maria, Winston Churchill would have been oblivious to what was obvious to everyone else. He was now eighty-eight years old, and his dementia had become severe. He no longer had lucid periods but sat staring stolidly ahead of him and hardly spoke at all. Karina Brownley, then only seventeen, was one of fifty guests aboard as the *Christina* cruised along the Amalfi coast. She recalled that on one evening they dined by the light of a silver moon. Aristotle, who was deeply superstitious, told them: 'You must understand that mermaids are both good and bad luck. Good luck if you find one in the sea. But bad luck if you bring her aboard. Never ever bring a mermaid on board. Remember that.' Maria appeared to hang on to his every word, occasionally glancing at Lee, who did not. When dinner was over Aristotle stood up and said, 'Lee and I are going to be unavailable for the rest of the evening. Please enjoy the many pleasures of the *Christina*. Good evening.'

'But will you be joining me later at the bar?' asked Maria.

'I seriously doubt it, my dear. But let's gather in the morning for breakfast.'

'So be it,' said Maria, resignedly, as Lee gave her a knowing smile. The next morning, at breakfast, Lee appeared to be radiant, but Maria, who had been publicly humiliated, left the ship at the next port. Lee, who must have realised that she too, in time, might be treated in the same fashion, later confessed, 'I am not a mean person, and that was cruel.'[169] Nonetheless, for the rest of the voyage she delighted in Aristotle's undivided attention and later told Agnetta Castallanos, 'Maybe for the first time, I thought, yes, this is what I want. Ari is what I want. Ari is what I deserve.'

Following the cruise, as Aristotle had anticipated, the affair became common knowledge and newspaper columnists were soon hinting at it. What he may not have anticipated, however, was that much of the comment, especially in America, was intensely hostile.

By 1963 Aristotle no longer had much real influence in Monaco, the principality of which he had once been the *de facto* ruler. He had always treated the laws and taxes of larger nations with derision and, despite his many homes ashore, he increasingly lived aboard the *Christina*. As Rainier continued to make him feel less welcome, he sought another refuge on land and discovered that the tiny island of Skorpios, in the Ionian Sea, was for sale. The seventy-four-acre atoll — shaped like a scorpion — was classed as uninhabitable because there was no reliable supply of potable water, so he was able to buy it for a mere $14,000. He solved the water problem by buying a mountain on a nearby island — at colossal expense — and piping the water across. He also imported sand for a beach and 200 different varieties of trees, some of which he planted himself. Three residences and a harbour were also built, but Aristotle never spent a night on Skorpios, preferring always to sleep on the *Christina*.

CHAPTER THIRTEEN
Omertà

Lee Radziwill was to find, as Maria and others had discovered, that Aristotle was a difficult man to marry. All the same, he was opposed to her remarrying Stas and tried to persuade her not to, warning her that it would 'change things' if she did. Aristotle denied that this was because of Maria, claiming that he only stayed with her because she threatened suicide every time he tried to drop her. When Maria saw a newspaper photograph of Aristotle and Lee in a nightclub she telephoned him at his office, screaming and threatening to throw herself off the *Christina*.[170] 'I can make you no promises,' he said, 'but I do care about you, Lee, and I do see a future for us. But, as you must know by now, I am not a man you can pressure.'

Lee found herself pulled in two directions as Stas, under pressure from his father, was adamant that that they must remarry. Pushback was also coming from the Kennedys who had heard rumours of her affair with Aristotle. Janet Auchincloss had appealed to Jack Kennedy to get the affair stopped and he had passed the problem over to his brother, Bobby. Having gone to great lengths to get Lee her annulment, Bobby was determined the remarriage should go ahead. If it did not, he feared it could damage his brother's chances of being re-elected in 1964. In July 1963, having returned from her cruise on the *Christina*, and accompanying President Kennedy to Berlin where he gave his famous 'Ich bin ein Berliner' speech, Lee Radziwill finally wed Stas for the second time — with the blessing of the Catholic Church — in London's Westminster Cathedral. By now, however, the marriage was clearly in trouble with Lee conducting two affairs and Stas involved with Charlotte Ford, the daughter of Henry Ford II.[171] Aristotle later told Peter Evans 'The Kennedys could accept me as Lee's lover: that was personal. What they couldn't accept was the idea that I might actually marry her: that was politics.'[172]

A few days after the remarriage, Jackie celebrated her thirty-fourth birthday at a house she and the President had rented on Squaw Island, near the Kennedy compound on Cape Cod, Massachusetts. She was pregnant and the announcement, a few months earlier, had created huge public interest. Not only was she young, beautiful and glamorous, she was going to be the first First Lady to give birth since 1893. Jackie's fame had reached mythic proportions and was eclipsing even her husband's. For five consecutive years Gallup polls had shown her to be the most admired woman in the world. In 1961, she had impressed General de Gaulle with her fluent French and knowledge of French history and culture, leading her husband to joke, 'I am the man who accompanied Jacqueline Kennedy to Paris — and I have enjoyed it!'

In 1962 she had taken television audiences on a tour of the White House, whose tired fabric she had recently refurbished at a cost of $2 million. The programme, still seen as a masterpiece of public relations, was watched by eighty million viewers and was syndicated to fifty different countries. William Shannon, a well-known columnist for the *New York Post*, wrote: 'Month after month, from the glossy pages of *Life* to the multicoloured cover of *Redbook*, Jack and Jackie smile out at millions of readers; he with his tousled hair and winning smile, she with her dark eyes and beautiful face. We hear of her pregnancy, of his wartime heroism, of their fondness for sailing. But what has all this to do with statesmanship?' Now, America and the world held their breath as her confinement approached.

The baby was due in September, but Jackie went into premature labour on 7 August and was taken to the Otis Air Force Base Hospital in Falmouth, Massachusetts, where her personal obstetrician performed an emergency caesarean section to deliver a baby boy. Because the child had breathing difficulties a priest was summoned to immediately baptise the child, named Patrick, but, despite every effort by the doctors, he died two days later of infant respiratory distress syndrome. Lee had been in Athens with Aristotle at the time. She had flown straight to America to support her family as soon as she knew the child was ill and had comforted Jackie following the death, returning to Athens a few days later. Aristotle had warned her that it would 'change things' if she remarried Stas, and he was as good as his word. She immediately sensed a new coolness and distance from him. He was now spending less time with her and more time with Maria.

In August, Lee and Aristotle were guests at the opening of a new Hilton Hotel in Athens. It was a highly publicised event and pictures of the couple were soon appearing in newspapers across the world. The secret was now out, and journalists openly wrote of an affair.

Among the Washington press corps there was, at that time, an unwritten rule that nobody wrote about the President's private life. Even William Randolph Hearst, the newspaper baron who had a reputation for attacking public figures, drew the line at politicians' sex lives, probably because he was himself vulnerable to those kinds of revelations. All of Jack Kennedy's political enemies would have heard the rumours of his philandering, but none were prepared to publicly call him out. This *omertà*, in fact, was so entrenched that a few newspapers, including *The New York Times*, would not write about Jack Kennedy's extra-marital affairs until thirty years after his death. Nonetheless, Jack was deeply worried when the Profumo scandal broke in Britain. Suzy Chang, a New York prostitute who had been living in London, was part of the vice girl ring that shook the British establishment to its core and helped bring down Harold Macmillan's government. Chang told investigators that she had slept with John Kennedy when he was a senator and had lunch with him at the 21 Club in New York. At least two American journalists knew about the allegations, and Bobby Kennedy had to use family influence with Hearst, their employer, to get details of the story spiked. J Edgar Hoover had also intervened to quash another story claiming that Jack had slept with a German-born prostitute, Ellen Rometsch, who was thought to be an East German spy.

While Jack's private life was off-limits, shenanigans

involving a foreign businessman and the President's sister-in-law were not. The influential *Washington Post* columnist, Drew Pearson, now demanded, 'Does the ambitious Greek tycoon hope to become the brother-in-law of the American President?' The story did not play well in the United States, where Aristotle was still considered to be little more than a rich foreign crook with a taste for high-profile mistresses. Jackie telephoned Lee to tell her that the pictures were splashed over every American newspaper, but Lee countered by claiming, untruthfully, that she and Onassis were 'just friends'.

Following the call, Lee reacted furiously, storming into a meeting between Aristotle and his Greek lawyer, Stelio Papadimitriou, and angrily accusing him of planting the stories in the media. Aristotle quietly reminded her that he did not expect his women to raise their voices to him, and then raised his own. Tantrums were a privilege he reserved for himself, and his temper was volcanic. 'I make news, and whoever is with me makes news. This is something you'll have to learn to live with, that is, if you want to be with me. Do you still want to be with me?' Overwhelmed, Lee nodded and said yes, she did.[173] 'And do you want to make news, Lee? Do you want people to notice you? Because you deserve to be noticed, Lee, if that is what you want. Is that what you want, Lee?' Once more, she nodded and said yes. This was a mind game that Aristotle had so often played, not only with mistresses but also with businessmen, bankers and politicians. He liked beating an opponent into total submission. What Lee should have understood was that once she had capitulated, he would lose interest and move on.

The only reason that Maria Callas had survived for so long was that she had never completely surrendered to him.

Jackie had been deeply affected by Patrick's death and became clinically depressed. Jack, who rarely showed emotion, was also very affected and openly wept over the child's coffin. Paradoxically, the tragedy brought them closer together and went some way to healing what had previously been a shaky marriage. While Jack's infidelities were habitual and constant, Jackie had also, on occasions, been unfaithful. In 1955, two years after her marriage, she'd had a brief relationship with the actor William Holden, who later boasted of introducing her to oral sex.[174] The dramatist and humorist Alan Bennet believed she slept with his co-star Peter Cook, in 1962, when the revue *Beyond the Fringe* was playing on Broadway: 'I may be libelling her, but I think Peter had an affair with Jackie Kennedy. I have an image of her standing next to Peter, stroking his arm, in the dressing room and he certainly went to parties with her.' At the same time, Jackie's spending, which would later become legendary, was already developing into a serious issue for her husband. During a meeting with a congressman in the Oval Office, a frustrated Kennedy showed him $40,000 worth of bills for Jackie's clothes. 'What would you do if your wife did that?' JFK asked him. That evening, Kennedy confronted Jackie, but she lamely pretended that she knew nothing about it.[175]

When Aristotle heard how upset she was, he offered her a cruise on the *Christina* to help her recuperate. Lee, who had failed to see what Aristotle really wanted, telephoned Jackie and said, 'Tell Jack

OMERTÀ

that Stas and I will chaperone you. It will be perfectly proper and such fun. Oh Jacks, you can't imagine how terrific Ari's yacht is, and he says we can go anywhere you want. It will do you so much good to get away for a while.'[176] Jack was predictably cool on the idea — Bobby even more so — but they cautiously agreed, sending the Under Secretary of Commerce, Franklin D Roosevelt Jr, and his wife Susan along as more reliable chaperones than Lee and Stas. Before Jackie left, Bobby took her aside and said, 'This business with Lee and Onassis. Just tell her to cool it, will you?'

Although the cruise was meant to be discreet, a crowd of reporters surrounded Aristotle as he boarded the *Christina* in Piraeus. 'She's the captain,' he told them, 'Mrs Kennedy's in charge here.' In Paris, Maria Callas learnt of the cruise, for the first time, when she saw the guest list in a newspaper.

The *Christina* called first in Lesbos, then Crete, but Aristotle remained out of sight. When they arrived at İzmir, Jackie asked him to be her personal guide, and he agreed — literally taking her by the hand — to the delight of the paparazzi whose photographs were wired around the world. In Paris, Maria told a friend, 'Four years ago, that was me by his side, being beguiled by the story of his life … although I'm sure he makes most of it up. Memories demand too much effort.' In Washington a Republican congressman was scathingly critical, not only of the Kennedys but also of Roosevelt, claiming that he shouldn't have accepted hospitality from a foreigner. The President telephoned his wife aboard the ship and suggested she return early. Johnny Meyer recalled, 'I think Jackie felt he was overreacting to the mudslinging of some cheesecloth congressman. Anyway, it was left that she should return on the seventeenth as planned.'

Aristotle, however, had never been more in his element. The most famous woman in the world was now his personal guest aboard the world's most luxurious yacht. He was completely captivated by her, and she was beginning to be captivated by him. This was what the *Christina* had been commissioned for, and the beautiful former frigate was paying him back in spades. Lee must have soon realised that Aristotle was slipping out of her grasp, but there would no longer have been anything she could do to prevent it. Early in the cruise, she had a row with Stas and he left the ship, flying home as soon as he could. One of the guests, Stelina Mavros, would recall, 'I remember we were all sitting on a curb watching people go by on one side of the street, and she and Ari were sitting together on the other side. I looked at Lee and she appeared to be confused and unhappy. She and Stas had, apparently, had a fight and he fled the cruise, headed back to England. So she was alone. At one point, she got up and sort of meandered across the street and sat with Ari and Jackie. Finally, she got up and crossed the street and joined the rest of us. It was as if she didn't know her place, where she was supposed to be.'[177]

In Washington, J Edgar Hoover, who had long mistrusted Aristotle, ordered the FBI to open a new file on him. One of Hoover's agents would later recall, 'Hoover instinctively disliked Ari. He was a great believer in no-smoke-without-fire theories and was convinced that the Greek was getting away with something. At the same time he must have been enjoying the President's discomfort. It was exactly the kind of situation that appealed to his sense of evil.' [178]

When Jackie returned to Washington, she admitted to friends that she regretted the bad publicity the cruise had caused — especially the criticism that Roosevelt had taken on her behalf — but she defended Aristotle, whom she described as '… an alive and vital person who has come up from nowhere'. Her husband insisted that Aristotle would not be welcome in the United States until after the 1964 election. 'Maybe you'll come with us to Texas next month?' he asked, and Jackie agreed.[179]

White House staff knew that the visit to Dallas was likely to be unpopular. Governor John Connally — who was no friend of Kennedy — had suggested that the planned motorcade be called off and, instead, the Kennedys be driven directly from the airport to the lunch venue. Kennedy's staff quashed this, however, and the route was agreed and published in two Dallas newspapers in advance. In our era, where extremism has fundamentally changed the political landscape, it seems incredible that a world leader would travel in an open car along a published route and pass empty buildings that had not been properly searched. Today, the President of the United States travels in a car so heavily armoured it is nicknamed 'the Beast'. But, in 1960s America, domestic terrorism was not considered a serious risk, despite four previous presidents having been assassinated.

As the motorcade passed Elm Street, shots were heard. A bullet passed through Jack's neck and struck Governor Connally. Neither were fatally wounded but, rather than speeding away, the car slowed down, giving Lee Harvey Oswald the chance to take another, carefully aimed shot which struck Jack's head and killed him instantly.

On CBS, Walter Kronkite told the nation, 'From Dallas, Texas, the flash, apparently official, at one o'clock pm, President Kennedy died at one o'clock Central Standard Time, two o'clock Eastern Standard Time, some thirty-eight minutes ago.' He then had to pause to compose himself, before announcing that Lyndon Johnson had been sworn in as the thirty-sixth President of the United States.

The most powerful man on earth had died with his brains in the lap of the most famous woman on earth. The images of Jack's assassination, along with those of Jackie in her bloodstained Chanel suit, mesmerised the world. For Americans, it was the single most shocking event since the Japanese attack on Pearl Harbor in 1941. The British philosopher and historian Isaiah Berlin wrote, '… the sense of something of exceptional hope for a large number of people suddenly cut off in mid-air is, I think, unique in our lifetime — it is as if Roosevelt had been murdered in 1935, with Hitler and Mussolini and everybody else still about and a lot of Chamberlains and Daladiers knocking about too.' Globally, an entire generation would always remember exactly where they were when they heard the news.

Aristotle was in Hamburg for the launch of a new 50,000-ton tanker, *Olympic Chivalry*. On hearing a bulletin, he immediately telephoned Lee who asked him to come to Washington. When he reminded her that he'd been told to stay out of America until 1964, she told him that was hardly relevant any more.

OMERTÀ

Within twenty-four hours he had received an official invitation and he was soon at the White House, where staff were astonished to see him walking through the Centre Hall hand-in-hand with Jackie. More searing images were to follow at the funeral as Jackie, her face covered in a black veil, placed a hand on her husband's coffin and John Junior, aged only three, saluted his father.[180]

That evening, Jackie and Bobby knelt to pray before Jack's grave in Arlington National Cemetery. Jackie laid lilies of the valley on the ground, and the two walked back to their car holding hands. They had always been friends but now, united in grief, they would become more than friends. Both knew that discovery would torpedo Bobby's political ambitions (he was married with eight children) and seriously tarnish Jackie's reputation. They were discreet, but FBI documents, released in 2007, confirm that they did have an affair. By 1964 they were spending so much time in each other's company that Bobby's wife, Ethel, took their children skiing while Bobby and Jackie holidayed with friends in Antigua.

Lyndon Johnson, who deeply disliked Bobby, asked J Edgar Hoover to investigate him during the 1964 Democratic Convention. The FBI duly reported: 'The subject seems to spend all his free time with Mrs John F Kennedy. Although it can't be confirmed at this time, they appear to be sharing the same hotel suite.' Franklin D Roosevelt Jr told the author David Heymann, 'The two of them carried on like a pair of lovesick teenagers. I suspect Bobby would've liked to dump Ethel and marry Jackie, but of course that wasn't possible.'

Bobby had a capacity for hatred that often shocked those who knew him, and he especially abhorred Aristotle Onassis. 'I've known that bastard for years,' he told a friend. 'He was a snake then and he's still a snake. Other than his bankroll, I don't understand what Jackie sees in him. If it were up to me, I'd sink his fucking yacht — and the goddamn Greek with it.' The historian Jeff Shesol wrote, 'Robert Kennedy, particularly early in his career, tended to see things in blacks and whites. You were either in his favour or you were entirely out of his favour.'

Bobby's first job, on graduating from university, had been to work for Senator Joseph McCarthy, an old friend of the Kennedy clan who had dated two of Bobby's sisters, Pat and Jean. When Joe Kennedy needed to find Bobby a job, all he had to do was lift the phone. The Senator for Wisconsin had lent his name to the notorious McCarthy era by making sensational but unsubstantiated charges of communist subversion. Aristotle Onassis was one of the foreign businessmen whom McCarthy suspected of trading with communist China (never proven), and Bobby would probably have seen FBI reports on Onassis at that time. Bobby left after six months, unable to get on with McCarthy's chief counsel, Roy Cohn, who would later become the lawyer not only of Donald Trump but also of the mafia boss Anthony 'Fat Tony' Salerno, the Gambino family boss Paul Castellano and, ironically, Aristotle Onassis.

Aristotle knew how Bobby felt, and told Johnny Meyer, 'He just sees me as the rich prick moving in on his brother's widow. Sooner or later, it'll come to a test of wills. I could bury that sucker (by revealing his affair with Jackie), although I'd lose Jackie in the process. But can't you just see the headlines?'[181]

Aristotle had returned to Europe before the funeral in time for the fortieth birthday of Maria Callas which they celebrated with a lavish party at Maxims. Despite the humiliations she had suffered, Maria's tenacity appeared to have paid off and, for the time being, she was once more, *maîtresse-en-titre*, and at the centre of his attention. Panaghis Vergottis, who was a friend of both Aristotle and Maria, recalled that she seemed to have buried the hatchet when she said to him, 'The shepherd, when the spring returns, thinks no more of the cold that has gone.' Vergottis was a rich 'old money' Greek shipowner who had known Aristotle since the 1930s, and he replied prophetically, 'When the spring returns, sometimes that is the best time to think of the cold to come.'

It had always been Maria's hope that he would marry her and allow her to retire as a singer but, when he failed to propose, she had returned to opera. Her divorce from Meneghini had cost her dear and she needed the money. She had not appeared in a full-scale opera for eighteen months, but she now agreed with Covent Garden's David Webster that she would sing *Tosca* if it was part of the current season and if Franco Zeffirelli directed. She hid this from Aristotle until the contracts had been signed, and then said, 'I need it Ari, I want to be *me* again.'

He did not, as she had feared, explode, but said, 'It's very short notice. Isn't it a risk?'

'I'm forty years old, Ari,' she replied. 'My whole life is a risk.'

Seven years earlier she had been the greatest prima

donna in the world. Inevitably, time had taken a toll on her voice but, in the event, *Tosca* was a triumph. The London audience knew she was past her prime, but they still loved her, giving her a standing ovation, and even the opera-hating Aristotle came to see the fourth performance. She immediately signed a contract to perform *Norma* in Paris. The opening night fell on the anniversary of the D-Day landings in Normandy and the Palais Garnier was filled with celebrities including Charlie Chaplin, the Aga Khan, Yves Saint Laurent, Jean-Paul Belmondo, Princess Grace, Jean Seburg, David Niven and a host of socialites and politicians. The French audience was less forgiving, however, and picked up on her rusty phrasing and timing. Finally, she broke on a high C and the catcalls began. Maria asked the orchestra to go back so that she could attempt the note again. Rudolf Bing would recall the silence which followed: 'the sort of quiet the mob probably made as the guillotine shivered before its descent'. This time she hit the note perfectly, but the heckling returned, and fights broke out between pro- and anti-Callas factions. Aristotle was, again, in the audience, and he was supportive, saying, 'You showed a lot of courage out there.'

'It was mostly impudence', she replied.

'I think we need to build some time together,' he said.

The construction work on Skorpios was now mostly complete and they would spend much of that summer on his private island. It was, probably, the closest that the couple had ever been.[182] Vergottis visited them there and the conversation turned to Maria's financial straits, which were serious. The three agreed to form a company for her, named Operation

OMERTÀ

Prima Donna, which would look for ship-owning opportunities. Vergottis had heard about a 28,000-ton bulk carrier being built in Spain. Because the vessel had been delayed, the buyer exercised their right to pull out. Consequently, the shipyard was desperate to sell to a new owner, and Vergottis knew he could get her cheaply: $3.6 million payable over eight years. Aristotle was cautious, saying to Maria, 'Ever since those damned American ships, I have made it a point of principle to never buy a leftover something from anybody.' Nonetheless, they agreed to go ahead, with Aristotle taking fifty per cent, and Vergottis and Maria taking twenty-five per cent each. After a little horse-trading, they got the ship for the bargain price of $3.4 million, and they celebrated at Maxims.

On her maiden voyage the ship developed engine problems and the superstitious Vergottis decided that she was unlucky. He offered to buy Maria out by converting her investment into an interest-bearing loan. Maria agreed but Aristotle, who had already transferred his shares to her and four of his nephews, was unhappy. Vergottis had also agreed to finance a movie of *Tosca*, directed by Zeffirelli, in which Maria would star. Aristotle was unhappy with this too; he first offered to finance the movie himself, but then was so critical of the producers that they pulled out altogether and the project fell through. Maria now decided to convert her loan back into the original twenty-five per cent shareholding but Vergottis, who by now had lost patience, refused. Aristotle, who may have intended the investment to be a final 'pay off' before parting with Maria, seemed determined to spar with Vergottis and none of the three would back down. Maria and Aristotle now sued Vergottis in the London courts and the case, predictably, drew a huge amount of publicity.[183]

Allegations of fraud and bad faith, laced with sexual overtones, now filled the newspapers. Both Aristotle and Maria found themselves on the witness stand being cross-examined on the exact nature of their relationship. At one point she said, 'I had the great joy of considering [Vergottis] more than my father because I never had a father or mother virtually. I was very happy with it and he knew it, and he considered me his greatest joy. He was very proud to travel around and participate in my glory. I am not trying to be funny.' In court, Aristotle tried to distance himself from Maria, downplaying not only the present but also the past, which led Maria to say, 'It wasn't a trial, it was a memorial service.' Her reputation was daily diminished with the press depicting her as a greedy woman with a rich and powerful lover who was trying to destroy a sick and elderly man.

Vergottis, who was seventy-eight and in poor health, won the case, but Aristotle and Maria lodged a successful appeal. Vergottis refused to concede and demanded a new trial. The case would drag on for a further eighteen months and ultimately be decided in the House of Lords, where Aristotle and Maria finally won. Their victory, however, was largely pyrrhic; the compensation they received could never be worth the public scorn and ridicule that both had been subjected to.[184]

On the island of Skorpios and in Paris, the long legal battle had, for its duration, reunited Aristotle and Maria. But now that it was over and the two exhausted victors had limped off the field, they began to drift apart. Maria had a new apartment on the avenue Georges-Mandel in Paris, paid for by Aristotle, and she often went weeks at a time without leaving it. Aristotle, clandestinely, had never lost contact with Jackie Kennedy. As Johnny Meyer put it, 'He won more tricks hiding his own intentions than by trying to discover what the fuck the opposition was up to.' He had always been a good poker player and, as one of his friends in Buenos Aires had observed, decades before, 'The only time you know what Onassis has got in his hand, is when he goes to the can!'

CHAPTER FOURTEEN
A Formidable Clan

In America, Jackie's popularity had begun to cool a little as newspapers refocused on her hemlines, her trips abroad and the cost of her secret service protectors. Her dispute with William Manchester had also played badly. Having first commissioned him to write *The Death of a President*, she and Bobby subsequently tried to suppress the book and it was finally published with 1,600 words removed. Americans seemed to wish that Jackie, like Queen Victoria, would always wear a widow's weeds.

In 1964 Jackie had a brief affair with Marlon Brando who later wrote, 'From all I'd read and heard about her, Jacqueline Kennedy seemed coquettish and sensual but not particularly sexual. If anything, I pictured her as more voyeur than player. But that wasn't the case. She kept waiting for me to try to get her into bed. When I failed to make a move she took matters into her own hands and popped the magic question, "Would you like to spend the night?" I said, "I thought you'd never ask".'[185]

At the same time, Lee, encouraged by her new friend, Truman Capote, was attempting to reinvent herself as an actress. Capote was then at the height of his fame having published *In Cold Blood*, while his Black and White Ball in New York had been dubbed the 'Party of the Century'.[186] When Lee took the role of Tracey Lord in a stage production of *The Philadelphia Story*, the tickets quickly sold out, but critics panned her wooden acting. Capote wrote a screenplay for her and used his influence to persuade ABC-TV to cast her in the lead role of *Laura*, which had been a successful movie for Gene Tierney in the 1940s. Once more, the adaptation was a popular success, but a critical disaster, and the reviews were excoriating. Capote tried his best to defend her on David Susskind's TV show: 'We had not foreseen the extent to which no matter what Lee did, the press was going to come down on her like hell ... because they really wanted to say nasty things about Mrs Kennedy and never could at that time because Jackie was still the widow lady, a little saint. There was, underneath all that adulation, a tremendous resentment and envy for this beautiful girl who had everything. And here was this other girl who wouldn't have got the part if she weren't Mrs Kennedy's sister ...'[187]

Aristotle thrived on publicity and loved to be written about, but he well understood that if his closeness to Jackie became common knowledge, public opinion might turn against her. Additionally, the Kennedys were still a formidable clan, and they might close ranks to exclude him. Since Jack's death, Bobby had become the *de facto* head of the family and one of Jackie's closest advisors. He already had his eye on the Democratic nomination for the 1968 presidential race, and he didn't want anything to tarnish the Kennedys' reputation. He had not changed his mind about Aristotle, referring to him derisively as 'the Greek' and saying he was 'a complete rogue on the grand scale'.[188]

By 1967 Jackie had been seen in public with several potential suitors, including Roswell Gilpatric, a former Secretary of Defence in the Kennedy administration, as well as the historian Arthur Schlessinger Jr, the film director Mike Nichols, and David Ormsby-Gore (Lord Harlech). Recently widowed, Harlech was an aristocrat and former British ambassador to Washington who had been a close friend of Jack. Journalists openly speculated that he would marry Jackie but, in truth, they were never as close as appearances might have suggested and Harlech may have simply been a convenient smoke screen. Harlech told a close friend that marriage was unlikely because: 'I'm not rich enough for her and it would have been like having a sixth child because she had to have the kind of adoration a child asks from you and the constant attention …' [189] Lee would tell her friend, Cecil Beaton, 'Of course she won't marry that fool, David, although he goes on about it the whole time.'[190]

What no journalist knew then was that — since the death of her husband — Jackie had secretly entertained Aristotle at her fifteen-room duplex on Fifth Avenue. Unlike Harlech, Aristotle was extremely rich and knew exactly how to give a woman 'the kind of adoration a child asks of you'. When Aristotle entertained her, at his avenue Foch house in Paris, the servants were kept in their quarters, and he served the meal himself. Initially, the relationship was platonic; he was still seeing Lee and had even made Stas a director of one of his companies, an appointment he gratefully accepted because his property fortune was now much diminished.

Both Jackie and her mother, Janet, were aware of the

relationship. While in London, Janet had heard that Lee, surprisingly, was staying at Claridge's and not at her nearby Mayfair home. She called, unannounced, at Lee's suite, only to find Aristotle sitting behind the desk in his dressing gown. Each demanded to know who the other was, and each was surprised by the answer. Lee had gone out, but, later that day, when Janet furiously challenged her daughter, she simply refused to talk about Aristotle.

A few weeks later, when Janet heard that Aristotle was in New York, she went to meet him at the Pierre Hotel, this time with an appointment. Her purpose was not to try and end the affair — she had too much respect for his wealth to want that — it was to try and ensure that Aristotle made the affair respectable by marrying Lee. She left believing that she had some kind of secret pact with him, but she may not have known that this was a businessman who signed contracts in disappearing ink.

In April 1967, a group of colonels overthrew the civilian government of Greece in a coup d'état which became known as the 'Greek Junta'. They expelled the young King Constantine and imposed a far-right, authoritarian regime which curbed civil liberties while detaining, torturing and exiling their political opponents. Western governments were outraged and, for seven years, Greece became a pariah state in the eyes of much of the world. Aristotle, who cared nothing for politics, saw the change simply as another business opportunity, and competed with his old rival, Stavros Niarchos, to benefit from government contracts. He set about cultivating the junta's dictator,

Georgios Papadopoulos, as a personal friend, giving him the use of his villa and even buying clothes for his wife. In Washington, London and Paris, however, this was seen as further evidence of Aristotle's 'shady' business tactics and it did nothing to improve his reputation.

In the summer of 1967, Fiat boss Gianni Agnelli and Taki Theodoracopoulos were sailing on the Ionian Sea in Agnelli's yacht, *Agneta*, when they decided to make an impromptu call at Skorpios. Aristotle was there and he welcomed them cautiously, taking them on a tour of the island in his buggy, but they found him to be uncharacteristically inhospitable: 'As we were coming down to the tiny harbour, we saw a woman leaving. I didn't recognize her but Gianni said to me, "You know who that was? It was Jackie." I said, "No, I didn't notice." She took off water-skiing and she stayed away the whole hour that I and Gianni — a couple of hours — were there. And then we felt that's why Onassis wanted to get rid of us because he was ill at ease ... this was a year and a half before it happened. So she was already there ...'[191] Agnelli would easily have recognised Jackie. In 1962, he had enjoyed a brief fling with her himself while she was holidaying in Italy away from her husband. He told his friend Frank Sinatra, 'I was in love with Jackie. But we decided to view our relationship as a summer romance.'[192]

Agnelli was right. Jackie had secretly joined Aristotle on Skorpios for a week's holiday telling no one — not even her mother and sister — where she was. As so often happened with his most important guests, he was impishly charming and mischievous, but he was also unfailingly attentive and indulgent, pandering to her every whim and spoiling her with every luxury that he could imagine. Every night at dinner, when she opened her napkin, a precious jewel fell into her lap. The public, however, knew nothing and, for the uninformed, the relationship seemed so improbable that suspicions never surfaced.

In January 1968, Janet's father died. Neither Jackie nor Lee had liked their maternal grandfather and he had never been invited to the White House. When Janet had tried to telephone Jackie to give her the news, she had a lot of difficulty tracking her down, and had been staggered when she finally traced her daughter to Greece, where she was staying with Aristotle. This was the first indication she'd had that both her daughters were close to him. A terse conversation followed, with Jackie telling her mother she wouldn't be attending the funeral. The antipathy must have been mutual because he didn't leave either sister a cent. For Jackie, this was a problem. Although her children had inherited millions in Kennedy trust funds, she had only received $70,000 from her husband's will. The Kennedys paid her an annual allowance of $175,000 (roughly $1.5 million in today's money) but Jackie was extravagant, and her annual spending came to considerably more.

In March 1968, Bobby declared his candidacy for the Democratic nomination in the forthcoming presidential race. Separating from his wife, Ethel, was now politically unacceptable, and he knew he would need the support of America's 'First Widow' to win. She gave it, fully, but privately she feared that Bobby, too, would be assassinated. In fact, the fear of assassination occupied her dreams along with a dread that her children would be kidnapped or harmed. At a dinner party, Jackie told Arthur Schlesinger: 'Do you know what I think will happen to Bobby? The same thing that happened to Jack ... There is so much hatred in this country, and more people hate Bobby than hated Jack. I've told Bobby this, but he isn't fatalistic like me.'[193] Two days later, Martin Luther King was shot dead in Memphis and serious rioting followed. Bobby was shaken but his resolve held. He would have preferred that Jackie end her friendship with Aristotle altogether but, aware of the threats that had been made, he settled for keeping it under wraps until the presidential campaign was over.

Typically, the *Christina* cruised in the Mediterranean, Aegean and Ionian Seas, but in May 1968 she was in the Caribbean, allowing Aristotle to more easily entertain American celebrities, including Cary Grant and Kirk Kerkorian, the businessman who built some of Las Vegas's biggest hotels. Another guest on that voyage was Joan Thring, the London-based manager of Rudolf Nureyev and Margot Fonteyn. Joan — who had once been an actress — was a feisty, straight-talking Australian whom Aristotle liked and trusted. Joan would later recall, 'Suddenly all the slipcovers were taken off the drawing-room sofas and things, and a lot of photographs of Jackie and Jack Kennedy suddenly appeared from nowhere, and we all laughed with each other because Ari never told you anything, it was very secretive, and he just went about doing whatever he was doing. He never said, "Well, Jackie's arriving tonight," or anything like that. So I said to them, "Guess who's coming to dinner — it must be

Jackie." They were all getting off that day so I went to see them off and then I came back and about an hour later I looked out of my window and there was Jackie arriving ...' But Thring was sure there was not yet any sex between Onassis and Jackie. 'She was with me all the time. And she certainly wasn't sleeping in his room because first thing in the morning she used to ring me — there were two kitchens on the yacht, one was French and the other Greek — and she'd say, "Oh, you must try scrambled egg from the Greeks this morning — it's delicious!" ... They never behaved as if anything was going on. There were no endearments or touching or anything like that ... I was absolutely convinced that nothing had gone on while we were there ... I think in the afternoons they spent an hour or two together, and they were working out some sort of agreement ... It was just all business talks and there weren't that many ... Most of the time we were there he didn't even have lunch with us.'[194]

Whatever negotiations may have taken place, Jackie agreed to nothing and, as Johnny Meyer observed, 'Although she knew they had a deal, she'd promised Bobby that she wouldn't make any waves until after the election. I think she figured it would be interesting to see the glimmer of uncertainty in Ari's eyes. It was a nice touch, keeping him waiting, turning the thumbscrews.'[195]

Jackie left the *Christina* at St Thomas on the same day that Bobby lost the Oregon primary to Eugene McCarthy; the first time that any Kennedy had lost a political election. The next day he travelled to Los Angeles where he was declared the winner of the crucial South Dakota and California primaries.

A little after midnight, while walking through the kitchen of the Ambassador Hotel, he was shot dead by Sirhan Sirhan. Jackie, who was asleep in her New York apartment, heard the news in the small hours of the morning in a telephone call from Stas in London where, five hours ahead of New York, the shooting was already on every news bulletin. What she heard devastated her. As she waited at the airport for Stas to arrive, she kept repeating, 'No! It can't have happened. It can't have happened. Tell me it hasn't happened.' Jackie, Stas and Roswell Gilpatric flew to Los Angeles in a private jet lent to them by Tom Watson of IBM. At the hospital, Bobby was being kept alive artificially, but it was clear that his injuries were fatal.[196] At his bedside, Ethel and Ted Kennedy were too distraught to make a decision, so it fell to Jackie to give the doctors permission to turn off the machines and allow him to die. Once again, she found herself aboard Air Force One, flying a Kennedy's body home for burial.

A few days later, at St Patrick's Cathedral, America's 'First Widow' again wore black and a heavy veil while, accompanied by her children, she walked up the aisle as if it were her own husband's funeral. Shirley MacLaine, who was aboard the train which took Bobby's coffin to Washington for burial at Arlington National Cemetery, described the scene. 'The two women, Mrs Ethel Kennedy and Mrs Jackie Kennedy, came through [the train], Jackie first, very regal, as only she can be, with this marvellous sense of sort of anticipatory dignity. She was always able, somehow, to anticipate when the train was going to lurch or when it would bump, and queenlike, take hold of something so that, when the bump came, she wasn't disturbed or dislodged.'[197] While she managed to hold herself together for the funeral, she was in pieces afterwards. According to Ros Gilpatric, 'After Bobby's death Jackie became alarmingly distraught, [she] seemed highly agitated, even unbalanced. Among other things she kept referring to Bobby as her husband. She became very imperious, barking orders as if she were still First Lady. It was as if Jackie could take one such tragedy, but not two.'[198]

'There was a terrible vacuum caused by Bobby's death,' said William vanden Heuvel, a close friend of Bobby's and a political aide. 'It was the finality that wasn't really there with Jack's death. After the President's death, Robert Kennedy was left to survive and to lead the generations, to be *pater familias*, and to be extraordinarily helpful to Jackie and the children. His death removed such a vitally important part of everybody's life, and I think the violence of America in 1968, the Martin Luther King assassination and then Bobby's assassination two months later, the street riots, all of that, it was that kind of violent year and I think she was very anxious to protect the children. Onassis was a powerful figure in the sense of a man with enormous wealth, who could give what almost no government could give, which was privacy. Whether it was a yacht or an island, it was privacy — and also out of the United States.'[199]

Jackie was now desperate, not only for emotional and financial support, but also for a safe haven, and where better than aboard a vast yacht, or on a private island? With Bobby's death, the last obstacle had been removed. Some biographers have suggested that Aristotle had a hand in Bobby's killing, but there is no credible evidence of that, while there is ample evidence that Sirhan Sirhan, who was convicted of the murder, acted alone. In 1988, shortly before she died, Christina Onassis told Peter Evans that in 1968 her father paid protection money to Mahmoud Hamshari — who later joined Black September — when he threatened to hijack aircraft belonging to Olympic Airways. It is possible this money was used to finance terrorism, but very unlikely that Hamshari or Black September killed Bobby.

Aristotle had flown to the United States as soon as he heard of the shooting. On arrival, Jackie took him to the Kennedys' family home in Hyannis Port, Massachusetts, where, to her relief, Joe and Rose Kennedy welcomed them both. Joe had been in poor health since suffering a stroke in 1961. Having outlived four of his children, he would die within a year. The couple had met Aristotle several times over many years and, unlike Bobby, rather liked him. Joe respected his success in business and appreciated the donations he had made to Bobby's campaign, while Rose liked his sense of humour. She would have known that the Greek Orthodox Church bears many similarities to the Catholic Church and marriages between the two faiths are permitted (she may not have known, however, that there is no such thing as a Greek Orthodox annulment). For her, this would have been crucial. She had refused to go to the wedding of her own daughter Kathleen 'Kick' Kennedy to William Cavendish, the Marquess of Hartington, because he was a protestant and would not agree to raise his children as Catholics. Kick's older brother, Joe, was the only member of her family to attend.[200]

Jackie's mother, Janet, reacted differently. She had always considered Aristotle to be vulgar, and her attempts to forge a pact with him over Lee had done nothing to change her mind. In her view, a shady Levantine businessman, no matter how rich, was no substitute for a president, and she made that clear. Back in Hyannis Port, on a second visit, Aristotle invited both Jackie and Ted Kennedy to join him on Skorpios.

Aristotle returned to Europe aboard the *Christina*, travelling with Joan Thring with whom he had a brief affair. Throughout the voyage he interrogated her about Jackie: 'I knew that whatever I said was important to him. Winning Jackie meant everything to him. It was the only time I ever sensed vulnerability in the man. It was an interesting new dimension.' Joan also recalled that he was now scathing about Maria, symbolically throwing her records into the sea and saying that her singing practice used to drive him mad.

When he returned to Greece, Maria Callas was ordered to stay away from the *Christina*. 'I want you to go to Paris and wait for me there.'

'Go to Paris in *August*? Are you mad?'

'I'm having company and you can't be aboard.'

By now, Maria had heard rumours of an affair with Jackie Kennedy, and her rows with Aristotle were becoming increasingly bitter. 'What are you?' Aristotle would say to her, 'Nothing. You just have a whistle in your throat that no longer works.'[201] His adored sister Artemis, who had never liked Maria Callas, became an ally of Jackie and entertained her at her Glyfada villa. The two had been friends since their first meeting. His children, Alexander and Christina, however, had always hoped that he would, one day, be reconciled with their mother, Tina, and they showed no more enthusiasm for Jackie than they had for Maria Callas.

Lee Radziwill had also heard the rumours and was devastated. She was still hoping that Aristotle might, one day, marry her and she felt that Jackie had betrayed her, especially as it was Lee who had first persuaded Aristotle to invite Jackie on a cruise. The resulting *froideur* between the once-close sisters was palpable, but they would not become entirely estranged until later.

The rumours were also surfacing in the United States, but the union seemed so improbable that few took them seriously. When Doris Lilly, a gossip columnist on the *New York Post*, predicted the marriage on the *Merv Griffin Show*, she was loudly booed by the audience and even jostled when she left the studio. Aristotle told another gossip columnist, Earl Wilson, that Lilly was 'flat-ass wrong'. Nonetheless, the evidence was growing. Marina Dodero had relatives who lived in the same apartment block as Jackie. 'Every day they would see that a present arrived for Jackie from Van Cleef or Cartier, or bouquets of flowers, every day, every day, and they knew it was from Mr Onassis. So I said, "I think there is a story going on between Jackie and Ari," and everybody laughed.'[202]

On 15 October the *Boston Herald Traveler* announced, unequivocally, that John F Kennedy's widow was going to marry Aristotle Onassis, and America began to digest the country's most shocking news story since Bobby's assassination. Franco

A FORMIDABLE CLAN

Zeffirelli would comment, 'When he [Onassis] had squeezed all the juice out of this orange [Maria] he would throw it away and get another one.' Maria now became an almost total recluse in her Paris apartment. She turned down offers to appear with Luciano Pavarotti and Plácido Domingo, losing her nerve at the last minute. She was persuaded to make a film of *Medea* with Pasolini, but it was a critical and commercial failure and there would only be one more public performance: a concert tour of several countries with her friend the Italian tenor Giuseppe Di Stefano. Although both were past their best, it was popular with audiences, if not with critics.

CHAPTER FIFTEEN
The Baroness Who Would Not be Bought

Both of Aristotle's children were now young adults but, as Alan Brien had feared, neither had developed into especially happy or well-adjusted people. Paul Ioannidis, who was Olympic Airways' chief pilot, recalled that Alexander had '... given me the impression that he had gone without a mother's love and family affection from a young age, which led him to seek this out in his personal life. He was quite young when he turned his attention to motorcycles, fast boats, fast cars, and subsequently aeroplanes and helicopters, which ended up becoming his passion. He did not talk much, and he sometimes would get lost in his thoughts. At other times, he could blow up at you.'[203] Ioannidis considered Alexander to be an excellent 'natural' pilot but found him reckless and prone to taking unnecessary risks.

At the age of eighteen, Alexander had dumbfounded his mother by dating one of her friends, Fiona von Thyssen, the third wife of the industrialist and art collector, Baron Hans Heinrich 'Heini' Thyssen-Bornemisza. A former model, who had once been ranked among the three most beautiful women in Britain, Fiona already had two teenage children and was sixteen years older than him.[204] She was an

THE BARONESS WHO WOULD NOT BE BOUGHT

Baroness Fiona von Thyssen (née Campbell).

aristocrat and member of Clan Campbell who had been the muse of Cecil Beaton, a favourite of *Vogue*, and a celebrated beauty.[205] Alexander fell in love with her at the age of twelve when he saw her getting out of a car in St Moritz. Fiona had married Heini the day after she first met him on a ski slope in 1956. Following their bitter 1965 divorce, she returned to London with her two children. Heini would marry twice more to make five wives in total, but Fiona never married again.

Both Alexander's parents deeply disapproved, but he continued with the relationship, despite their determination to end it. Tina told him she'd heard that Fiona had slept with an older man for £50 when she was only seventeen. Aristotle was subtler: he bought Alexander a villa in Athens, hoping it would divert him, or at least make the couple beholden to him. Fiona, however, refused Alexander's demand that she move in with him, believing that if she did, she would become another Onassis object, 'to be manipulated, brutalised and treated on any level and on any terms he chooses. I suspect that very few people in his life had told him to go and stuff himself, although my intent was not to just tell him to stuff himself: I just wouldn't allow myself to be bought as his son's mistress ... Ari didn't want to have a son who was going to threaten him on any level. He was jealous of his attractiveness and his charm. His reactions to Alexander's success were not the normal reactions of a father towards his son. He did everything to humiliate him ... he simply didn't want Alexander to be cleverer wiser or better educated than he was.'

Aristotle was, undoubtedly, jealous of his son. Fiona

von Thyssen was exactly the kind of trophy mistress he liked to target himself: beautiful, sophisticated, mondaine and already a baroness, the sort of woman who turned heads as soon as she entered a room, or even a yacht! Fiona, however, proved herself to be a shrewder judge of character than either Maria or Jackie. In the event, she remained loyal to Alexander until his untimely death in 1973.[206] She also persuaded him to reconcile his differences with his sister, Christina, whom he had not spoken to for several years.

Alexander's early sexual experiences were bizarre. Raised largely by tutors and servants, he spent a lot of time with Jacinto Rosa, his father's Paris-based chauffeur. Rosa taught him to drive and also taught him a lot about engines and mechanical things. 'Many times he asked me to drive him to the Bois de Boulogne, where he liked to spy on the prostitutes working with their clients in cars,' Rosa recalled. 'Sometimes I tried to tell him what's better to do and what was better not to do, but I had to be diplomatic because he would not have accepted any kind of reprimand from one of his father's employees.' Alexander would later describe himself as having never known a day when he was not 'intimidated by the old man's wealth'.[207]

Aristotle was fatalistic and was certain that God had granted him a son for the sole purpose of perpetuating his empire, but that did not mean the boy saw much of him. Both parents were absent for long periods, and when his father did find time for him, he seesawed between unrestrained praise and scathing criticism — often delivering both in public.

Aristotle gave even less time to his daughter, Christina. She was the second child he had never wanted, and he had beaten her mother bloody when she refused to have an abortion. Although he could, at times, dote on her, and even named his yacht after her, he took little interest in her day-to-day upbringing. She found him so frightening that she once peed herself in his presence. While Alexander was reasonably attractive and could communicate — even charm people — when he chose to, Christina was painfully shy, introverted and plain. As she matured, she became a deeply unhappy and psychologically disturbed young woman. Artemis tried her best to talk both siblings into accepting Jackie, but to no avail.

Internationally, the reaction to the wedding was as bad as it had been in America. There was universal condemnation of Jackie, who appeared to be betraying her husband's memory by marrying a vulgar tycoon. Even General de Gaulle, who had liked Jackie and praised her demeanour following Jack's assassination, privately commented, 'fundamentally, she's behaving like a movie star, it will all end on the yacht of a millionaire'.[208] The Vatican was initially silent, but a monsignor later condemned Jackie as having 'knowingly violated the laws of the Church'. A solitary voice spoke up for her: Cardinal Cushing, Archbishop of Boston, defended the marriage, but received so much hate mail that he took early retirement.

Such were the auguries for the most controversial wedding of the twentieth century. For Aristotle, it was the culmination of a lifelong dream to beat the *haut monde* at their own game and marry into America's royal family. For Jackie, it meant security, wealth and an escape from America. It is inconceivable that she did not have misgivings, but she went ahead. Public opinion in America, along with the disapproval of the Kennedys, meant a wedding there was unthinkable, so, the ceremony took place on 26 October 1968 in the tiny church of Panayitsa on Skorpios, Aristotle's private island. As few Greeks would be attending, Aristotle insisted upon a priest 'who understands English and doesn't look like Rasputin'. He also sent Johnny Meyer to the United States to see Gloria Swanson who, he feared, might tell journalists she'd had affairs with both the groom and the bride's former father-in-law. Swanson was insulted by the suggestion and never mentioned either man, even in her memoirs.

Donald McGregor, who had been about to fly an Olympic Airways Boeing 707 from New York to Athens, was told to offload all ninety-three passengers and fly Jackie and her entourage to a Greek military airbase where an amphibious aircraft would take them to Skorpios. In Paris, Richard Burton and Elizabeth Taylor were holding a party to celebrate the release of their film, *A Flea in Her Ear*. They invited Maria Callas, via their mutual friend Rex Harrison. Burton told him, 'I just heard the news from New York. She'll need a bit of cheering up, I fancy.'[209]

It rained, but Artemis assured everyone that rain was a lucky omen. Only Jackie and Aristotle appear to be happy in the photographs; their four children seem less so. Christina wept, but not from a surfeit of joy. Jackie wore a gown by Valentino and Aristotle a dark blue suit. Jackie's stepfather, Hugh Auchincloss, gave her away for the second time and the couple, naturally, honeymooned aboard the *Christina* although, for the first few days, she remained anchored at Skorpios.

Jackie began married life by summoning her interior decorator, Billy Baldwin, from New York and tasked him with redesigning their house. Given a cabin on the *Christina*, he privately told her he thought the ship was 'the epitome of vulgarity and bad taste'. He conceded, however, that there was a certain masculine charm about the library which 'almost made up for the horrors of the rest of the ship'.[210]

Four days after the wedding, Ted Kennedy's worst fears were confirmed when Aristotle announced his investment in Project Omega, a $400 million infrastructure deal he had concluded with his now close friend, the dictator George Papadopoulos. Aristotle modestly called it 'the biggest deal in the history of Greece'. His staff joked that he was the only man who could handle two honeymoons at the same time: one with Jackie and one with Papadopoulos. Outside Greece, many governments feared that Aristotle was giving the colonels a worrying new level of credibility.

On the tiny island of Skorpios, Jackie was left alone for long periods while Aristotle was absent on lengthy business trips. Within eleven days he was secretly having dinner with Maria Callas in Paris. In America, the negative feelings about her marriage were getting worse. In Las Vegas, Joan Rivers was openly mocking the couple accompanied by gales of laughter: 'Come on, be honest, would you sleep with Onassis? Well, she has to do something. I mean, you can't stay in Bergdorf's shopping all day.' Aristotle was unconcerned, and he told Johnny Meyer, 'She's got to reconcile herself to being Mrs Aristotle Onassis because the only place she'll find sympathy from now

THE BARONESS WHO WOULD NOT BE BOUGHT

The wedding took place in the tiny church of Panayitsa on Skorpios, Aristotle's private island.

on is in the dictionary between shit and syphilis.'[211]

For all this, the couple made no attempt to hide their physical attraction. In the restaurant of Claridge's, and elsewhere, they would sit at a corner table holding hands.[212] Aristotle's secretary confirmed that they often behaved 'like teenagers, unable to keep their hands or lips off each other's bodies. Artemis would smile at me when they did that in front of her …'[213] They enjoyed impromptu and spontaneous sex in aeroplanes, in boats and even on beaches, oblivious to who might see or even photograph them. Aristotle was, anyway, an exhibitionist who liked his sex acts to be observed; he frequently copulated in random cabins of the *Christina* — or in rooms of his homes — with the door open.

Jackie was unable to persuade Aristotle to get rid of the portrait of Tina which hung in his bedroom aboard the *Christina*, she only managed to get it moved to another part of the ship. It soon became obvious to her that a corner of his heart was still reserved for his first wife. She told Artemis that it upset her to see that 'beautiful face' and she knew that Aristotle was still a little in love. Divorcing Tina had never been part of his plan; he thought he could have an open marriage with her and that she would tolerate his affairs if he turned a blind eye towards hers. But, when he publicly humiliated her with Maria Callas, he overstepped the mark and lost her. For many years, both he and his children secretly hoped that they would remarry. Jackie probably divined this too late, after she had become his second wife. Before long, however, Jackie would realise that her real rival was not Tina, but Maria. Artemis was her brother's most loyal supporter, but even she could not pretend that he was blameless. She told Jackie, 'He may not be faithful, but he is considerate and discreet.'[214]

Jackie no longer felt safe in America, and she'd been humiliated by all the negative press she received there and across Europe. She moved backwards and forwards between the 'Pink House' on Skorpios, and the Onassis compound of villas in Glyfada. There was not much company for her, and even when Aristotle was on Skorpios, they spent less time together as she lived in the Pink House, and he preferred to eat and sleep on the *Christina*. In Paris, a city Aristotle often visited, he began to spend more time with Maria and was soon, effectively, courting her once more.

Aristotle had purchased Maria's apartment on the avenue Georges-Mandel using two of his Panamanian companies, and he paid all the household expenses. This was a tactic he often used: owning a mistress's property meant, by extension, that he owned the mistress and could behave as he wished. In his mind, mistresses and wives were always business transactions: assets on the balance sheet rather than emotional ties. The apartment was near to his own home on the avenue Foch.

At first, Maria refused to speak to him or let him into the apartment. He took to whistling below her window, as if they were teenagers. When that drew no response, he threatened to drive his Rolls-Royce into the building, and she finally relented. Once in her company he began to complain about Jackie's behaviour: she was still writing letters to Roswell Gilpatric and had begun to spend more time in New York, leaving him to entertain his guests alone.

Although it was less than a month since the marriage, he claimed that she now meant 'nothing' to him. When he tried to take Maria to the bedroom, she threw him out. As he walked away, she shouted abuse at him from the window, reminding him that it was the anniversary of Jack Kennedy's death.

She did not, however, stop him from visiting again and from this day he did so regularly. To begin with, Aristotle was careful not to be discovered: he told Maria to turn down the lights when he came and the appointments were always made through his secretary, never directly. He made a point of never discussing business with Jackie — 'It would bore you, honey' — but he did with Maria: 'Their relationship went beyond sex,' his secretary said. 'He needed her to discuss his problems, his innermost thoughts and feelings. Had Jackie been able to assume that role, perhaps he would not have craved Maria. I do not know why he went to Maria so often. All I know for certain is that he went.'[215]

What Aristotle may not have fully understood was that Jackie was still a deeply damaged woman. She knew how to hide her feelings behind a mask of politesse and charm, but the mask occasionally slipped. On the anniversary of Jack's death, the same night on which Aristotle secretly resumed his affair with Maria, Jackie was alone with Artemis on Skorpios. She was obviously out of sorts and when Artemis asked her what was wrong, she burst into tears. 'I'm having a very bad day. I know I should be happy now, but all I can think about is my first husband and what happened to him in Texas. Sometimes I think I will never be able to be truly happy again.'[216]

THE BARONESS WHO WOULD NOT BE BOUGHT

In those early years Jackie immersed herself in Greek culture, having lessons in the language, visiting museums and galleries and engrossing herself in the history of the art and literature of her new home. As far as possible she stayed away from places where she might be recognised. Once, while she was visiting friends of hers on the island of Patmos, a cruise ship arrived and some of the passengers spotted her, literally chasing her down the street and demanding photographs. She had to take refuge in a church to avoid them.

When Aristotle was on Skorpios, he still showered her with jewellery and gifts, but she would not have known that the jewels had first been given to Maria. He had kept them in a safe in his Glyfada villa since the last time she had stormed off the *Christina*. Gore Vidal recalled talking to Maria about them in Rome: 'She was getting ready to make *Medea*. And Pasolini was there [but] all she wanted to talk about was Jackie. Very funny about her. The jewellery that Jackie had got: "I know those jewels, they're nothing, they're second-rate except the ruby earrings are quite good. I remember those and I almost took them but they really weren't right for me." The rest of it, she said, was just trash. Then she said, "But of course, she wouldn't know the difference, would she?"' [217]

In public, however, both Aristotle and Jackie appeared to be comfortable and at ease with each other. The writer, Patrick Leigh Fermour, recalled meeting them at an embassy dinner: 'I sat next to Jackie and was fascinated by her. Her face was somehow rather wildly put together, eyes very wide apart but captivating and unusual. Her voice was so quiet it was almost a coo: "Oh, yaiss …" She reminded me faintly of a sort of quiet, intelligent and beautiful-mannered little girl, the sort that wants to please and wins all hearts … Onassis, opposite, seemed the acme of boisterous vigour and much nicer than I had imagined he would be … there was a great feeling of cheerful interruptions and laughter. Later, after coffee and more delicious drinks, I remember [Aristotle] singing some very out-of-date Athens music-hall songs, the older the better, and illustrating dance steps by demonstration and even joining hands on shoulders.'[218]

Aristotle's children, however, resolutely rejected Jackie. Alexander, in particular, would try to avoid even being in the same room as her. Aristotle's secretary recalled one embarrassing scene when Aristotle wanted Alexander to see them both off before they flew to New York, but, when the time came for them to leave, Alexander could not be found. For once, Jackie was visibly angry: 'I was surprised when Mrs Jackie said, "I do not know why your children are so rude to me." Usually she was so careful in the way she treated her husband. "I have done nothing to deserve such rude treatment".

'"Worry only about your own children, not mine, my dear," he told her nastily, as he walked so fast to the plane that there was no way she could keep up with his pace.'[219]

Mutual dislike of Jackie could unite Alexander and Christina in a way that few other things did, 'When Christina called to speak to Alexander or went into his office to speak to him, they always spoke about their father, discussing his moods and his plans.

They liked to know exactly where he was and with whom and for how long. But when the two of them started to discuss Jackie, their voices changed. They were no longer concerned, loving children; they were scheming, unhappy stepchildren. If anything, their dislike for Jackie drew them closer together, as she was the common enemy they both wanted to defeat. So often, they spoke of the time when Jackie and their father would separate, always keeping hope alive in each other.'[220]

They made an exception, however, for Jackie's children, Caroline and John, both of whom they liked. Aristotle could be better with other people's children than he had been with his own. He had divined, correctly, that Jackie would not marry him unless he proved he was going to be a good stepfather. Consequently, he'd made a great effort to win Jackie's kids over, even cancelling business meetings to spend time with them.

In America, the Kennedys' gilded reputation was about to be tarnished. Journalists had long known that Teddy Kennedy was an alcoholic. One journalist had even privately described him as an accident waiting to happen. In July 1969, while driving home from a party, his car skidded off the Chappaquiddick Island bridge, near Martha's Vineyard, and landed nose-first in the water before flipping over. He escaped but his passenger, Mary Jo Kopechne, died. Kennedy did not report the accident to the authorities until the following morning, by which time the girl's body had already been found. He was only convicted of leaving the scene of an accident, but the twin suspicions that he'd needed time to sober up, and that he'd been having an affair with the girl, would always hang over him. He managed to hold on to his seat in the Senate, but irreparable damage was done to his reputation and that of the Kennedy clan, including Jackie.

Strains in the marriage were now clearly and publicly visible. Jackie had an enquiring mind; well-read and well-educated, she liked to discuss history and culture with those who shared her interests. Aristotle had little interest in either and was irritated by such talk. His private secretary, Kiki Feroudi, witnessed one of their increasingly frequent rows. One evening, Aristotle was with his friends Miltos Yiannacopoulos and Yiannis Georgakis when Jackie, who had been reading a book about Socrates, asked Yiannis Georgakis whether he thought that Socrates had really existed or whether he was invented by Plato. Aristotle exploded, shouting at her: 'What is the matter with you? Why do you have to talk about such stupid things? Don't you ever stop to think before you open your mouth? Have you ever noticed the statue of a man with a moustache that is in the centre of Athens? Are you too stupid to know that is a statue of Socrates?' Jackie, burst into tears and ran outside into the rain. Aristotle rarely apologised, but a few days later he bought her an expensive gold bracelet, from the Athens jeweller Zolotas. According to Kiki, he had 'acted like a true Greek man who liked to scream and say whatever he wanted. For her part, Mrs Onassis acted like a true Greek wife …'[221]

By now, Jackie must have been having serious doubts. Not only would she have been on the receiving end of her husband's drunken rages, but it is also probable that she was beaten. Aristotle boasted, more than once, that all Greeks beat their wives: 'He

THE BARONESS WHO WOULD NOT BE BOUGHT

Maria Callas filming on location.

who loves well beats well'. His first wife had warned Meneghini that Aristotle was a brutal drunk. Unlike the relationships with Tina and Maria, however, this one had no sado-masochistic element.

Maria was deeply superstitious and rarely took important decisions without consulting astrologers or fortune tellers. While filming *Medea* in Türkiye she met a local clairvoyant who spoke only Turkish. Her driver had to translate, and he hesitated before telling her that, according to the reading of her palm, she would die young but would not suffer.[222] 'Destiny is destiny,' she said, resignedly.

On her return to Paris, she told reporters, 'I had a certain relationship with Onassis but fortunately for me it's all over. It was a period of my life that I want to forget.'[223] This was not true; she and Aristotle were lovers again and were soon being seen together in public, dining together at Maxims, his favourite restaurant. It was not, however, an exclusive arrangement: she was also seen in public with other admirers including the actors Omar Sharif and Raf Vallone. Paradoxically, this gave her a better press than she'd received before. No longer seing her as a 'sad' figure, Italian journalists now wrote, 'The value of Maria Callas, on the contrary, has risen dramatically. Once upon a time, everyone pitied her; in the Parisian salons she was spoken of as the *Pauvre Marie*. Now she's more desirable and high society names compete in inviting her, her presence is enough to determine the international success of a social evening.'[224]

For all this, privately, she was deeply unhappy. When Aristotle returned to Athens for a week-long cruise with Jackie on the *Christina*, she fell into a depression, begging friends not to leave her alone. Finally, she took an overdose of sleeping pills and had to be rushed to the American hospital, where she was stomach-pumped and revived. Although it was not her first suicide attempt, she publicly claimed it was an accident and sued two newspapers who carried the story.[225]

This was not the only cry for help to have an impact on Aristotle. Stavros Niarchos had long been his bitter rival, not only in business but also in love and in status. Each time Aristotle launched a super-tanker, Niarchos would launch a bigger one. When either announced a major contract, the other would always try to announce a better one. When Aristotle married the younger daughter of a shipping tycoon, Niarchos married his older daughter. When Aristotle built a private yacht 325 feet long, Niarchos built a bigger one, 379 feet long. Finally, when Aristotle bought the private island of Skorpios, Niarchos promptly bought the larger private island of Spetsopoula and built a home there. The rivalry was as bitter and vicious as any in history but, for Aristotle, Niarchos may have served an important purpose: he needed enemies as much as he needed friends. It was enemies that brought all his energy, cunning and invention into play, giving him a level of motivation that went beyond the normal boundaries of ambition and greed. For Aristotle, marrying Jackie would be his crowning glory, the thing that Niarchos could never match. For once, he had completely outmanoeuvred his old rival.

Eugenia Livanos was the third wife of Stavros Niarchos and the older sister of Aristotle's first wife, Tina. They married in 1947 and had four children, but he divorced her in 1965 to marry Charlotte Ford, a former lover of Stas Radziwill, who was thirty-two years younger than him and already pregnant with his child. The marriage to Ford lasted barely a year and when it was over Niarchos was reconciled with Eugenia, who moved back into his house on Spetsopoula. Greek law did not recognise their divorce so, technically, they were still married. Over dinner one evening in August 1970, Niarchos telephoned Charlotte in Paris and invited her to the island with their daughter, Elena. Eugenia, who had heard the call, went to her room and took an overdose of the barbiturate Seconal. A maid found her an hour later in a coma. Instead of calling a local doctor, Niarchos telephoned his sister in Athens asking her to call a doctor who worked in the Niarchos shipyards. He took three hours to reach the island (a local doctor would have taken an hour) and Eugenia died within thirty minutes of his arrival. He refused to sign a death certificate as Eugenia had clearly not died of natural causes. The police, seeing bruises on her throat and abdomen, opened an inquiry.[226]

Greece was still under the rule of the military junta. Niarchos was forbidden to leave the country and Greek newspapers forbidden to report the death. That did not stop the Niarchos family leaking a story to the international press that she had taken twenty-five Seconal tablets. The public prosecutor recommended that Niarchos be charged with involuntary manslaughter, which carried a maximum penalty of eighteen years in prison, but he never faced trial. There were three different autopsies, one found that her death had been caused by injuries, and two found that she had died from an overdose. Niarchos, who claimed that the injuries were the result of him trying to revive her, was on the verge of investing $200 million in one of the colonels' most important infrastructure projects. After a long delay, and disagreements between the rival colonels, the government ratified Niarchos's investment and the charges were dropped. The suspicion would remain, however, that Niarchos had — at the very least — contributed to his wife's death, if not directly caused it.

Aristotle Onassis was not the only one to denounce Niarchos, but Alexander supported his uncle. Johnny Meyer recalled, 'Ari wanted to keep Eugenia's death an issue ... Tina took the two youngest Niarchos kids to stay with her in England. It was Alexander who finally convinced his father to drop the whole business. It was the first time I'd ever seen him square up to his old man. He told him to drop it because he was hurting nobody but the kids. "Their mother's dead and all you can think about is getting even with their father" he said. Ari eventually backed off.'[227] Christina, however, remained deeply suspicious of her uncle.

Aristotle wanted Christina, now nineteen, to marry into shipping nobility, favouring Peter Goulandris who was twenty-three, good-looking and — more importantly — from a family who ran four shipping lines with vessels worth more than $1.5 billion. 'Some marriages are made in heaven, the best ones are made in Skorpios,' he said. However, Christina told a friend, 'Love is a quest, not a business deal. I learned for myself that to begin to feel is to begin to hurt.' She decamped from Skorpios to Monte Carlo where she met Joseph Bolker by a hotel pool. He was an urbane forty-eight-year-old, twice-divorced American with two daughters and what Christina described as a 'dinky fortune made in real estate'.

Bolker began a relationship with her, but soon found she was an insistent and unstable girlfriend. When he returned to the United States, she astounded him by turning up on his Los Angeles doorstep unannounced and demanding to move in with him. He telephoned her mother, Tina, in the south of France, and got an even more surprising response. 'I do not want my daughter living with a man she is not married to. Christina must return to Europe immediately or make it legal.' When Bolker pointed out to Christina, as gently as he could, that he was twenty-seven years older than her and not in love, she demanded, 'What's wrong with me? Why won't you marry me? Aren't I good enough for you?' Later that evening he found her in the bedroom having taken an overdose. One of his neighbours was a young doctor who managed to bring her round but, once coherent again, she threatened to keep taking overdoses until he married her. In the end, Bolker gave in, and they were married in Las Vegas.

Aristotle already knew a lot about Bolker, as he spied on both his children and even bugged their phones, but he still exploded at the news that Christina was already married. Another man might have been plunged into despair but Aristotle, who always needed enemies, seemed to relish fighting Bolker, especially as he'd been forced to back off his traditional enemy, Stavros Niarchos. His relationship with Jackie was already starting to flag and he was having to make excuses to reporters about her frequent absences. As one of his aides put it, 'He needed to test his edge on other kinds of men once in a while just to know that he still had it.'

He began by preventing Christina from receiving $75 million in a trust fund which had been due on her twenty-first birthday. Next, he dispatched one of his most trusted confederates, Johnny Meyer, to California. Officially, Meyer described himself as a public relations man, but in reality 'Pick up the Cheque Johnny' was a behind-the-scenes fixer, skilled in the black arts of schmoozing, cajoling, glad-handing and — on occasions — frightening the rich and powerful. He had learnt his trade first as a Hollywood publicist, and later as a henchman of Howard Hughes. In 1947, when Hughes was being investigated by the Senate, Meyer was subpoenaed to explain his staggeringly high expense account.[228] The formidable New York lawyer Roy Cohn would later recall, 'Johnny Meyer was a truly enterprising man, one of a very small group of people in life who surround themselves with very rich and powerful people … whenever a problem came up or something had to be done … checking somebody out or getting the dirt on somebody, Johnny was always there, ready to act with a wide circle of contacts upon whom he could call.'229

Meyer met the couple at the Polo Lounge of the Beverly Hills Hotel. Bolker was cautious and feared for his safety, having been warned by Christina that Meyer 'took care' of a lot of situations for her father in very definite ways. Meyer's opening shot was a simple one: Christina would get the $75 million as soon as the couple divorced. Bolker gamely countered that he was quite capable of supporting his wife and she didn't need the trust fund. Meyer's next play was more invidious, claiming that having 'a Jew in the family' might cause Aristotle to lose important contracts in Saudi Arabia which would spook his lenders, 'Nervous banks are bad news, Joe. It'd do more than scrape the paintwork if they called in their loans.' Bolker calmly countered with, 'I really don't think the Saudis have any animosity towards Jewish Americans.' The lunch ended cordially but inconclusively. This, however, was only the beginning.230

Five weeks after the wedding, Christina met her mother in New York and was told, 'You must prove to him [your father] that you're right and he's wrong. Just stand up to him.' Tina also secretly gave her $200,000, no small gesture from a woman who was notoriously careful with money. According to Fiona von Thyssen, 'To get Tina to break into a five-pound note was a goddam miracle.' What she did not tell her daughter was that her motives were less noble than they appeared. Tina, herself, was secretly planning a betrothal which would wound Aristotle more deeply than even Christina's. Tina's childless marriage to 'Sunny' Blandford had quickly run into the sand and, for several years, she had lived apart from him at her home in Paris, while he remained at Blenheim. In 1971, the French courts had granted them a divorce, following Sunny's discovery that Tina was having an affair with her brother-in-law, Stavros Niarchos. Under French law, Tina would keep her own considerable wealth, but would get little or nothing from her second husband.

Tina kept the wraps on her third wedding until the last possible minute. Her mother, Arietta, had played a considerable role in the marriage. The Livanos family, who were shipping royalty, had always seen themselves as a dynasty and, to them, marriage was a natural way of strengthening their links with other shipowners. With one daughter dead and another divorced, marriage to Stavros Niarchos seemed, by their lights, to be a wise precaution. The ceremony took place in Paris on 22 October, eighteen months after Eugenia's death. Tina's son, Alexander, only learnt about it from a courier-delivered letter which he was handed one hour after the ceremony. Christina learnt about it from a message left with the concierge desk at Bolker's Los Angeles apartment. The news devastated not only Aristotle but also Christina, who had always suspected that Niarchos caused her aunt's death. For a woman whose emotional stability had, at best, been tenuous, this event blew it to smithereens. Bolker recalled, 'It was a very emotional time, a lot of yelling and screaming, a really bad scene'. He was convinced that Tina had 'married Niarchos just to hurt Onassis — a revenge situation. She [Christina] believed that Niarchos killed her aunt, Eugenia, and was going to kill her mother'.

A friend of Christina's said, 'The marriage seemed to Christina an act of madness, the greatest disloyalty to the memory of her aunt and an outrage to her father's pride. She couldn't shake the notion that something real bad was going to come out of it. It was just the worst time for her. The battle of wills with her father, her growing suspicion that she had made a big mistake marrying Joe, had taken a lot out of her. And now there was this shit. Tina couldn't have contrived a situation more likely to unglue her daughter's fragile state of mind.' In the turmoil that followed, Christina again attempted suicide. [231]

While recovering, at Bolker's suggestion, she flew to London to see her personal doctor, and found a staunch ally in Fiona von Thyssen, her brother's lover. Fiona had just made an unpleasant discovery of her own. One of Aristotle's people — also a friend of Alexander's — had recently been a house guest at her home in Wilton Place, and he'd carelessly left a sheaf of papers behind. They were transcripts of telephone conversations between Aristotle and Johnny Meyer (Aristotle obsessively recorded everything), and it was clear they had considered harming Bolker. Alexander was so concerned that he deposited documents with several people that would incriminate his father should anyone be hurt. Christina poured her heart out to Fiona, admitting that she no longer loved Bolker and the marriage had been a mistake. Fiona advised her to return to California and tell Joe she wanted a divorce, before Aristotle turned the whole affair into a media circus.

A few weeks later Christina and Joe Bolker announced that they were divorcing; their marriage had lasted just ninety days. Aristotle had won the battle but further damaged his relationship with Christina, who now began to date a procession of trust fund heirs, playboys and sportsmen. Aristotle had been shaken to the core by the two betrothals, neither of which he saw coming. Christina's divorce allowed him to recover some of his pride, but there was nothing he could do about Tina's wedding to his arch enemy. In defeat, he always needed someone to blame and, this time, he turned his venom on his wife, Jackie. An autograph dealer in New York had got hold of a letter from Jackie to Roswell Gilpatric written during her honeymoon on Skorpios. The day after it was published, Gilpatric's wife sued for divorce. She denied the divorce was linked to the note but told the *Chicago Daily News* that her husband and Jackie were: '... very, very close. I have my own feelings about that but I won't go into them. Just say it was a particularly warm, close, long-lasting relationship.'

When read today, Jackie's note seems little more than a warm goodbye to an old friend, but amid the fevered speculation that then surrounded everything connected to Aristotle Onassis, it was seen as evidence that his marriage was shaky.

> Dearest Ros — I would have told you before I left — but then everything happened so much more quickly than I'd planned. I saw somewhere what you'd said and I was touched — dear Ros — I hope you know all you were and are and ever will be to me — with my love, Jackie.

THE BARONESS WHO WOULD NOT BE BOUGHT

Aristotle knew that that the two had been lovers before he married Jackie, but his Greek pride found this public humiliation difficult to accept. His close, old friend and business associate Costa Gratsos had always disliked Jackie and had strongly disapproved of the marriage. So much so that for a while the two men hardly spoke to each other. Now, Aristotle admitted to him, 'My God, what a fool I have made of myself.'[232]

Aristotle could be thin-skinned, always feeling he had to retaliate when slighted, especially in public, and this time he responded in kind. He had been covertly seeing Maria Callas for some time, but now he openly courted her again, allowing their photograph to be taken while they dined together in Paris. When Maria was staying on Tragonisis, a private island belonging to the Embiricos shipping family, Aristotle flew in by helicopter to present her with a set of antique earrings, and he allowed journalists to photograph them kissing. *Time* magazine reported, 'Responding like a dalmatian to the fire bell, Jackie flew to Greece, to Onassis, to the yacht *Christina*, and to squelch rumours.' Unknown to *Time*, however, Jackie had begun to spend more time in New York and Aristotle was frequently told that he could not stay at her Fifth Avenue apartment because it was, once more, being redecorated. 'She has a thing about decorating,' Aristotle told Willi Frischauer. While in Rome, he guaranteed the attention of paparazzi by throwing a glass of champagne over them as he dined with Elizabeth Taylor, who was not accompanied by her then husband, Richard Burton. In conversation with Johnny Meyer, he emphasised that his rekindled relationship with Maria Callas was now, once more, in the open: 'Everybody here knows three things about Aristotle Onassis. I'm fucking Maria Callas, I'm fucking Jacqueline Kennedy — and I'm fucking rich.'

Aristotle paid Jackie $30,000 per month as an allowance — roughly the equivalent of $215,000 today — but she far exceeded it. After getting a $9,000 bill from the couturier Valentino, he reduced her allowance by a third and kept closer tabs on her spending. When she lost $300,000 speculating on the stock market, he refused to make good the shortfall. As the marriage cooled, he began to use a technique he'd perfected over many years: he briefed journalists against her, planting stories in the media about her extravagance and profligacy. Worse still, he tipped off photographers with the precise time and place where Jackie would be sunbathing, naked, on Skorpios. Using powerful lenses from boats offshore, they got multiple nude images of her which appeared in the American pornographic magazine, *Hustler*. It was an early example of revenge porn.

In 1971, Christian Kafarakis, who had worked on the *Christina* as a steward, cooperated in a book which claimed that — prior to the marriage — Aristotle had signed a 170-clause contract with Jackie detailing every aspect of their relationship, all the way down to the precise number of days they would spend together and even which rooms they would occupy.[233] Most biographers doubt his allegations on the grounds that Kafarakis produced no evidence other than personal hearsay, and it seems unlikely that a steward would have been able to read the whole of such an important and detailed document. He might have heard snatches of conversation, but little more. It also seems unlikely that Aristotle, who had always been recognised as a virtuoso negotiator, would agree to such ridiculous clauses. Additionally, under both Greek law and the law of most American states, such a contract would have been unenforceable.

Peter Evans, Aristotle's official biographer, gives a more convincing account of the negotiations prior to the marriage. Edward Kennedy, who represented Jackie, agreed with Aristotle that Jackie would receive $3 million for herself and $1 million for each of her children, and she would receive a further $150,000 per year for life to replace the allowance she had received from the Kennedy family. In exchange for this she would waive her rights under Greek law to a percentage of his wealth for her and her children. On top of the guaranteed figure, she received further discretionary allowances which brought the monthly sum up to $30,000.

Aristotle wanted to tap Jackie's New York telephone, but his people gave up when they found that her secret service agents kept a close eye on her apartment, making it very risky to try and break into it. When Jackie ran up a $300,000 legal bill trying to shake off a persistent photographer, Aristotle choked at the cost and hired Roy Cohn (Bobby's old nemesis) to challenge the fees. Cohn successfully got the bill reduced, but Jackie was furious, telling friends that Aristotle was a skinflint and a haggler. Cohn noted that his client felt 'a lot of displeasure at Mrs Onassis' way of doing things and what he thought was a lack of judgement ... all of these things were building up to a point of great grievance in him'.

During Easter the *Christina* cruised the Caribbean and Jackie joined the ship at Puerto Rico. Among the guests was Aristotle's old flame Geraldine Spreckels, along with her current husband, Andrew Fuller. Despite their brief, chaotic and unconsummated romance, Aristotle and Geraldine had remained friends since first meeting in New York in the 1940s, and Aristotle confided in her that he was already thinking of divorcing Jackie.[234]

CHAPTER SIXTEEN
A Son Is Lost

Alexander had no formal schooling; he was educated by a private tutor and failed the entrance exam to a Paris Lycée at the age of sixteen. Aristotle gave him a job in his Monaco headquarters, paying him only $12,000 per year, but Alexander showed little enthusiasm or aptitude for the work. His father, who seemed to fear competition from his son, often publicly berated and belittled him, despite considering him heir to his empire.

Alexander's only passion, apart from Fiona von Thyssen, was for mechanical objects; especially cars, boats and planes. He learnt to fly at the age of nineteen and proved himself to be a competent, if occasionally reckless, pilot. His eyesight wasn't good enough for him to get an Airline Transport Pilot's Licence, but he did get a commercial licence and amassed 1,500 flying hours on a variety of light aircraft. In 1971, Aristotle allowed Alexander to form a subsidiary of Olympic Airways, called Olympic Aviation, which operated light aircraft and helicopters. Here, Alexander could indulge his passion for planes and learn to run a business.

Aristotle had never felt the same affinity for aircraft as he had for ships. He'd been an enthusiast for

Zeppelins until the *Hindenburg* disaster, but avoided flying for several years after, only returning to it when he had to. Even his ownership of Olympic Airways had been an uncomfortable fit; he revelled in the prestige but never really came to terms with the complexities and subtleties of such a tightly regulated industry. When he commissioned the *Christina*, however, he saw an opportunity to put her in a different league from any other yacht. If she carried an amphibious aircraft, then he and his guests would, literally, be able to go anywhere. Additionally, even when the aircraft wasn't being used, its mere presence on her deck put the *Christina* in a class of her own.

After the Second World War the Italian plane maker, Piaggio Aero, was looking for a gap in the market for small commercial aircraft. Their facilities had been reduced to ruins by Allied bombing and their resources were limited, so only something ingenious and relatively inexpensive would fit the bill. Enrico Piaggio, the founder's son, was a brilliant engineer with a commercial flair. Among other things, he had designed the first Vespa scooter; a huge commercial success and a design icon to this day. Piaggio saw a small but important market for an amphibious passenger aircraft. Unlike flying boats, amphibians can operate from either land or water, but they are difficult aircraft to get right. The Piaggio P.136, which first flew in 1948, could carry up to five passengers with luggage and had a range of up to 900 nautical miles. *Flight International* praised its handling characteristics and Aristotle bought two, frequently carrying one aboard the *Christina*. The plane could be carried on deck and launched or recovered, using ship's gear, when needed. It could also reach Skorpios, which was too small to have its own airfield.

Both the amphibians had been transferred to Olympic Aviation although, by now, they were getting old. Alexander warned his father that they had become 'death traps' and recommended replacing them with helicopters, but Aristotle was unconvinced. Alexander was beginning to make a success of the new company, although his father refused to give him any credit for it. The problem seemed to be that he wanted Alexander to be just like him but, when the boy started to succeed on his own terms, it didn't sit well with his father. As Johnny Meyer put it, 'He was jealous of his youth, he was as jealous as hell of the Baroness, but he still loved the kid. Only he wanted him to be a replica of himself, a made-over Ari. He couldn't bring himself to let the kid evolve his own ethos, work out his own life.'

Alexander took a leaf out of his father's book when he began recording their telephone conversations and playing them back to Fiona. 'Listen to him. It's two o'clock in the afternoon over there, and he's completely pissed out of his mind.'[235] Their relationship had become a well-kept secret, they were rarely seen out together, and Alexander exploded if they went anywhere where there were photographers. Fiona found the secrecy intolerable and, after four and a half years, she ended the relationship.

Aristotle was delighted and, for a while, father and son were reunited in a round of lavish parties, cruises and dinners, always accompanied by beautiful and eligible women. Clandestinely, however, Alexander and Fiona were soon lovers again. Together, they hatched a plan which would, ultimately, give Alexander his independence: Fiona would buy a house in Switzerland, while Alexander would go to university and get a degree. Even if Aristotle totally disinherited him, he would be able to get a decent job and maintain a living. Realistic or not, they convinced themselves that it could work.

In New York, Aristotle was again talking to Roy Cohn, but this time with more purpose. He had now come to the firm conclusion that he wanted a divorce. He had already consulted Greek lawyers, but he needed to tie up any loose ends regarding his assets in America. The marriage, he told Cohn '… had gotten down to a monthly presentation of bills'.

In January 1973, Aristotle and Alexander dined together in Paris. Alexander had still made no mention of his plans with Fiona, but Aristotle told his son that he was definitely going to divorce Jackie. This would have been welcome news: Alexander had never got on with his new stepmother and avoided her as much as he could, just as he now avoided his mother to whom he had not spoken a word since her wedding to Niarchos. Aristotle was in a celebratory mood and made a further concession to his son: he could sell the remaining Piaggio amphibian and replace it with a helicopter, once Aristotle had used it for the final time on a forthcoming trip to Miami. Following the dinner, Alexander phoned Fiona, who was holidaying in Mexico with her children. 'The old man's seeing sense at last. He's divorcing the Widow and selling the albatross.' [236]

Later that month, Alexander was back in Athens

checking out a new pilot on the Piaggio. Donald McGregor, who usually flew the plane, was temporarily grounded while he recovered from an eye operation and Donald McCusker, who'd recently been hired, needed to be certified on the Piaggio so that he could fly the plane until it was sold in Miami. Alexander was to be his instructor and Donald McGregor would be on board as an observer. McCusker was an experienced American pilot with plenty of time on amphibians. He only needed to familiarise himself with the Piaggio, so the flight appeared to be routine. The aircraft had just come out of maintenance, requiring the pilots to do a thorough pre-flight inspection, but Alexander had forgotten his printed checklist and had to do the checks from memory. McGregor recalled that Alexander was usually a stickler for detailed inspections: 'I know that when he checked me out he chewed me up for not making a visual check.'

Had the pilots been more thorough, they would have seen that a catastrophic mistake had been made by the engineers who'd overhauled the aircraft. The control wires to the ailerons had been reversed, meaning that when the pilot commanded left bank, he got right bank, and vice versa. As soon as the aircraft left the ground the right wing dropped, possibly because of wake turbulence from the Boeing 727 which had taken off in front of them. McCusker, who was flying from the left-hand seat, tried to correct and inadvertently increased the bank angle causing the right float to strike the ground, followed by the aircraft cartwheeling. Alexander, sitting in the right-hand seat, took the full force of the impact. All three men were taken to hospital. McGregor and McCusker were both seriously injured but would recover in time. Alexander, however, had received a heavy, crushing blow to his temple. Surgeons operated to remove blood clots but found there had been huge and irreparable brain damage.

Aristotle and Jackie were in New York when they received the news. Aristotle immediately chartered an entire airliner to bring one passenger, the prominent neurosurgeon, Alan Richardson, from London to Athens. On arrival, Richardson confirmed the prognosis of the Greek surgeons, that there was irreversible brain damage. Fiona von Thyssen had also chartered a jet to bring her from Switzerland. She recalled, 'There was little evidence of his injuries, and he was not bandaged. Except for scratches on his hand, he looked unmarked.' Aristotle flew in another neurosurgeon, this time from Boston. At the same time, he arranged for a sacred icon, believed to have miraculous powers, to be brought from one of the islands and placed beside Alexander's bed. The American surgeon confirmed that Alexander was in a deep, irreversible coma, and unable to breathe without life support. There was no possible hope of a recovery. Aristotle finally bowed to the inevitable and told the doctors to wait until the boy's sister, Christina, arrived from Brazil, and then turn off his life-support system.

Christina arrived in the early evening and spent some time with her brother before he was allowed to die. Aristotle, utterly overwhelmed by events, walked the streets of Athens looking for the church where he had prayed when his grandmother died. It was nearly dawn when he found it and prayed again. The loss of a child for any parent is, perhaps, the most devastating of all bereavements, but it was more so for Aristotle. He had always been deeply fatalistic and superstitious. God had granted him a son to perpetuate his empire and now, for reasons he could not fathom, God had taken him away. It was impossible for him to accept that Alexander had died because of a simple engineering error compounded by an oversight. Even less possible was accepting that his own people could have made such a basic mistake. For Aristotle, there had to be a deeper explanation, and someone had to take the blame. His suspicions fell on the colonels who were still governing Greece, and the CIA. He convinced himself that Alexander had been deliberately murdered as revenge for past business dealings. He offered a million dollars for information, tried to have McCusker charged with manslaughter, and even brought out his own expert from Britain to examine the wreckage of the aircraft. The expert reconfirmed the findings of the earlier inquiry — that the control wires had been crossed — and no evidence was ever produced of foul play.

McCusker was pursued relentlessly by Aristotle's lawyers, but Aristotle refused to settle his claim for compensation, even when American lawyers threatened to seize one of Olympic Airways' aircraft. Johnny Meyer recalled, 'Right to the end he had this conviction that the CIA had killed his son, and as long as he could keep McCusker on the hook something was sure to come out.'[237] The case dragged on for years and Olympic Airways were unable to settle McCusker's claim until after Aristotle's death; they finally gave him $800,000.

Aristotle would never be the same again: a part of

him had died with his son. Friends and employees recalled how, in the past, he had often worked through the night in his cabin aboard the *Christina*. Now, he just paced the decks through the hours of darkness, staring out to sea, as if afraid to sleep. Hélène Gaillet, the New York-based photographer who knew Aristotle well, recalled, 'Ari was a man who had decided that nothing was that important anymore. It was as if some essential part that held things together had gone out of his life.' He began to lose interest in his business; the thing that had consumed his every waking hour before. It had brought him so much wealth and glamour, but it could not replace what had been taken away. He even lost interest in his divorce from Jackie: the details had been agreed in principle, but it was never concluded. He would remain legally married to her until his death, at which point, she again became a widow.

Alexander was buried in a family tomb on Skorpios. When Aristotle was there, he walked endlessly along the beaches, or spent hours beside Alexander's grave. Night after night he would sit beside the mausoleum, weeping, with two glasses of ouzo, one for Alexander and one for himself. Sometimes he would even have a dinner table set there and dine with Artemis or Jackie. In his despair, he turned to Maria more than Jackie. She was the one woman whom he had always been able to share his problems with, and now he poured his heart out to her. 'They [his enemies] would rather see me suffer than kill me,' he told her, still convinced that Alexander had been murdered and more than ever convinced that God was punishing him by taking his only son.

A SON IS LOST

In a revealing TV interview in New York, Maria Callas told Barbara Walters, 'I thought that when I met a man I loved, that I didn't need to sing. Because I think that the most important thing in a woman is to have a man of her own and to make him happy. Because I don't think that singing is a woman's job ... Any man who is in love with you the way that he was, I'm sure he was, did not want me to sing. But I had to sing as we both, or I, could not make up our minds about marriage. I also had a husband, remember, who was making a lot of trouble and once you get married and divorced you are very, very ... I, at least, am very frightened of getting married a second time, I don't think I ever will. I don't like using the word never because you never know ... I think love is so much better when you're not married. Why should I marry? Give me one good reason why I should marry? A man has every right to be able to fall in love with someone else. There are no chains for love. I left him [Aristotle Onassis] of my own accord. We both agreed to that. Because we loved each other maybe too much ... I hoped a lot, I put a man on a pedestal.'

Within a few short years, both Aristotle and Christina would be buried alongside Alexander. Several months later, in an uncharacteristic and previously unthinkable gesture, Aristotle invited Tina and her third husband, Stavros Niarchos, to visit Alexander's grave with him. The Niarchos yacht, *Atlantis*, was newer and a little bigger than the *Christina*: she had to be, as the two men had been lifelong rivals and each always had to go one step beyond the other. The two ships met and anchored, at sea, at a point halfway between the two private islands. Geraldine Fuller (née Spreckels) recalled, 'It was a very strange meeting in the middle of the ocean, these two enormous yachts ... as if two warlords were meeting to sign a peace treaty in neutral waters or something.'

Aristotle was, by now, a changed man but a little of the insecurity that had always driven him was still there. When he and his guests were invited onto the *Atlantis* for lunch, the crew were drawn up in a guard of honour. They wore very smart uniforms, unlike the *Christina*'s crew, who often wore simple T-shirts with the name of their ship emblazoned on them. That evening, all the guests dined ashore on a local island. On their return Aristotle invited everyone onto his yacht for a nightcap, and there were his crew, suddenly resplendent in immaculate and brand-new uniforms. Geraldine Fuller recalled, 'We were met by Ari's captain and crew absolutely impeccably turned out in tropical uniforms and peaked caps; the captain wore more braid than any admiral I've ever seen in my life. Where Ari got those uniforms from in the middle of the Aegean, I don't know ... when Stavros's sailors looked smarter than his, he simply couldn't bear it.'

In London, Lee Radziwill's marriage was also coming to an end. Stas's business partner, Felix Fenston, had died, and their business empire had plunged in value following a slump in London property prices. Their successful partnership had always been based on Fenston's shrewd business mind along with Stas's charm and social connections. On his own, Stas was soon facing bankruptcy. Lee was openly conducting an affair with Stas's friend, the American artist, Peter Beard, and Stas had begun divorce proceedings which were finalised in 1974. Jackie had always liked Stas and took his side. The divorce was the final straw in dividing the sisters, who rarely met or spoke to each other afterwards.

Aristotle's superstitious nature was also coming into play, exacerbated by Christina, who was more fatalistic than even her father. He had bought a new Lear Jet to be flown by his two favourite pilots, the Koutis brothers. While approaching Nice Airport at night, they had crashed into the sea and both had been killed although, mercifully, there were no passengers aboard. The cause of the accident was almost certainly pilot error, but Aristotle suspected foul play or the hand of the CIA. The ancient Greeks believed you cannot escape your fate, and the Onassis family believed it too. Christina, supported by Costa Gratsos, convinced her father that Jackie had brought a curse to the family which had killed the Kennedys, the Koutis brothers, her aunt, her mother and her brother. 'Before she came to us, she was by her American husband's side when he died ... Now the curse is a part of our family, and before long she will kill us all ...'[238] Christina would not have known that Giovanni Battista Meneghini had put a curse on her father many years ago.

Aristotle and Jackie continued to drift apart. She now wanted to build a house in Acapulco, the scene of her honeymoon with Jack Kennedy, but Aristotle saw this as the final straw. Their arguments became louder, more bitter and more public. On a flight to New York they openly quarrelled, with Jackie reminding him of every lapse in taste and social gaffe that she'd seen over five years. He eventually moved to the other end of the aircraft to avoid her and began redrafting his will, trying to ensure that as much as possible went to his surviving child and as little as possible to Jackie. His wife was bequeathed a lifetime income of $200,000 per year with Caroline and John getting $25,000 per year until they were twenty-one. She would only receive this, however, if she did not challenge his will or resort to the courts, in which case she would forfeit her annuity, and his executors and heirs were instructed to fight her 'through all possible legal means'. At the same time, he set up a foundation in Alexander's name to do good works although, like so many of Aristotle's schemes, it was not as altruistic as it first appeared. Set up in Liechtenstein, the foundation would also help him to untangle his complex web of assets and investments lodged in tax havens across the world.

When they arrived in New York Aristotle appeared to be unwell. He was pallid, he no longer walked erect, and his speech sounded slurred, even when he hadn't been drinking. With his legendary stamina disappearing, he consulted doctors who diagnosed myasthenia gravis, an autoimmune disorder which, they assured him, could be controlled with drugs. The prognosis seemed hopeful: although the condition was incurable, it didn't usually kill sufferers unless there was some kind of comorbidity. Aristotle's general health was excellent, so, initially, he was not over-concerned.

Although he was now a shadow of his former self, flashes of the old Aristotle occasionally reappeared. At the Crazy Horse Saloon in Paris, he invited the photographer Roger Picard to follow him to the men's room where he

A SON IS LOST

allowed his penis to be photographed. 'There it is,' he roared, 'that says it all. Sex and money — that is my secret.'

Stavros Niarchos was not the only former enemy with whom he now wished to bury the hatchet. He returned to Monaco and invited Rainier to dinner aboard the *Christina*. A rapprochement was agreed, but a few days later Aristotle found his jaw was so weak he had difficulty eating. It was an early indication that the drugs were not working as intended. While his health deteriorated, he began to take a much greater interest in his daughter, Christina, who would now inherit most of his estate. She was sent to New York to 'learn the ropes' under the supervision of Costa Gratsos. 'She's going to be fine,' Costa assured him, 'Already I trust her intuition more than my intelligence, probably even more than your sorcery.' Others, however, were less otpimsitic: in crucial business meetings she often did not utter a single word, a flash back to the long silences of her childhood.

In August, the Onassis family traditionally gathered in Skorpios but, this year, Christina was absent. When calls and messages went unanswered, she was eventually traced to the Middlesex Hospital, where she'd been admitted under a false name having taken a massive overdose of sleeping pills. Her mother flew straight to London and spent forty-eight hours at her bedside, occasionally sleeping in an armchair in the waiting room. Christina recovered but Tina was not in a very secure state of mind herself. Her marriage to Stavros Niarchos had broken down and she was considering a divorce. She had also discovered that under Greek law a brother-in-law cannot marry his sister-in-law, so her marriage was, anyway, illegal. This gave her an easy exit but a troubling one because, like Aristotle, she was superstitious and fatalistic. She now began to wonder if events in her life, including the deaths of her sister and her son, were divine retribution. These fears, combined with the loss of her once famous looks, were preying on her mind as she reached her mid-forties, and they had been exacerbated by her own addiction to barbiturates.

A few weeks later, a maid found Tina dead in a bedroom of her Paris home. Her husband, Stavros Niarchos, was sleeping in the room next door. Niarchos's London office later put out a statement saying that she had died from a blood clot in her leg that had moved to the heart. In Paris, Tina's secretary said that she had died from a heart attack or pulmonary oedema (fluid on the lungs). Christina, who was in New York, flew straight to Paris. By the time she arrived newspapers were already comparing Tina's death to that of her sister, Eugenia. The French media were soon speculating that Tina had, in reality, died from an overdose of sleeping pills. In America, the journalist Bernard Valéry — who had known the family for decades — was writing in the *New York Daily News* (with certainty) that she had died from an overdose of barbiturates and tranquillisers.

Christina was immediately suspicious; unlike her brother, she had always believed that Niarchos was responsible for her aunt Eugenia's death. She obtained, with Aristotle's support, a magistrate's warrant ordering a post-mortem examination. Johnny Meyer recalled, 'Ari went along with it. I don't think it had anything to do with trying to hurt

A SON IS LOST

Niarchos. He just wanted to put the zipper on the rumours for Christina's sake. She seemed so shaken that he actually feared that she would try to kill Stavros.'

Two pathologists appointed by the public prosecutor's office confirmed that Tina had, in fact, died from acute oedema of the lung. In London, *The Times* reported that there was no evidence of violence and that the public prosecutor had issued a burial permit. Nonetheless, despite the unequivocal verdict of the doctors, suspicions would persist among her friends and among some journalists that she did, in fact, die from her own hand.

Tina was buried in Lausanne, next to her sister. At the funeral, Niarchos was in tears. Aristotle was absent, but Christina and Sunny Blandford held each other at the graveside and wept inconsolably. Following the burial, Niarchos, unfeelingly, put out a statement suggesting that Christina's earlier suicide attempt had been a factor in Tina's death: 'Tina never recovered from the depression into which these blows plunged her.'

Maria Callas now took daily calls from Onassis, who was even more distraught. But Maria's own health was failing, she had labyrinth vertigo, which affected her reflexes, and she temporarily lost her sight, which terrified her. While on tour, the pain from her hernia, worsened by singing, gave her internal bleeding, causing her to lose weight. 'Though I love to be thin,' she wrote to her doctor, 'I got frightened I was so thin and wan.'[239]

On Skorpios, Aristotle was weak but could still summon the energy to entertain guests. He drove

Geraldine Fuller around the island and showed her Alexander's grave, telling her that his son was, '... just as living to me as you are. He comes to me often. Unfortunately, until I die I cannot go to him.' That evening, the two of them dined alone on the *Christina*. 'This is the only place on earth on which I don't feel alien,' he told her.

By November, he was being treated in a New York hospital. Christina was there with him and finding a new closeness to her father that she hadn't previously known. His businesses were beginning to falter as he spent less and less time overseeing them. The 1970s oil crisis had caused ocean freight rates to tumble and precipitated a global recession. At the same time, Olympic Airways was losing money heavily and needed a cash injection to keep it afloat. Greece had finally returned to democracy, meaning that Aristotle could not squeeze concessions out of the new government as easily as he could under the colonels, most of whom were now in prison. He took a bold gamble by grounding the airline and freezing salaries, hoping to put pressure on the new government, but they responded firmly by renationalising the company. In December, against his doctors' advice, he flew back to Athens for face-to-face talks, but he was no longer the tireless and brilliant negotiator he once had been. He was finally forced to concede that, after twenty years, he had lost control of Olympic Airways. Jackie, who had been in New York, left for a skiing holiday in Switzerland and journalists quickly noted that she had not been at her husband's side during the crisis. The strain of the negotiations may well have weakened him further.

A SON IS LOST

His divorce from Jackie was now forgotten but, once again, he asked Christina to marry the shipping heir Peter Goulandris, and this time she agreed. A few weeks later Aristotle collapsed with severe abdominal pain. His doctors diagnosed gallstones but were reluctant to operate because of his weak state. Jackie flew from New York to Athens and Christina returned from Gstaad, where she had been holidaying with Goulandris. At the Athens villa a team of specialists who'd been flown in from as far afield as Paris and New York were trying to come to a consensus. One recommended an immediate operation; another said the patient was too weak to survive the surgery. His body weight had dropped forty pounds in eight weeks, his voice had almost disappeared, and he was very feeble. Christina was distraught although Jackie remained calm; a state of mind which Aristotle's family saw as indifference.

Aristotle himself took the decision to fly to Paris and have the operation in the American Hospital at Neuilly. Jackie and Christina accompanied him on the plane and in the limousine that took him from the airport to his Paris home. When they arrived, to find a horde of reporters and photographers on his doorstep, he insisted on taking the last few steps himself: 'I want to walk from this car under my own steam. I don't want those sons of bitches to see me being held up by a couple of women.' That evening he told Johnny Meyer, 'Soon I shall be in Skorpios with Alexander. You know I am dying, Johnny.'

Meyer joked, 'You're crazy, Ari. Whoever heard of anybody dying of droopy eyelids.'

The following day he was taken to hospital and

operated on to remove his gall bladder. He survived the operation, but only just. For the next few days, he was kept alive by a ventilator and fed intravenously. At first, the family would not let Maria Callas see him, although Christina later relented and allowed her to spend a few minutes at his bedside. She claimed he managed to speak to her, saying, 'I loved you, not always well, but as much and as best as I was capable of. I tried.'[240] On 15 March 1975, Aristotle Onassis died.

Jackie was back in New York when she heard the news. She telephoned Ted Kennedy, pleaded with him to accompany her, and then flew to Paris with him and her mother, Janet. At the airport they were met only by Jacinto Rosa, the Onassis family chauffeur, and a throng of journalists and photographers. She made a brief statement: 'Aristotle Onassis rescued me at a moment when my life was engulfed with shadows. He meant a lot to me. He brought me into a world where one could find both happiness and love. We lived through many beautiful experiences together which cannot be forgotten, and for which I will be eternally grateful.' Perhaps unintentionally, she had damned Aristotle with faint praise. 'Meant a lot to me' is usually the kind of epithet given to a friend or colleague, rather than a husband. These measured and understated words would reinforce the view that she only married him for his money.

At the hospital chapel, in line with Greek tradition, Aristotle lay in an open coffin with an icon on his chest. Jackie made the sign of the cross and said a prayer but showed no visible signs of emotion behind her veil. The dignity and self-control she had displayed at her first husband's funeral had been part

A SON IS LOST

of the legend that made her America's queen. But here, surrounded by Greek family and in a Latin country, her demeanour seemed cold-hearted. At the avenue Foch, Christina brushed off Jackie's efforts to console her. Aristotle's family would not forget that she had been three thousand miles way when he died and had taken forty-eight hours to return. Christina, who was in a deep depression, was sedated and one of her wrists was bandaged, leading to suspicions that she might, again, have made an attempt on her own life.

Jackie forbade Lee to attend the funeral, not wanting to remind either press or public of her sister's affair with Aristotle. 'Jackie finally has what she wanted,' Lee told a friend. 'She's walking in black behind another coffin.'[241] Three days later a large entourage of family and friends flew to Athens on a specially chartered Olympic Airways Boeing which carried Aristotle's coffin in its hold. On arrival, Jackie and Christina walked from the plane arm-in-arm while Ted Kennedy stayed a couple of paces behind. Jackie bore a grim half-smile with her eyes hidden behind dark glasses, but Christina looked tired and drawn. A procession of cars would take the mourners to the small fishing village of Nidri from where Aristotle's body would be taken by boat to Skorpios. During the journey, Ted Kennedy crassly tried to bring up 'financial matters' with Christina, causing her to get out of the car and join her aunts' car, immediately behind.

On Skorpios, the coffin, made from one of the island's walnut trees, was carried up the hill to the chapel, past lines of sailors and staff holding candles. In the harbour, the *Christina* lay at anchor with her flag at half-mast. Aristotle was laid to rest in a concrete tomb next to Alexander, as he had wished.

CHAPTER SEVENTEEN
The Aftermath

Christina took control of her father's empire with more determination and skill than many of her friends and family would have given her credit for. She even managed to make tax arrangements that her father would have been proud of. She was also determined to settle scores with Stavros Niarchos, whom she detested and held responsible for both her mother's and her aunt's deaths. As a shipping heiress, Tina had been extremely wealthy in her own right with a personal fortune estimated at $270 million. Christina launched a lawsuit to have her mother's marriage to Niarchos declared void on the grounds she had wed her brother-in-law, which was illegal in Greece.

By April, *The New York Times* had revealed that Aristotle had been planning to divorce Jackie and had instructed Roy Cohn to begin proceedings. It also reported that Christina was 'bitterly hostile to Mrs Onassis'. Under pressure from Jackie, Christina put out a statement of denial, but it was seen as so weak and contrived that it merely reinforced the rumour. Behind the scenes, Christina and Jackie were parleying a settlement for Aristotle's estate. The negotiations dragged on for eighteen months, but they finally

THE AFTERMATH

agreed on a figure of $26 million. It was substantially more than the amount left to her in Aristotle's will, but both knew that would be unlikely to hold up in court and neither wanted to wrangle in public. At the same time, Christina's lawyers agreed an out-of-court settlement with the Niarchos lawyers to return all of Tina's money and jewellery to Christina. Finally, she quietly called off her engagement to Peter Goulandris. She had only agreed to the marriage to please her father, and her fiancé's family had also cooled on the idea as freight rates weakened. In the wake of the 1970s oil crisis, the global shipping industry was going through one of its periodic recessions. One Athens shipbroker had said that it would have been 'the biggest merger of white elephants in the world.'

Tragically, she was increasingly relying on barbiturates for sleep and amphetamines for energy, and both had become an addiction. She also binged on Coca-Cola and junk food, meaning that her weight fluctuated and often ballooned. These habits, combined with the low self-esteem she had always suffered from, were weighing upon her fragile mental health. Following her divorce from Bolker, she would wed three more times — all following short engagements — but none of her marriages would last more than three years. In 1985, her third husband, the French pharmaceutical heir, Thierry Rousel, would provide her with a daughter, Athina. Today, she is Aristotle's sole living descendant and the inheritor of his remaining fortune.

As for the *Christina*, the exquisite yacht that had been Aristotle's real home and the backdrop for so many episodes of his life, she was bequeathed to Jackie and Christina — if they wanted her — or the Greek government, if they did not. In the event, neither woman, nor the government, wanted to take on her annual running cost of circa $600,000, and she lay rotting in Piraeus for decades. Her once pristine hull was stained orange by rust, junk littered her decks, and her staterooms were filled with dust and debris. In 1996, Alexander Blastos bought her, but the cheque bounced and he went to prison for wire fraud. In 1998, John Paul Papanicolaou, a Greek ship-owning friend of the Onassis family, bought her and restored her. Today, she sails the world's oceans once more, and is available for charter — for those who can afford her — at a rate of €700,000 per week. She still has the original swimming pool, along with Aristotle's bust of Churchill, and her bar stools are still covered in the foreskins of whales.

In 2013, a long lease on the island of Skorpios was sold by Athina Onassis to the daughter of Dmitry Rybolovlev, a Russian oligarch, who plans to develop the island as a resort. The legality of the purchase is being investigated by the Greek government: Aristotle stated in his will that the island should remain with his family for as long as they could afford to maintain it, and if they could not, it should be donated to the Greek state.

Maria Callas lived for little more than a year after the death of Aristotle. Lonely, depressed, addicted to Mandrax and in declining health, she wrote to a friend, 'I am a person without identity. I was born of Greek parents, yet I have never felt absolutely Greek. I was born in America, yet I am not an American. I lived the most crucial period of my career in

THE AFTERMATH

Italy, I married an Italian but, of course, I am not an Italian. I now live permanently in Paris, but this doesn't mean I feel French. What the hell am I, after all? What am I? I am alone, always alone.'[242]

At the age of fifty-three, Maria Callas was found dead in her Paris apartment on 16 September 1977. She had died, in her sleep, from heart failure. Her sister was the only relative to attend her funeral, and her ashes were taken to Greece and scattered over the Aegean Sea.

Jackie Kennedy Onassis returned to her apartment in New York, the city where she had grown up and the place where she had always been most comfortable. New Yorkers are among the few people in the world who don't visibly react when they see a celebrity; here she could travel by yellow cab, shop in her favourite stores and eat in her favourite restaurants without being mobbed. She got a job as an editor for Viking Press, a happy fit for her as she had always loved books and literature and she worked well with authors. Over the next twenty years she would commission more than 100 books for a variety of publishers. She dated several men, and finally found happiness with Maurice Tempelsman, a Belgian-American businessman and diamond merchant who had been managing her finances for several years. She died from non-Hodgkin lymphoma in 1994 at the age of sixty-four.

On 19 November 1988, when Christina Onassis was thirty-seven years old, a maid discovered her dead in the bath of her house in Buenos Aires. The autopsy found no evidence of suicide, drug overdose or foul play, but gave the cause of her death as acute pulmonary oedema. She is buried in the Onassis family plot on Skorpios, alongside her father and brother.

Christina's then three-year-old daughter, Athina, was raised by her father and his second wife. In 2005, Athina married the Brazilian showjumper and Olympic medallist, Álvaro de Miranda Neto, but they divorced in 2017 without any children. In 2006, on her turning twenty-one, Athina Onassis' lawyers tried to install her as president of the foundation that her grandfather had created in the name of her uncle, Alexander. The board turned her down on the grounds that she had no connection with the Greek culture, religion, language or shared experience, that she never went to college and had no work experience. She is alleged to have told her stepmother that if she could burn all the Onassis money, she would.[243]

Jackie Kennedy Onassis became a successful literary editor, commissioning more than 100 books.

Postscript

In the 'Me Too' era and 'fourth wave' of feminism, we have re-evaluated sexual politics, especially the power-structured relationships of sex and gender. In our times, celebrities who beat their partners can expect to see their reputations vanish overnight. The Women's Movement, which began in the 1800s, had entered its second wave by the 1960s, with a new focus on women's sexual liberation, reproductive rights, job opportunities, violence against women, and changes in custody and divorce laws. The sixties were, arguably, the final years in which such an unapologetic pirate, chauvinist and wife-beater as Aristotle Onassis could flourish.

Today, there are more billionaires than ever before, and some are richer than Onassis, but we live in a very different age. The ultra-rich of our times are frequently shadowy, secretive figures who live incognito behind dark glass and elaborate security. Their super-yachts, often painted black, ride anonymously at anchor while their owners, whose names we rarely know, are discreetly brought ashore surrounded by security guards.

Aristotle Onassis belonged to a different age, perhaps the last in which wealth could so easily be flaunted and success measured in column inches. He was, in many respects, the last tycoon.

References

Chapter One

1 Jackie Kennedy was only two inches taller than Aristotle Onassis. However, unlike Maria Callas, she did not always wear flat shoes in his company. Combined with backcombed hair, this made her appear much taller.

2 Ben Macintyre, *The Times,* 16 March 2018.

Chapter Two

3 Hardy, Frank, *Onassis, An Extraordinary Life*, New York Creative Publishing, 2013.

4 Fleming, Katherine Elizabeth, *Greece: A Jewish History*, Princeton University Press, 2008.

5 Some accounts suggest that Aristotle Onassis was born in 1900. He appears to have given different dates of birth to different people at different times. In Buenos Aires, he may have exaggerated his age to get work and a passport, or he may have reduced his age to avoid military service (Argentinian citizenship procedures were then perfunctory). However, had official records shown that he was more than seventeen at the time of the fall of Smyrna, he would almost certainly have been sent to an internment camp. I have assumed, therefore, that he was born in 1906, the year shown on his Greek passport and engraved on his tomb. Towards the end of his life, however, he told friends, 'To be honest, I'm not sure how old I am for even my papers lie.'

6 Some accounts suggest that Aristotle and the lieutenant became lovers. I could find no evidence of this, but they clearly did become friends and Aristotle was distressed when he later heard of the lieutenant's death.

REFERENCES

7   Evans, Peter, *Ari, The Life and Times of Aristotle Onassis*, Summit Books, 1986.

8   Hardy, Frank. *Onassis, An Extraordinary Life*, New York Creative Publishing, 2013.

9   Aristotle bought the island in 1963 for $11,000. In 2013, his granddaughter, Athina Onassis, sold a lease on Skorpios to the family of Dmitry Rybolovlev for $153 million. Aristotle Onassis, his son Alexander, and his daughter Christina are all buried there.

Chapter Three

10   Petsalis-Diomidis, Nicholas, *The Unknown Callas: The Greek Years*. Amadeus Press, 2001.

11   Spence, Lyndsy, *Casta Diva*, The History Press, 2021.

12   Ibid.

13   Stancioff, Nadia, *Callas Remembered*, New York: Dutton, 1987.

14   *The Norman Ross Show*, 17 November 1957.

15   Interview in *Oggi* magazine, 1957.

16   Petsalis-Diomidis, Nicholas, *The Unknown Callas: The Greek Years*. Amadeus Press, 2001.

17   Ibid.

18   Meneghini was writing in 1981, after the deaths of both Aristotle and Maria. He never forgave either of them for the affair which ended his marriage, and he remained bitter for the rest of his life.

19   Maria Callas, from an earlier recording in Tony Palmer's TV movie *Callas*, 1978.

20   Her cancellation record, however, compared to those of other sopranos, was better than average. The truth may be that she was too inclined to perform when feeling under the weather.

Chapter Four

21   Evans, Peter, *Ari, The Life and Times of Aristotle Onassis*, Summit Books, 1986.

22   Schettini, Christiana, *A Social History of Prostitution in Buenos Aires*. 2017.

23   Fernande Grudet (1923–2015) known as Madame Claude, was the head of a French network of call girls who worked especially for dignitaries and civil servants.

24   https://www.biography.com/business-figure/aristotle-onassis

25   The citizens of Buenos Aires were known as porteños because so many of them had arrived from Europe by sea.

26   Douglas, Nigel, 'Claudia Muzio', in *More Legendary Voices*, André Deutsch, 1994.

27   In the 1950s, Maria Callas would also be dubbed 'La Divina'.

28   Evans, Peter, *Nemesis*, HarperCollins, 2004.

29   Evans, Peter, *Ari, The Life and Times of Aristotle Onassis*, Summit Books, 1986.

30   The Greek historian, Spyros Azthrahas, coined the term the 'dispersed city' for the 120 inhabited islands in the Ionian and Aegean Seas which were linked only by maritime trade

31   *ARGENTINA: Abdication of a Tycoon*, Time magazine, 16 May, 1949.

Chapter Five

32   Hardy, Frank. *Onassis, An Extraordinary Life*, New York Creative Publishing, 2013.

33   Michalakopoulos was an influential liberal politician who had, himself, been prime minister of Greece from October 1924 to June 1925. Throughout his career he remained a close associate of Eleftherios Venizelos.

34   Constantine 'Costa' Gratsos was Aristotle Onassis' oldest and most trusted friend.

35   Evans, Peter, *Nemesis*, HarperCollins, 2004.

36   Evans, Peter, *Ari, The Life and Times of Aristotle Onassis*, Summit Books, 1986.

REFERENCES

37   Ibid.

38   Garraty, John A, *The Great Depression*, Anchor, 1986.

39   Lowenstein, Roger, *History Repeating, Wall Street Journal*, Jan 14, 2015

40   In 1970, a Canadian board of inquiry found that an Onassis vessel involved in a major oil spill had no functioning radar or echo sounder, a defective compass and no qualified navigators apart from the captain 'and there are even doubts about his ability'.

Chapter Six

41   Bradford, Sara, *America's Queen*, Penguin, 2000.

42   Ibid.

43   Kashner, Sam. *The Complicated Sisterhood of Jackie Kennedy and Lee Radziwill, Vanity Fair*, 2016.

44   Taraborrelli, J Randy, *Jackie, Janet & Lee*, St. Martin's. 2018.

45   Bradford, Sara, *America's Queen*, Penguin, 2000.

46   John P Marquand was best known for his Mr Moto spy stories. In 1938 he won a Pulitzer Prize for *The Late Mr Apley*. The American class system was a recurrent theme in his work.

47   Bradford, Sara, *America's Queen*, Penguin, 2000.

48   *Daily Mail,* 28 May 2014.

49   Joe Kennedy Jr, the eldest son, had been killed in action during the Second World War.

50   Bradford, Sara, *America's Queen*, Penguin, 2000.

51   Pamela Harriman née Digby (1920–1997) was an English-born socialite whose great-great aunt was the nineteenth-century adventurer and courtesan Jane Digby. Pamela married Randolph Churchill, followed by Leland Hayward and Averell Harriman. Related to the Churchills by marriage and not blood, she nevertheless bore a striking resemblance to Winston Churchill. Randolph proposed to her at their first meeting, having been turned down by

eight women in the space of two weeks. She named her only child Winston and had affairs with many prominent men, including Stavros Niarchos.

52   Beauchamp, Carrie, *Vanity Fair*, 13 February 2009.

53   'The medical records collected by his physician, Janet Travell, show that Kennedy's health was even more problematic than previously understood. Between May 1955 and October 1957, while he was launching his vice presidential and presidential bids, he was secretly hospitalised nine times for a total of forty-four days, including two weeklong stays and one nineteen-day stretch.' Dallek, Robert, *An Unfinished Life: John F. Kennedy, 1917–1963*. Little Brown, 2003.

54   *Why England Slept* had originally been a thesis for JFK's Harvard degree and was a justification of the appeasement policies of Chamberlain, and other British leaders. JFK believed that if England had confronted Germany earlier, the results might have been disastrous.

55   Bradford, Sara, *America's Queen*, Penguin, 2000.

56   Ibid.

57   Ibid.

58   Dallek, Robert, *An Unfinished Life: John F. Kennedy, 1917–1963*. Little Brown, 2003.

59   Bradford, Sara, *America's Queen*, Penguin, 2000.

60   Ibid.

61   Ibid.

Chapter Seven

62   In 1956, an Australian expedition confirmed that there are no islands at this location, but they found two previously undiscovered islands, further to the south, to which the name has since been applied.

63   Aristotle was trying, at the time, to avoid alcohol, but his usual habit was to drink a lot of whisky and he frequently got drunk.

64   Götaverken became bankrupt in 1989. Today, the shipyard only undertakes maintenance and repairs.

REFERENCES

65   Dedichen, Ingeborg and Pessar, Henry, *Onassis, mon amour*. Éditions Pygmalion, 1975.

66   Ibid.

67   *Business History Review*, Harvard College, 2014.

68   Theodoracopulos, Taki, *Mancode* magazine, *Monte Carlo by Sir Taki*, 2017.

69   Simon never married. It was later alleged by her secretary that she gave a gold key to her bedroom to any man she was attracted to, including George Gershwin.

70   Swanson, who died in 1983, was married six times, twice to the same man.

71   Evans, Peter, *Ari, The Life and Times of Aristotle Onassis*, Summit Books, 1986.

Chapter Eight

72   This quote was made famous in the 1974 movie *The Godfather Part II*, but it was originally credited to the sixth-century BC Chinese general, Sun Tzu.

73   Stavros Niarchos was married five times, the third time to Eugenia Livanos. His fifth and final wife would be his sister-in-law (and Aristotle's first wife) Tina Livanos: they married following her divorce from the Marquess of Blandford (her second husband) in 1971. Greek shipping families liked to remain close.

74   Evans, Peter, *Ari, The Life and Times of Aristotle Onassis*, Summit Books, 1986.

75   Ibid.

76   Ibid.

77   *Chicago Tribune*, November 1989.

78   Since 2001, the Château de la Croë has been owned by the Russian businessman, Roman Abramovich.

79   Evans, Peter, *Ari, The Life and Times of Aristotle Onassis*, Summit Books, 1986.

80   Ibid.

Chapter Nine

81   ARAMCO was an acronym for the Arabian American Oil Company, now known as Saudi Aramco.

82   *Washington Post*, 2 August 1978.

83   Interview with Robert Mahue, May 2006.

84   *New York Times*, 16 November 1954.

85   Evans, Peter, *Ari, The Life and Times of Aristotle Onassis*, Summit Books, 1986.

86   The television audience for MGM's live broadcast of the wedding was estimated at 30,000,000. They were given TV rights in exchange for releasing Kelly from her contract.

87   *Daily Mail*, 17 April 1956.

88   La Pausa, in Roquebrune-Cap-Martin, was originally built by the Duke of Westminster for his mistress, Coco Chanel.

89   Wendy Russell was an American philanthropist, socialite, former fashion model and celebrated beauty.

90   Evans, Peter, *Ari, The Life and Times of Aristotle Onassis*, Summit Books, 1986.

91   Ibid.

92   Colville, Jock, *Fringes of Power*, Weidenfeld & Nicolson, 1956.

93   Ireland, Josh. *Churchill and Son*, John Murray 2021.

94   Hastings, Max, *Finest Years — Churchill as Warlord, 1940–1945*. HarperPress 2009.

95   Evans, Peter, *Ari, The Life and Times of Aristotle Onassis*, Summit Books, 1986.

96   Dallek, Robert, *An Unfinished Life: John F. Kennedy, 1917–1963*. Little Brown, 2003.

97   Evans, Peter, *Ari, The Life and Times of Aristotle Onassis*, Summit Books, 1986.

REFERENCES

98   Bradford, Sara, *America's Queen*, Penguin, 2000.

Chapter Ten

99   Because Onassis hid his money and his companies in so many different tax havens, it is difficult to be certain of his precise wealth but, after the Suez crisis, he was certainly the world's largest private shipowner and, by any measure, spectacularly wealthy.

100   'Panamax' vessels are limited to a beam of 106 feet and a draught of 39.5 feet. Their height is also limited to 109 feet by the Bridge of the Americas.

101   Evans, Peter, *Ari, The Life and Times of Aristotle Onassis*, Summit Books, 1986.

102   Ibid.

103   Spence, Lyndsy, *Casta Diva*, The History Press, 2021.

104   Shaw, George Bernard, *Pygmalion*, 1916.

105   Feroudi Moutsatsos, Kiki, *The Onassis Women: An Eyewitness Account*, G P Putnam's Sons, 1998.

106   Schwarz, Charles, *Cole Porter: A Biography*, W H Allen, 1978.

107   *The Press: Elsa at War, Time*, 7 November, 1944.

108   *The Spectator*, December 2012.

109   McLean, Adrienne, *Being Rita Hayworth*, Rutgers University Press, 2004.

110   Galatopoulos, Stelios, *Maria Callas*, Simon & Schuster, 1998.

111   Feroudi Moutsatsos, Kiki, *The Onassis Women: An Eyewitness Account*, G P Putnam's Sons, 1998.

112   Evans, Peter, *Ari, The Life and Times of Aristotle Onassis*, Summit Books, 1986.

113   Ibid.

114   Spence, Lyndsy, *Casta Diva*, The History Press, 2021.

115 Ibid.

116 Meneghini, Giovanni Battista, *My Wife Maria Callas*, Farrar, Straus & Giroux, 1982.

117 Evans, Peter, *Ari, The Life and Times of Aristotle Onassis*, Summit Books, 1986.

118 Montague Browne, Anthony, *The Long Sunset*, Cassell, 1995.

119 Spence, Lyndsy, *Casta Diva*, The History Press, 2021.

120 Evans, Peter, *Ari, The Life and Times of Aristotle Onassis*, Summit Books, 1986.

121 Meneghini, Giovanni Battista, *My Wife Maria Callas*, Farrar, Straus & Giroux, 1982.

122 Evans, Peter, *Ari, The Life and Times of Aristotle Onassis*, Summit Books, 1986.

123 This ancient Greek proverb is sometimes translated into English as, 'Those whom the gods wish to destroy, they first make mad.'

124 As leader of the Greek Orthodox Church, Athenagoras was a proponent of unity among Christian faiths. He had spent many years in the United States, spoke fluent English and was less parochial than his predecessors. In 1964, he would meet Pope Paul VI in Jerusalem and they would jointly revoke their churches' mutual excommunication decrees of 1054.

125 Sherman Adams, an aide to Eisenhower, resigned because he had accepted gifts, including a vicuna coat, from the industrialist Bernard Goldfine.

126 Evans, Peter, *Ari, The Life and Times of Aristotle Onassis*, Summit Books, 1986.

Chapter Eleven

127 Otzen, Ellen, quoting Nico Mastorakis, BBC, 15 March 2015.

128 Spence, Lyndsy, *Casta Diva*, The History Press, 2021.

REFERENCES

129   Sirmione is on the shores of Lake Garda; there is no Lake Sirmione.

130   Meneghini, Giovanni Battista, *My Wife Maria Callas,* Farrar, Straus & Giroux, 1982.

131   Ibid.

132   Interview in *Epoca*, September 1959.

133   Meneghini, Giovanni Battista, *My Wife Maria Callas,* Farrar, Straus & Giroux, 1982.

134   Bing, Rudolf, *5,000 Nights at the Opera,* Doubleday, 1972.

135   Jascha Heifetz, a Russian-American, was regarded by critics as the greatest violin virtuoso since Paganini.

136   Evans, Peter, *Ari, The Life and Times of Aristotle Onassis*, Summit Books, 1986.

137   Ibid.

138   *La Stampa*, 17 September 1959.

139   *The Stage* 8 October 1959.

140   *Il Mundo*, October 1959.

141   Spence, Lyndsy, *Casta Diva,* The History Press, 2021.

142   Ibid.

143   Evans, Peter, *Ari, The Life and Times of Aristotle Onassis*, Summit Books, 1986.

144   Spence, Lyndsy, *Casta Diva,* The History Press, 2021.

145   'William Hickey' was the by-line of any journalist published in the *Daily Express*'s popular gossip column. Named after the eighteenth-century diarist William Hickey, the column was first established by Tom Driberg in May 1933.

146   *The Independent*, 19 October 2014.

147   The couple divorced in 1971, a year before Sunny inherited either the title or the palace. Sunny married four times in all, the last time at the age of eighty-two.

148   Pearson, John, *The Private Lives of Winston Churchill*, Simon & Schuster, 1991.

149   *Evening Telegraph*, 15 January,1960.

150   Spence, Lyndsy, *Casta Diva*, The History Press, 2021.

151   Sutherland, Robert, *Maria Callas: Diaries of a Friendship*, Constable, 1999.

152   Spence, Lyndsy, *Casta Diva*, The History Press, 2021.

153   Ibid.

Chapter Twelve

154   Taraborrelli, J Randy, *Jackie, Janet & Lee*, St. Martin's Publishing Group, 2018.

155   Ibid.

156   Bradford, Sara, *America's Queen*, Penguin, 2000.

157   Taraborrelli, J Randy, *Jackie, Janet & Lee*, St. Martin's Publishing Group, 2018.

158   Ibid.

159   Ibid.

160   Bradford, Sara, *America's Queen*, Penguin, 2000.

161   Ibid.

162   *Daily Mail*, 12 July 2013.

163   Taraborrelli, J Randy, *Jackie, Janet & Lee*, St. Martin's Publishing Group, 2018.

164   Waxman, Olivia B, *Time*, 3 August 2018.

165   Spada, James, *Peter Lawford: The Man Who Kept the Secrets*, Bantam, 1991.

166   Taraborrelli, J Randy, *Jackie, Janet & Lee*, St. Martin's Publishing Group, 2018.

167   Ibid.

168   Ibid.

REFERENCES

169   Ibid.

Chapter Thirteen

170   Bradford, Sara, *America's Queen*, Penguin, 2000.

171   In 1965, Charlotte Ford would become the fourth (but not final) wife of Stavros Niarchos.

172   Evans, Peter, *Ari, The Life and Times of Aristotle Onassis*, Summit Books, 1986.

173   Papadimitriou, Stelio, *The Other Onassis*.

174   *Chicago Tribune*, 18 June 1996.

175   Dallek, Robert, *An Unfinished Life: John F. Kennedy, 1917–1963*. Little Brown, 2003.

176   Evans, Peter, *Ari, The Life and Times of Aristotle Onassis*, Summit Books, 1986.

177   Taraborrelli, J Randy, *Jackie, Janet & Lee*, St. Martin's Publishing Group, 2018.

178   Evans, Peter, *Ari, The Life and Times of Aristotle Onassis*, Summit Books, 1986.

179   Ibid.

180   Ibid.

181   Haymann, C David, *Bobby and Jackie*, Simon and Schuster, 2009.

182   Evans, Peter, *Ari, The Life and Times of Aristotle Onassis*, Summit Books, 1986.

183   Ibid.

184   Ibid.

Chapter Fourteen

185   Haymann, C David, *Bobby and Jackie*, Simon and Schuster, 2009.

186   Davis, Deborah, *Party of the Century*, John Wiley & Sons, 2006.

187   Bradford, Sara, *America's Queen*, Penguin, 2000.

188   Evans, Peter, *Ari, The Life and Times of Aristotle Onassis*, Summit Books, 1986.

189   Bradford, Sara, *America's Queen*, Penguin, 2000.

190   Beaton, Cecil, *Diary*, 6 June 1968.

191   Bradford, Sara, *America's Queen*, Penguin, 2000.

192   Porter, Darwin and Prince, Danford. *Pink Triangle*, Blood Moon Productions, 2014.

193   Bradford, Sara, *America's Queen*, Penguin, 2000.

194   Ibid.

195   Evans, Peter, *Ari, The Life and Times of Aristotle Onassis*, Summit Books, 1986.

196   Bradford, Sara, *America's Queen*, Penguin, 2000.

197   Haymann, C David, *Bobby and Jackie*, Simon and Schuster, 2009.

198   Ibid.

199   Bradford, Sara, *America's Queen*, Penguin, 2000.

200   Both William Cavendish and Joe Kennedy Jr would be killed in action within a few months of the wedding. Kathleen died in a plane crash in 1948.

201   Stassinopoulos, Arianna, *Maria: Beyond the Callas Legend*. Simon & Schuster, 1981.

202   Bradford, Sara, *America's Queen*, Penguin, 2000.

Chapter Fifteen

203   Ioannidis, Paul J, *Destiny Prevails: My life with Aristotle, Alexander, Christina Onassis and her daughter, Athina*, Significance Press, 2015.

204   In the 1950s, Fiona Campbell-Walter, Barbara Goalen and Anne Gunning were considered to be Britain's most beautiful and sought-after models.

205   In 1963, Baroness Fiona von Thyssen was famously profiled by Alan Whicker in a TV documentary entitled *The Model Millionairess*.

REFERENCES

206 Evans, Peter, *Ari, The Life and Times of Aristotle Onassis*, Summit Books, 1986.

207 Ibid.

208 Nancy Mitford to Cecil Beaton, 24 October 1968: 'When the General saw widow Kennedy two years ago he said to Gaston [Palewski] 'Au fond c'est une vedette — tout ça finira dans le yacht d'un millionaire.' Cecil Beaton Collection, St John's College, Cambridge.

209 Evans, Peter, *Ari, The Life and Times of Aristotle Onassis*, Summit Books, 1986.

210 Ibid.

211 Ibid.

212 Bradford, Sara, *America's Queen*, Penguin, 2000.

213 Feroudi Moutsatsos, Kiki, *The Onassis Women: An Eyewitness Account*, G P Putnam's Sons, 1998.

214 Ibid.

215 Ibid.

216 Ibid.

217 Bradford, Sara, *America's Queen*, Penguin, 2000.

218 Ibid.

219 Feroudi Moutsatsos, Kiki, *The Onassis Women: An Eyewitness Account*, G P Putnam's Sons, 1998.

220 Ibid.

221 Ibid.

222 Maria Callas died in her sleep at the age of fifty-three.

223 *La Stampa*, 16 March 1970.

224 *La Stampa*, 3 February 1970.

225 Spence, Lyndsy, *Casta Diva*, The History Press, 2021.

226 *Time*, 31 August 1970.

227 Evans, Peter, *Ari, The Life and Times of Aristotle Onassis*, Summit Books, 1986.

228 In the 2004 movie, *The Aviator*, Johnny Meyer was played by Adam Scott.

229 Evans, Peter, *Ari, The Life and Times of Aristotle Onassis*, Summit Books, 1986.

230 Ibid.

231 Ibid.

232 Feroudi Moutsatsos, Kiki, *The Onassis Women: An Eyewitness Account*, G P Putnam's Sons, 1998.

233 Kafarakis, Christian, *Le Fabuleux Onassis*, Productions de Paris-N.O.É, 1971.

234 Evans, Peter, *Ari, The Life and Times of Aristotle Onassis*, Summit Books, 1986.

235 Ibid.

Chapter Sixteen

236 Ibid.

237 Ibid.

238 Feroudi Moutsatsos, Kiki, *The Onassis Women: An Eyewitness Account*, G P Putnam's Sons, 1998.

239 Spence, Lyndsy, *Casta Diva*, The History Press, 2021.

240 Ibid

241 Bradford, Sara, *America's Queen*, Penguin, 2000.

Chapter Seventeen

242 Spence, Lyndsy, *Casta Diva*, The History Press, 2021.

243 *The Last Onassis, Vanity Fair,* 29 January 2018.

Bibliography

Bing, Rudolf, *5,000 Nights at the Opera*, Doubleday, 1972.

Bradford, Sara, *America's Queen*, Penguin, 2000.

Colville, Jock, *Fringes of Power*, Weidenfeld & Nicolson, 1956.

Dallek, Robert, *An Unfinished Life: John F. Kennedy, 1917–1963*. Little Brown, 2003.

Davis, Deborah, *Party of the Century*, John Wiley & Sons, 2006.

Dedichen, Ingeborg and Pessar, Henry, *Onassis, mon amour*. Éditions Pygmalion, 1975 (not published in English).

Douglas, Nigel, *More Legendary Voices*, André Deutsch, 1994.

Evans, Peter, *Ari, The Life and Times of Aristotle Onassis*, Summit Books, 1986.

Evans, Peter, *Nemesis*, HarperCollins, 2004.

Fleming, Katherine Elizabeth, *Greece: A Jewish History*, Princeton University Press, 2008.

Feroudi Moutsatsos, Kiki, *The Onassis Women: An Eyewitness Account*, G P Putnam's Sons, 1998.

Galatopoulos, Stelios, *Maria Callas*, Simon & Schuster, 1998.

Garraty, John A, *The Great Depression*, Anchor, 1986.

Hardy, Frank, *Onassis, An Extraordinary Life*, New York Creative Publishing, 2013.

Hastings, Max, *Finest Years — Churchill as Warlord, 1940–1945.* HarperPress 2009.

Haymann, C David, *Bobby and Jackie,* Simon and Schuster, 2009.

Ioannidis, Paul J, *Destiny Prevails: My Life with Aristotle, Alexander, Christina Onassis and her Daughter, Athina,* Significance Press, 2015.

Ireland, Josh, *Churchill and Son*, John Murray 2021.

Kafarakis, Christian, *Le Fabuleux Onassis*, Productions de Paris-N.O.É, 1971.

McLean, Adrienne, *Being Rita Hayworth*, Rutgers University Press, 2004.

Meneghini, Giovanni Battista, *My Wife Maria Callas,* Farrar, Straus & Giroux, 1982.

Montague Browne, Anthony, *The Long Sunset,* Cassell, 1995.

Pearson, John, *The Private Lives of Winston Churchill,* Simon & Schuster, 1991.

Petsalis-Diomidis, Nicholas, *The Unknown Callas: The Greek Years.* Amadeus Press, 2001.

Porter, Darwin and Prince, Danford. *Pink Triangle*, Blood Moon Productions, 2014.

Schwarz, Charles, *Cole Porter: A Biography*, W H Allen, 1978.

Spada, James, *Peter Lawford: The Man Who Kept the Secrets,* Bantam, 1991.

Spence, Lyndsy, *Casta Diva,* The History Press, 2021.

Stancioff, Nadia, *Callas Remembered*, Dutton, 1987.

Stassinopoulos, Arianna, *Maria: Beyond the Callas Legend.* Simon & Schuster, 1981.

Sutherland, Robert, *Maria Callas: Diaries of a Friendship,* Constable, 1999.

Taraborrelli, J Randy, *Jackie, Janet & Lee*, St Martin's Publishing Group, 2018.

Index

Agnelli, Giovanni (Gianni) 210
Alexander, Queen 78
Anargyros, Soterios 47
Anatolia 15–17
Arabian-American Oil Company (ARAMCO) 105–109, 128
Astor, Chiquita 75
Atatürk, Mustafa Kemal 17, 21, 24–25
Athenagoras I 148–149
Auchincloss, Hugh D 69–70, 225
Auchincloss, James Lee 70
Auchincloss, Janet Jennings 70
Augustus, MS 77–78

Bartlett, Charlie 73
Beard, Peter 258
Beaton, Cecil 208, 222
Beaverbrook, Lord 121, 132–133
Bennet, Alan 194
Berlin, Isaiah 198
Beyond the Fringe 194
Bing, Rudolf 43, 154, 202
Bolker, Joseph 239–241
Boston Herald Traveler 218
Bouvier, Jacqueline *see* Kennedy Onassis, Jacqueline
Bouvier, John Vernou (Black Jack) 66–69, 67 (image), 75

Bouvier, Lee *see* Radziwill, Lee
Brando, Marlon 115, 206
Brien, Alan 134–135, 161
British United River Plate Telephone Company 44
Bryde, Ingevald Martin 77
Burton, Richard 10, 111, 225, 245

Callas, Maria
abortion 12, 165, 167–168
affair with Aristotle Onassis 12, 136–150, 139 (image), 145 (image), 169 (image)
death 271
early life in Greece 35–40
early life in USA 32–35
prima donna 34–35, 40–43
suicide attempt 12
Camelot 8, 10
Canadian National Steamship Company 60–61
Canfield, Augustus Cass 172
Canfield, Michael 171–181
Capote, Truman 71, 206–207
Castallanos, Agnetta 162, 184, 188
Catapodis, Spyridon 109
Cavendish, William 216
Chang, Suzy 192
Charteris, Frances Laura 178
Château de la Croë 98, 133–134, 161, 164
Christensen, Lars 79

291

Christina (yacht) 11, 13, 110–114, 113 (images), 116, 121, 142
Churchill, Pamela *see* Digby, Pamela
Churchill, Randolph 117, 121–123, 123 (image), 128
Churchill, Winston 117–125, 120 (images), 131
Claridge's 157, 183–184, 209, 228
Cohn, Roy 200, 247, 252
Connally, John 197
Constantine II, King 209
Cook, Peter 194
Cushing, Richard James (Cardinal) 75, 224

Daily Express 162
Daily Mail 61
Dallas Morning News 158
de Gaulle, Charles 190, 224
de Hidalgo, Elvira 36–37
de Monléon, Rose 177
de Montigny, Irma 83
Death of a President, The 206
Dedichen, Hermann 78
Dedichen, Ingeborg 77–91
Demiri Yolu 19, 45, 147
Dietrich, Marlene 73
Digby, Pamela 73, 122–123, 123 (image)
Dodero, Alberto 53, 90, 94, 96
Drake, Betsy 111

Edward VII, King 78
Edward VIII, King 136, 171–172

Elizabeth II, Queen 74, 116–117
Evans, Peter 45, 57, 134, 147, 247
Evening News 158
Evening Standard 132
Fenston, Felix 177, 258
Feroudi, Kiki 234
Fields, Gracie 144
Flea in her Ear, A 225
Ford, Charlotte 190, 237
Freud, Sigmund 28
Fuller, Geraldine *see* Spreckels, Geraldine

Gaillet, Hélène 256
Gallipoli, Battle of 21
Gaono, Juan 47
Garbo, Greta 111, 131
Gardner, Ava 131
Georgakis, Yiannis 167, 234
George, Lloyd 21
George, Prince, Duke of Kent 171–172
Getty, John Paul 86
Ghiringhelli, Antonio 43, 154
Gilpatric, Roswell 208, 214–215, 229, 244
Götaverken 79
Goulandris, Peter 239, 265, 269
Graf Zeppelin 62
Grace, Princess 115–116, 131
Grant, Cary 111, 212
Gratsos, Constantine 'Costa' 57–59, 88–89, 101–102, 125–126, 128, 155, 245

INDEX

Greek Junta 209
Guns of Navarone, The 166
Haakon VII, King 78
Haden, Ernst 84
Harewood, Lord 38
Harriman, Pamela *see* Digby, Pamela
Harriman, Averell 122
Harrison, Rex 225
Hindenburg 62, 249
Holden, William 194
Hoover, J Edgar 104, 192, 196, 199
Husted, John 170
Hustler 246

ITT 44
İzmir, *see* Smyrna

Jhare, Andres 84
Johnson, Lyndon 198–199
John XXIII, Pope

Kafarakis, Christian 246
Kalogeropoulos, George 32–35, 38
Kalogeropoulos, Litsa 32–37, 153
Kalogeropoulos, Maria *see* Callas, Maria
Kalogeropoulos, Vassilis 32–33
Kalogeropoulos, Yakinthi (Jackie) 32, 36–37
Karamanlis, Constantine 129
Karataş 15, 147
Kelly, Grace *see* Grace, Princess
Kennedy Jr, John 76, 199, 260

Kennedy Jr, Joseph (Joe) 179, 216
Kennedy, Caroline 76, 178, 260
Kennedy, Edward 226, 233–234, 247, 266
Kennedy, Ethel 199, 211, 214
Kennedy, Eunice 72
Kennedy, John Fitzgerald (Jack)
accent 10
affairs 174, 178, 192–194
assassination 197–198
early life 10, 72–73
marriage to Jacqueline Bouvier 72–76, 76 (image), 126, 174, 178–179, 183 (image), 190–191, 194, 197–198
Kennedy, Joseph (Joe) 72–73, 124, 126, 200, 216
Kennedy, Kathleen (Kick) 73
Kennedy, Patrick 191, 194
Kennedy, Robert Francis (Bobby) 72, 181, 189, 192, 195, 199–201, 207, 211–215
Kennedy, Rose 13, 73, 216
Kennedy Onassis, Jacqueline (Jackie)
accent 10
affairs 70, 72, 194, 199, 206, 210, 244
career 71
discredited in media 12–13, 246
early life 66–76, 67 (image), 71 (image)

engagement to Aristotle
Onassis 7–8, 9 (image),
124–125, 182, 195–196,
201, 205, 207–208,
212–213, 216–218, 224
engagement to John F
Kennedy 72–74
marriage to Aristotle
Onassis 225–237, 245–248,
248 (image), 245–248,
248 (image), 259–260,
264–268, 271
marriage to John F Kennedy
72–76, 76 (image), 126,
174, 178–179, 183 (image),
190–191, 194, 197–198
spending 12, 49, 194, 211
Kolin, Grace 177
Konialides, Constantine 47–48, 62
Konialides, Nicolas 47, 62, 85, 91
Kronkite, Walter 198

Lake, Veronica 89
Lamazzi, Giovanna 167
Lawford, Peter 182
Lee, Janet Norton 66–69, 67 (image), 75, 170, 208–209, 217
Livanos, Athina (Tina) 93, 95 (image), 97, 113 (images), 131–132,
Livanos, Eugenia 93, 95 (image), 97, 101 (image), 137, 237
Livanos, Stavros 90, 92–93

MacLaine, Shirley 214
Mahue, Robert 107–108
Manchester, William 206
Marquand Jr, John P 70–71
Marquand, John P 70
Maud of Wales 78
Maxims de Paris 83, 183, 201, 203, 235
Maxwell, Elsa 135, 142, 143 (image)
McCarthy, Joseph 200
McCusker, Donald 253–255
McGregor, Donald 130, 225, 252–253
Meneghini, Giovanni Battista 39–43, 39 (image), 136–150, 139 (image), 147–148, 150–153
Metaxas, Ioannis 63
Meyer, Johnny 45, 138, 165, 195, 205, 226, 240–241, 251, 255, 262
Michalakopoulos, Andreas 57
Monroe, Marilyn 115, 135–136, 182
Montague Browne, Anthony 123, 143
Montague Browne, Nonie 144, 146
Mount Athos 148
Muzio, Claudia 48–49, 52, 54 (image)
Nansen, Fridjof 29
New York Times, The 8, 110, 192, 268

INDEX

Niarchos, Eugenia *see* Livanos, Eugenia
Niarchos, Stavros 11, 90, 94, 96–98, 100, 101 (image), 107, 209, 236–238, 242–243, 257–258, 268
Nichols, Mike 208
Nixon, Richard 107–108
Nobleza Piccardo 47
Olympic Airways 129–130, 184, 249–250
Olympic Aviation 249
Olympic Challenger 102, 109
Onassis, Alexander 49, 97, 159–161, 160 (image), 218, 220–223, 232–233, 238, 249–256
Onassis, Aristotle Socrates (Ari)
 affair with Maria Callas 12, 136–150, 139 (image), 145 (image), 169 (image)
 early business ventures 44–54
 early life 16–31, 61 (image)
 engagement to Jacqueline Kennedy 7–8, 9 (image), 124–125, 182, 195–196, 201, 205, 207–208, 212–213, 216–218, 224
 illness and death 260, 263–267
 in Argentina 11, 44–54
 in Greece 55–58, 63–64, 129–130, 186, 209–210, 226, 264
 in Monaco 13, 103–104, 112, 114–116, 130, 162, 188
 in United States 87–89
 Liberty ship scandal 98–101
 marriage to Athina Livanos 93–94, 96–98, 100 (image), 102, 104 (image)
 marriage to Jacqueline Kennedy 225–237, 245–248, 248 (image), 245–248, 248 (image), 259–260, 264–268, 271
 Saudi Arabian deal 105–109
 shipowner 53, 59, 65 (image)
 Suez Crisis 127–128
Onassis, Artemis 17, 19, 85, 137, 186, 217, 224–225, 228–230
Onassis, Athina Hélène 269
Onassis, Callirrhoe 18
Onassis, Christina 14, 49, 98, 159–162, 163 (image), 218, 223–224, 232–233, 239–244, 254, 261
Onassis, Gethsemane 18, 26
Onassis, Helen 18
Onassis, Homer 22
Onassis, Merope 18, 85
Onassis, Penelope 15
Onassis, Socrates 15, 17, 19, 22–23, 25, 27–28, 55–56, 60
Onassis, Tina *see* Livanos, Athina
Opera News 35
Ormsby-Gore, David 208
Oswald, Lee Harvey 198
Ottoman Empire 20–21

Papadimitriou, Stelio 193
Papadopoulos, Georgios 210, 226
Papas, Irene 166
Parker, John L 25
Pascal, Gisèle 115
Pasolini, Pier Paulo 34, 231
Pavlova, Anna 52
Pearson, Drew 193
Perón, Eva 94, 96
Perón, Juan 94
Piaggio P.136 250–253
Pius, Pope XII 75
Preston, Alice Gwynne (Kiki) 171–172

Radziwill, Anna Christina 179–180
Radziwill, Lee 12, 66, 69–72, 170–188, 171 (image)
Radziwill, Stanislas (Stas) 170–183, 171 (image), 214
Rainier, Prince 103–104, 115–116, 188, 261
Reeves, Emery 118
Rhinelander, Jeanne 133, 156
Rivers, Joan 226
Roosevelt Jr, Franklin D 195, 199
Rousel, Thierry 269–270, 272
Russell, Wendy 118–119

Saud, King 108
Saudi Arabaian Maritime Company (SAMCO) 106
Schlessinger Jr, Arthur 208, 212
Serafin, Tullio 38, 41
Skorpios 13, 29, 188, 225
Skouras, Spyros 88, 90, 157
Smyrna 16–29, 195
Société Anonyme des Bains de Mer (SBM) 103–104, 130
Somerset, David 173–174
Spencer-Churchill, John (Sunny Blandford) 163–164, 242, 263
Spreckels, Geraldine 89, 248, 257–258, 263–264
Stage, The 157
Stromboli (eruption of) 7, 146, 166
Swanson, Gloria 73, 89, 126, 225

Tatler 163, 173
Taylor, Elizabeth 225, 245
Tebaldi, Renato 43
Templesman, Maurice 271
Theodoracopulos, Panagiotis (Taki) 88, 185, 210
Thring, Joan 212–213, 217
Thyssen-Bornemisza, Hans Heinrich (Heini) 220–221

INDEX

Time 182
Times, The 263
Tomasso di Savoia 30, 31 (image), 103
Trivella, Maria 36

Vanderbilt, Consuelo 164
Venizelos, Eleftherios 56–57
Vergottis, Panaghis 201–204
Vidal, Gore 174, 178, 231
Visconti, Luchino 42
von Post, Gunilla 74, 126

von Thyssen, Fiona 220–223, 221 (image), 241, 243, 251–252, 254
Vogue 68, 222

Washington Times-Herald 71
White, Sam 132
White House, The 10, 182, 90–191
Why England Slept 74

Yrigoyen, Hipólito 59

Zeffirelli, Franco 201, 203, 218–219